# *Foundations of* CLASSICAL OIL PAINTING

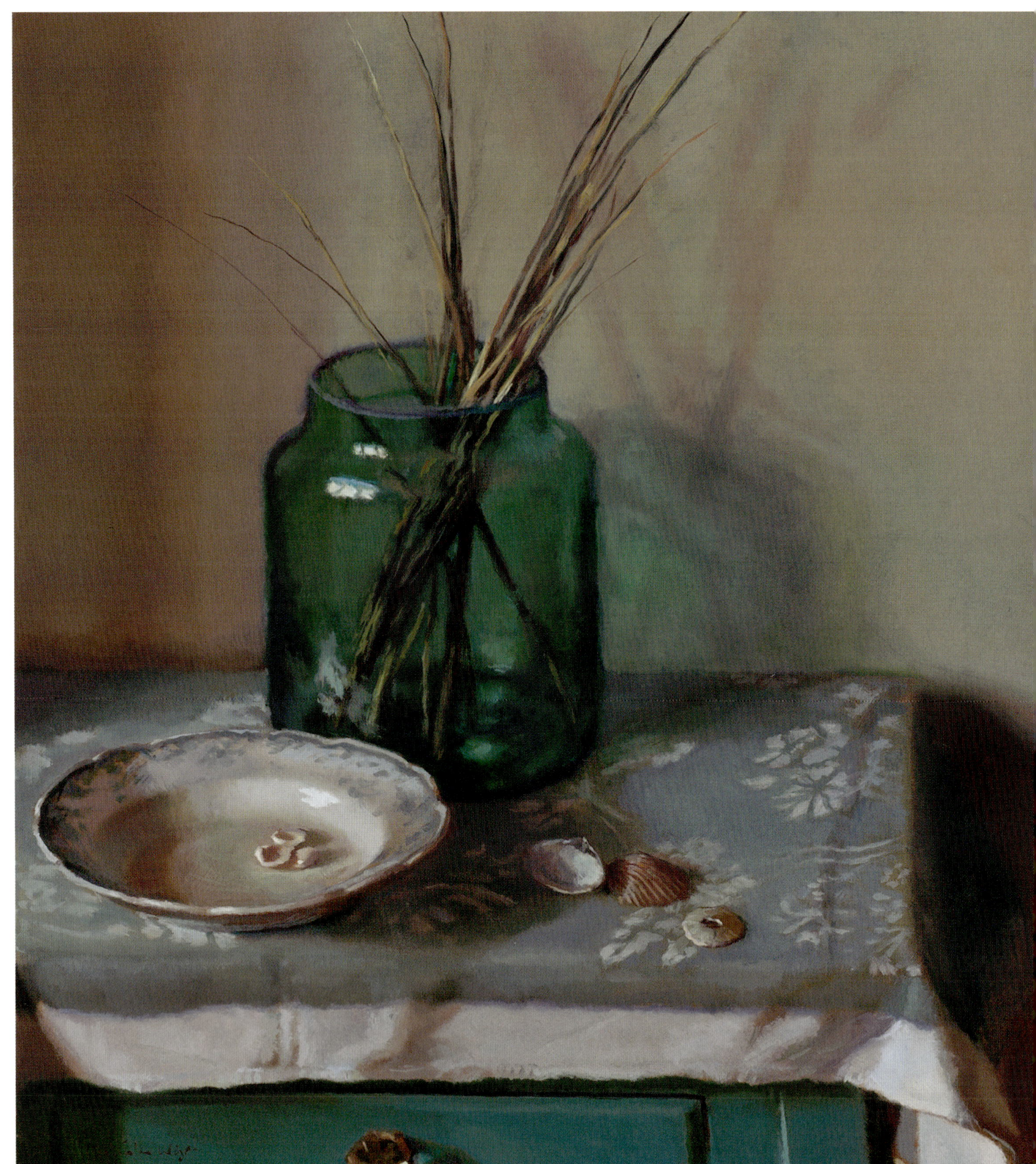

**Glass and Shells**
Lea Colie Wight
Oil on linen
20" × 18" (51cm × 46cm)

# *Foundations of* CLASSICAL OIL PAINTING

How to Paint Realistic People, Landscapes and Still Life

LEA COLIE WIGHT

CINCINNATI, OHIO
artistsnetwork.com

# CONTENTS



## *Materials*

SURFACE
stretched canvas

OIL PIGMENTS
Magenta
Permanent Rose or Quinacridone Red
Alizarin Crimson
Cadmium Red Deep
Cadmium Red Medium or Cadmium Scarlet
Cadmium Orange
Cadmium Yellow Light or Lemon
Yellow Ochre
Indian Yellow
Cadmium Green Light
Viridian
Phthalo Green
Cerulean Blue
Ultramarine Blue
Dioxazine Purple
Cobalt Violet Deep
Burnt Sienna
Black
Titanium White

BRUSHES
Silver Brush #5001 hake flat or mop brush
Silver Brush #7110 sable cat's tongue sizes 4, 6 and 8
Silver Brush #1034 long bristle filbert sizes 2, 3, 4 and 6
Silver Brush #1003 extra-long bristle filbert size 6
Rosemary brush #278 size 2, 4 and 6

OTHER
nitrile or vinyl gloves
odorless mineral spirits or Gamsol
paper towels
stand oil
spray Retouch varnish

**Dress Fitting**
Lea Colie Wight
Oil on linen
20" × 18" (51cm × 41cm)

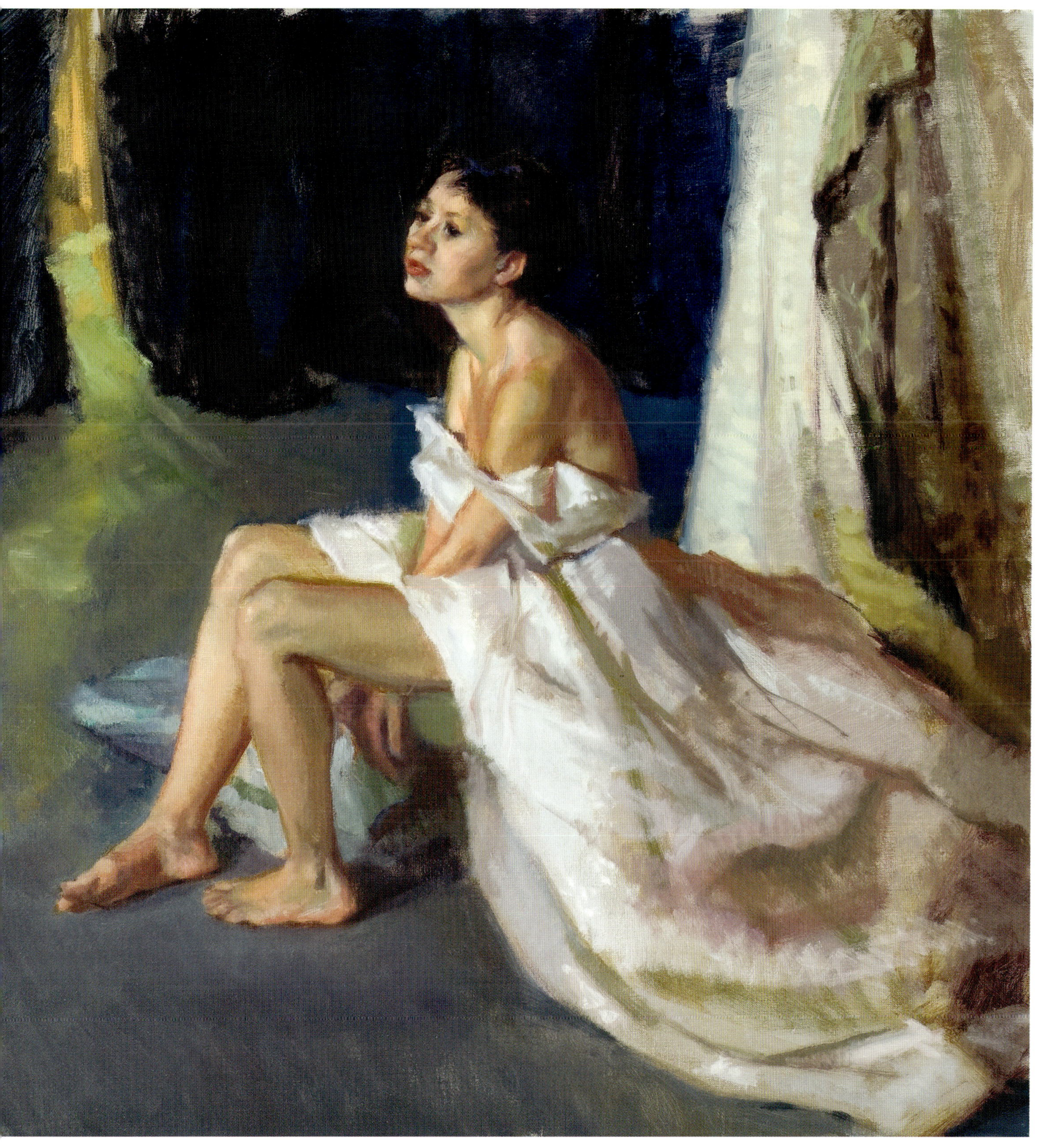

# INTRODUCTION

Nearly all of us are born with the tools necessary to become artists. Some of us can even become great ones. We often take these tools for granted, even though we use them every day.

You've probably heard people say, "I can't even draw a straight line!" Well not only are the majority of us indeed capable of drawing a straight line, we also have the ability to compare the length of lines, their relative thickness and the degree of angles. We know whether a door is wide enough, or if it would be a tight squeeze to fit through. We can see the difference in proportion and shape between an oval ball and a round ball. We can tell what is in shadow and what is in light. We can see that the color of the sky at midday is different than its color at sunset.

This instinctive awareness of relative values, colors, shapes and proportions is one of the greatest tools at your disposal as an artist. Work hard to develop it, and your confidence and artistic ability will continue to grow. The lessons and exercises covered in this book will help you identify and build on the skills you already possess, while laying a solid foundation for the fundamental techniques necessary to create a successful painting, regardless of the subject or medium.

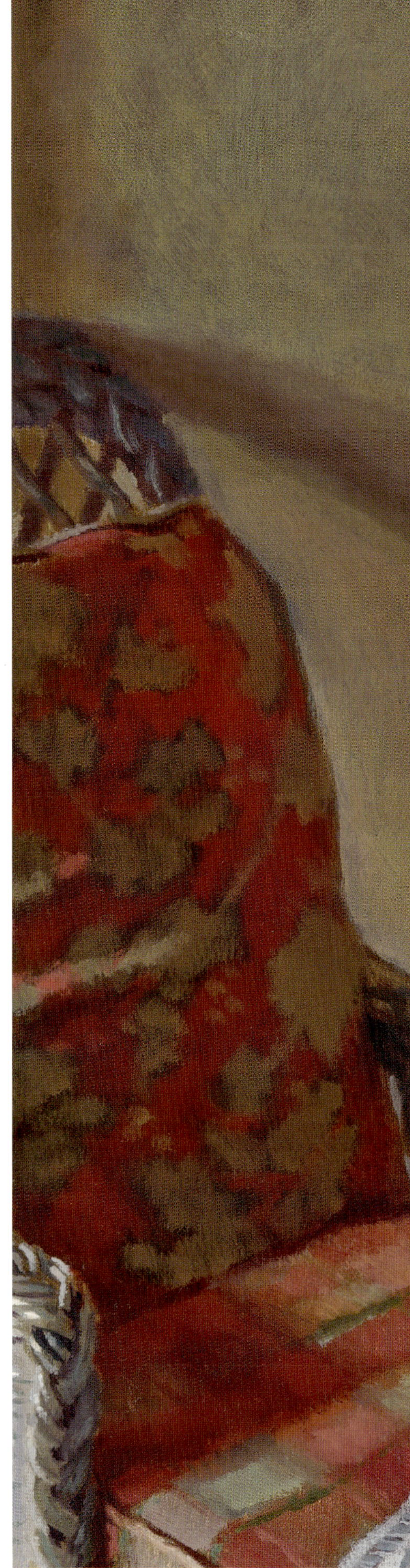

**Stillness**
Lea Colie Wight
Oil on linen
20" × 18" (51cm × 41cm)

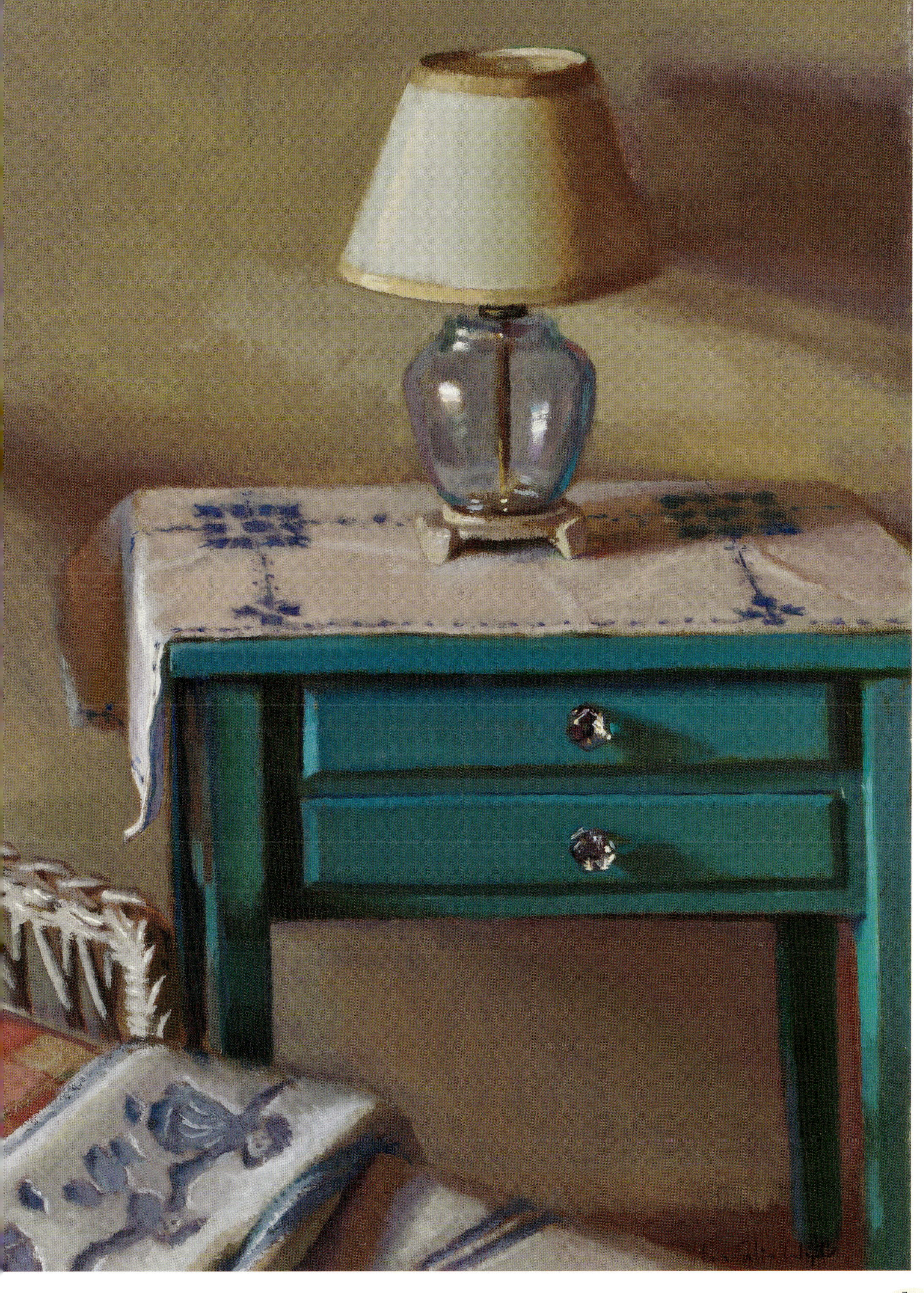

# MATERIALS

If you're just beginning your artistic journey, the following information will outline the basic supplies you'll need to get started. If you've been painting for years, perhaps you'll find some new materials to explore.

## PAINTS

There are various brands and qualities of oil paints available at many different price points. Brands like Vasari, Rublev and Michael Harding stand apart because they are handmade and provide intense pigmentation and consistency. Winsor & Newton and Gamblin's professional paint cost a bit less and are good brands.

I recommend sticking with professional-grade paints regardless of which brand you choose. Anything labeled as student or economy grade will be full of filler and consequently weak. You'll have to use a lot more paint to get good coverage and will end up going through your tubes much faster. It has been my experience that using the very best paint you can afford is actually more economical in the long run.

## BRUSHES

There are many brush types, shapes and sizes to choose from. Oil brushes are traditionally long handled. My favorites are Silver Brush natural hog bristle filbert brushes in various lengths and sizes. I use filberts because I prefer to use the side of the brush and can lay in paint either broadly or in a line. Other brushes I regularly use are Silver Brush cat's tongue sables in various sizes, a Silver Brush 7100 Renaissance and a Rosemary & Co. Series 278 long filbert (for later stages of painting).

Clean your brushes at the end of each painting day, and be sure to let your brushes dry with the ferrule pointed down to prevent paint build up. Mineral spirits and paint thinner can both be used for cleaning brushes. I use The Masters Brush Cleaner and Preserver by General Pencil Company.

## SOLVENTS

Turpentine is a traditional solvent. Like most solvents, it's toxic and emits a strong odor. Always use an air purifying unit, even when working with odorless solvents. Gamsol by Gamblin is a good non-toxic alternative.

## MEDIUMS

Mediums are used primarily to change the consistency of oil paint. Stand oil is my medium of choice. It can also be used for "oiling out" in the painting process. This involves applying a thin layer of oil film to the dry canvas to bring the colors to a fully saturated look.

## VARNISH

Retouch varnish is used as a temporary overall varnish once a painting is dry. A final coat of permanent varnish should not be applied for several months. If you paint very thickly with a lot of medium, even more time is advised before the final coat. Retouch varnish can also be used as a substitute to oiling out, but it may leave freckles of varnish. If this happens, brush them out.

## SURFACES AND SUPPORTS

Stretched linen, stretched canvas and Gessobord all lend themselves well to oil painting. Many artists, myself included, like to work on a middle-tone surface because you can see light and dark values in the first notes.

## EASELS

There are studio easels in all price ranges and to suit all needs. I have a David Sorg counterweight easel as well as a simple wooden single-staff easel. For landscape painting, I use a portable French easel. Keep your preference of canvas size in mind and make sure your easel will accommodate.

### *Tip*

Viva Strong & Soft paper towels work best for wiping your brushes during painting. They are the most like cotton—thick, absorbent and leave very little lint. Be careful though, Viva Vantage paper towels do not have the same qualities. Blue Shop Towels by Scott work great, too. In my opinion, the best thing to use for wiping brushes are cotton paint rags because they are reusable. I cut up old T-shirts for this purpose.

## TABORET

A taboret is a small portable stand or cabinet with drawers and shelves for storage. They come in all shapes and sizes. Spend some time thinking about your present needs as well as what you may need in the future. Do you need a taboret that will easily fold up for storage? How large a surface do you need? Will you need side extensions to allow for more materials? Ask other artists about their experiences.

## STUDIO SETUP

A studio setup depends on the size of the space, the configuration of the room and the lighting. Northern light is ideal because it is the most consistent. Southern light moves all day. Painting hours are also curtailed in Eastern or Western light exposure as the sun moves across the sky.

Having the luxury of northern light simply isn't possible for many artists, but there are solutions. If your studio has no outside light at all, there are artificial lights on the market that can be adjusted for cool and warm light. The ilumi light bulb is around $40 and allows a rainbow of color possibilities.

Initially it is important to have one light source illuminating your subject. This allows you to see clear light and shadow separation. Whatever light you're working with, place your easel at an angle to the light source so you will have less of a problem with glare. Try to make sure you have enough room to stand several feet away from your easel and subject.

## ADDITIONAL SUPPLIES

- Nitrile or vinyl gloves to protect your hands
- Tube wringer—a great tool for getting the last bit of oil paint out of the tube
- Clamps
- Model timer
- Tape to mark your model's position
- Container for oily rags
- Air purifier—note whether it is for chemicals and what size room it covers

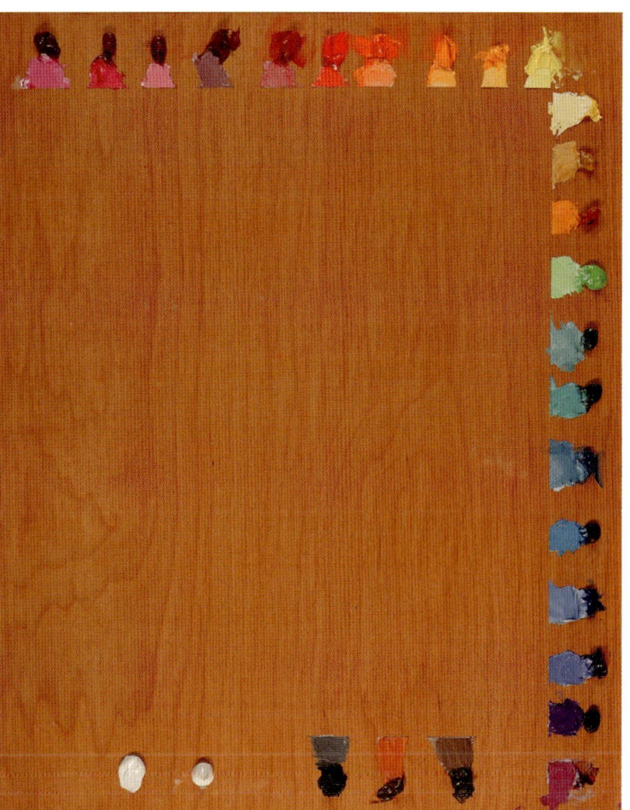

### *My Palette*

I use maplewood palettes from New Wave Art. I use a highly chromatic palette, which can be expensive to set up. With that in mind, I've indicated a modified palette by placing any nonessential colors in parenthesis, starting clockwise from the top left:

Magenta
Permanent Rose or
Quinacridone Red
Alizarin Crimson
(Cadmium Purple)
Cadmium Red Deep
Cadmium Red Medium or
Cadmium Scarlet
Cadmium Orange
(Cadmium Yellow Deep)
(Cadmium Yellow Medium)
Cadmium Yellow Light or Lemon
(Naples Yellow)
Yellow Ochre
Indian Yellow

Cadmium Green Light
Viridian
Phthalo Green
Cerulean Blue
(Prussian Blue)
Ultramarine Blue
(Cobalt Blue)
Dioxazine Purple
Cobalt Violet Deep
Burnt Sienna
(Burnt Umber)
Black
Titanium White
(Flake White)

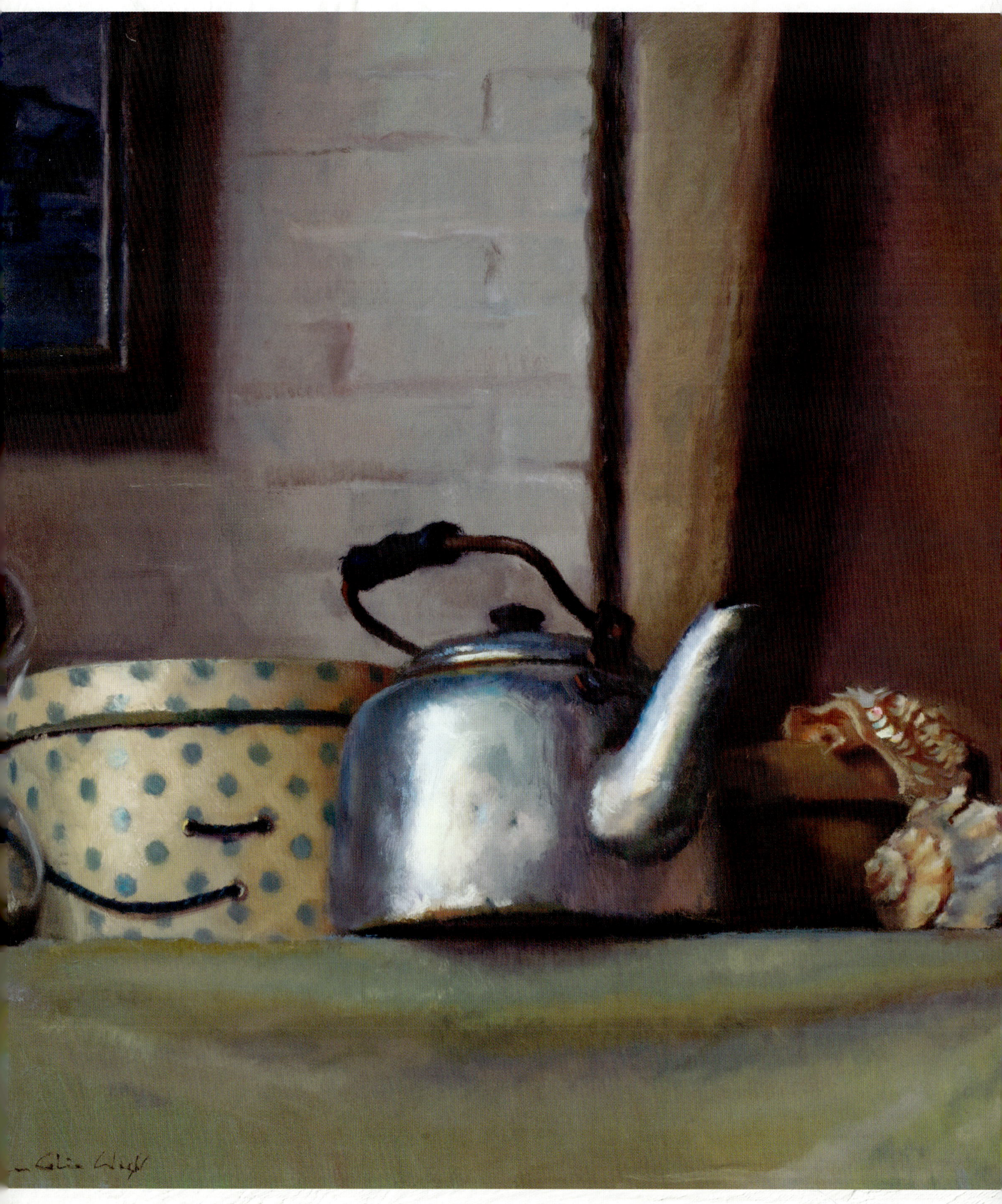

# 1 VALUE *and* COMPOSITION

A good composition is essential to a good painting, and a strong composition is achieved through value. Since the two go hand-in-hand, this chapter will focus on both.

When you are walking through a gallery, what pulls you toward a particular painting? Once you're standing in front of the painting, you can appreciate all the beautiful detail, but it is the powerful composition that draws you close enough to see it. And what creates powerful compositions? Values.

Composition tells the viewer what to focus on—the important elements in the painting. It leads the viewer through the painting, lingering on certain areas before moving to the next. It can be energetic or calm. The areas of different values create this. A pinpoint of light within a dark mass draws your eye in, while a strong sweeping arc of dark carries your eye along it. A dark strip of land within a field can convey isolation, whereas a busy jumble of contrasting values can show the excitement and activity of a city street. However, even a hectic scene still needs focal points to guide the viewer.

Study the Old Masters—they understood the value of composition. And the next time you're walking through an art museum, really think about what it is that draws you to certain paintings.

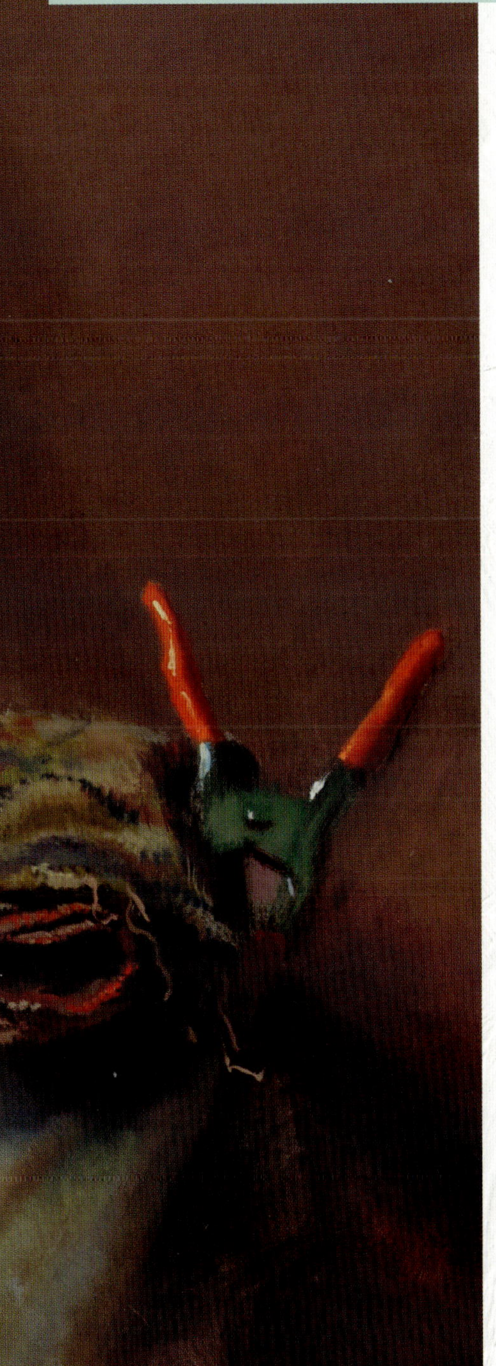

**Studio Still Life**
Lea Colie Wight
Oil on linen
18" × 24" (46cm × 61cm)

# VALUES

The ability to show correct value relationships is one of the most important components in painting. Remember, if your value isn't right then your color isn't right.

The prevalent painting system throughout this book is based on macro to micro for all skills, and that holds true for values.

The basic rule of nature is that when there is a single light source there is a clear division between things in the light and things in the shadow regardless of color. A single light source can be an artificial light shining on your subject, the sun outside or light coming in through windows on only one side of a room. Nothing in the light will be as dark as anything in the shadows. Squint at your entire composition. Expect to see the division between light and shadow and you will most likely see it.

To simplify the study of values it's easier to take color out of the equation. That's why most basic value illustrations are in shades of gray.

Begin with simple setups. Make sure there is one light source so you have a minimum of atmospheric light affecting your subject. Begin your setup exercises using a middle value backdrop and bottom surface for your object.

Make sure you have clear, simple plane differences in your object. Do this by adjusting the angle of your light.

Move to more and more complex compositions as time goes by.

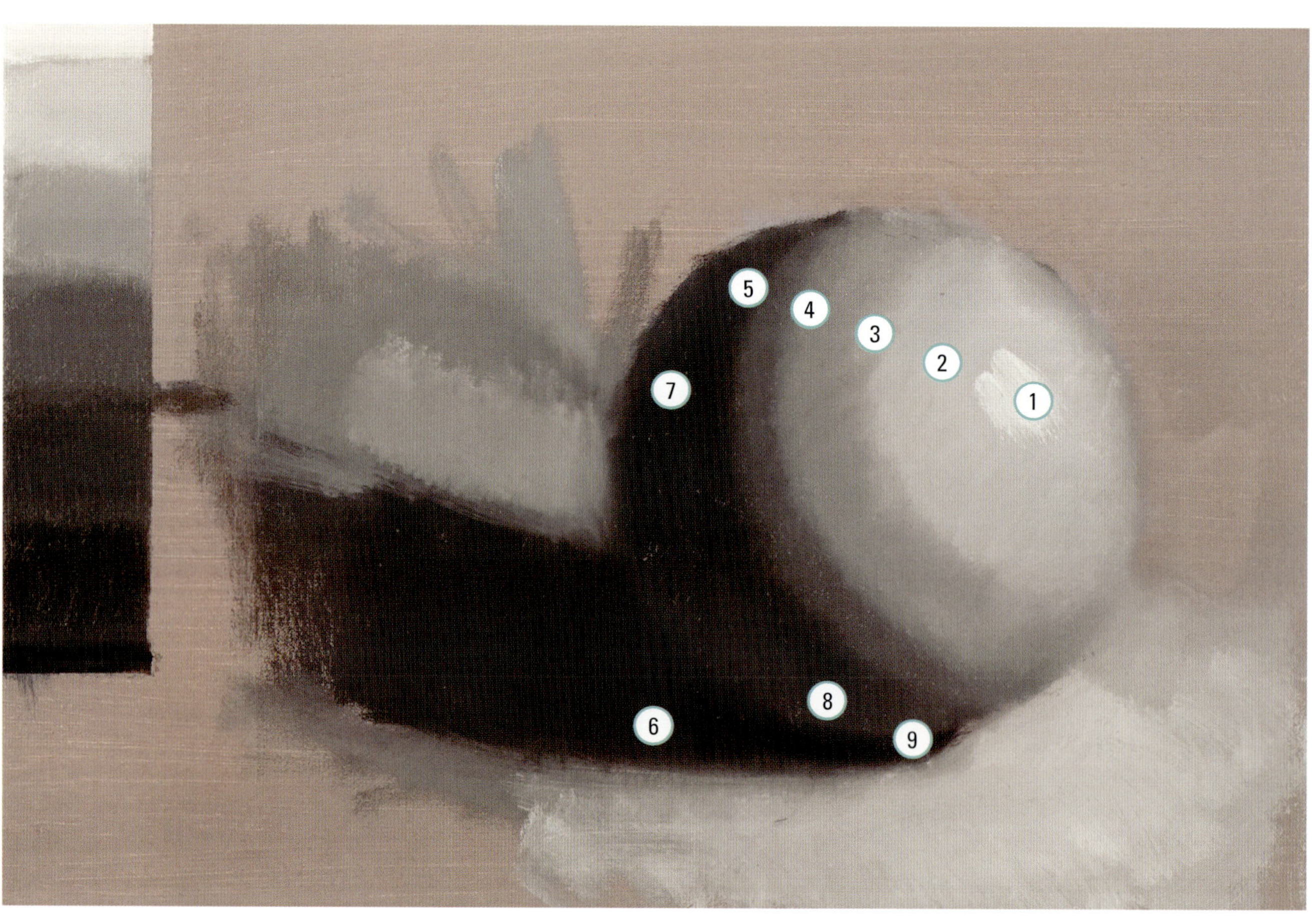


SIMPLE VALUE RELATIONSHIPS

This ball in light illustrates the simplest value relationships within an object. In painting, understanding this simple breakdown will allow you to begin your painting with a solid, accurate road map to build on. Be especially careful of reflected light. Because it is surrounded by darker values, it can seem lighter than it really is.

1. Highlight; 2. Light light; 3. Middle light; 4. Dark light; 5. Terminator; 6. Dark dark; 7. Middle dark; 8. Reflected light; 9. Dark accent

**SIMPLE VALUES DESCRIBE FORM**
This illustration shows the same simple values used to describe form.

1. Highlight; 2. Light light; 3. Middle light; 4. Dark light; 5. Terminator; 6. Dark dark; 7. Middle dark; 8. Reflected light; 9. Dark accent

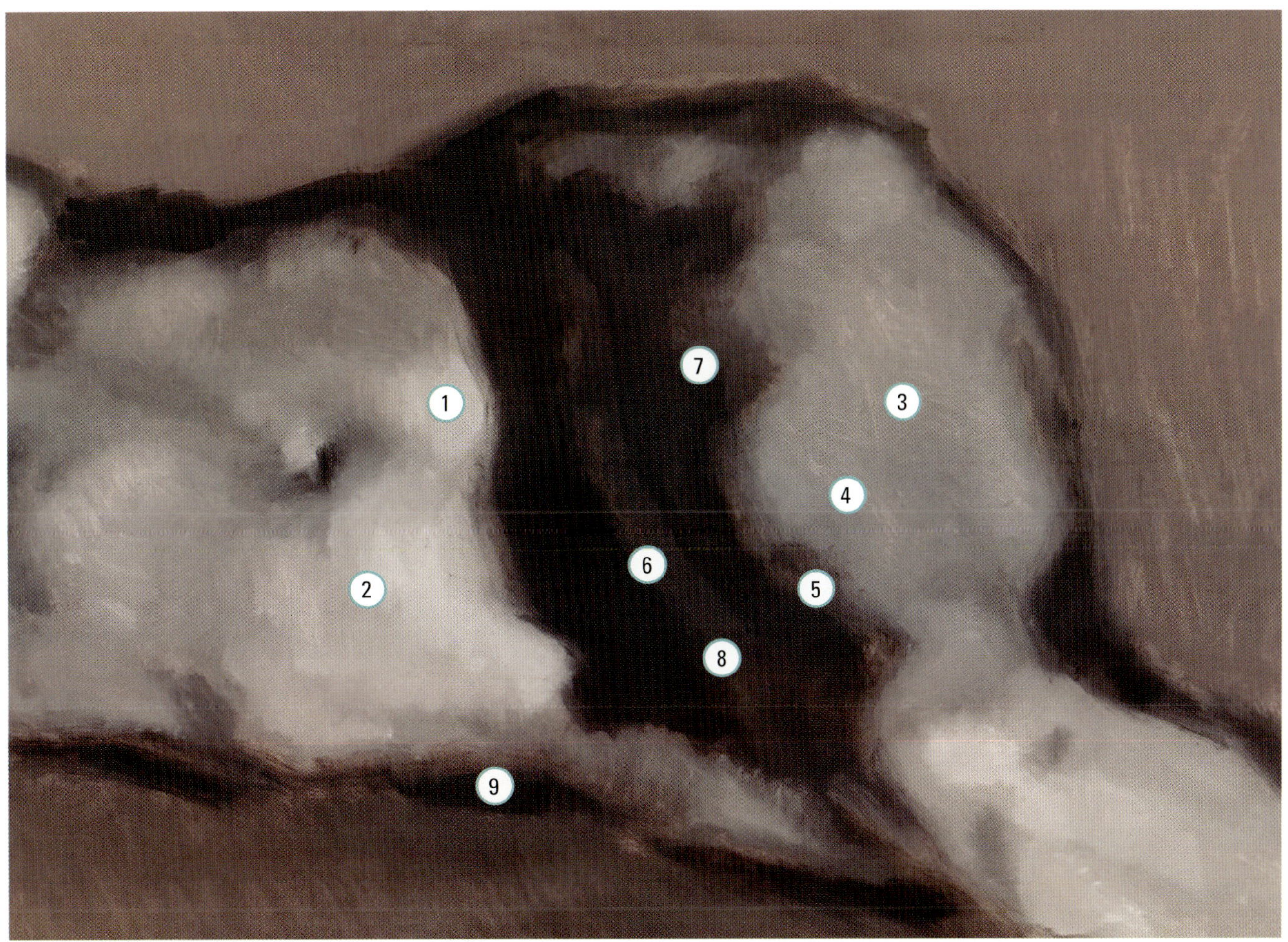


## *Squint!*

The easiest way to see and judge values is to squint down until your object separates into light and shadow. Use this to compare your painting with your subject. Squint at your subject and notice when the values in an area unify, then look at your painting. The values should unify at the same degree of squinting.

Squint your eyes as you switch your gaze from your painting to your subject and back again. Details in the shadows will disappear turning into one simple value. The shadows in both your painting and your subject should do this at the same level of squinting. If the values within an area on your subject merge as one, but that same area on your painting still shows two values within that area, then that means your values don't match.

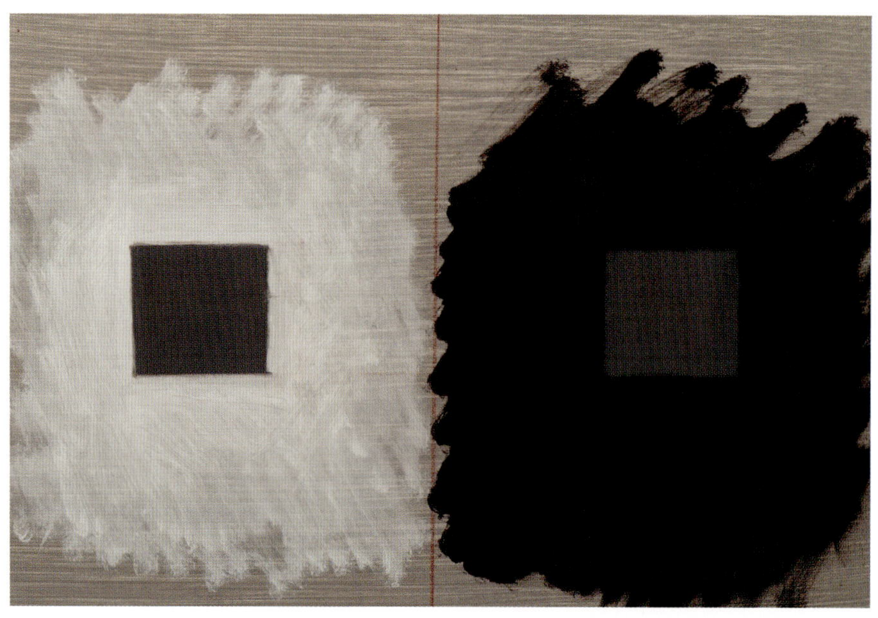

### REFLECTED LIGHT

Here, the value is the same within both gray squares. The placement against white and black is what makes us perceive it as different. A value in shadow can look lighter than it is because of the dark surrounding it. It will be deceiving especially if you stare. This awareness is very helpful when dealing with the challenge of reflected light. Remember this when judging values. The more complex your composition is, the more essential this skill.

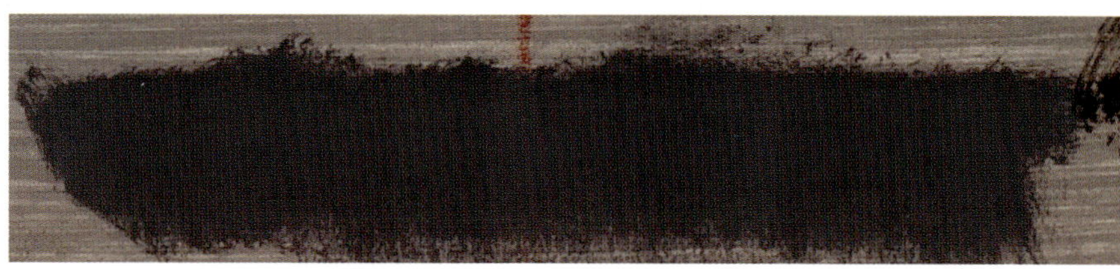

### TRUE VALUE

This is the actual value of both squares. When you squint at the squares above, the right square values are mostly merged as one. There's much higher contrast for the square on the left.

### LOOKS CAN BE DECEIVING

Reflected light is often found within the shadow of an object whether it's the human form or the side of a building. Because reflected light is surrounded by a darker value, it can appear to be much lighter than it actually is. One of the most common errors in painting is looking only within the shadows to judge reflected light instead of looking at the larger relationship between the entire object in light and in shadow. It's easy to be deceived into painting the reflected light much brighter than it is.

I tried to come as close as I could to painting the same value within each square. The paint I used for each is pictured directly below each swatch.

# EXPANDED VALUE RANGES

The illustration below shows a more complex object broken down into values. In most painting compositions there will be many more values than just the ones present on a simple single object.

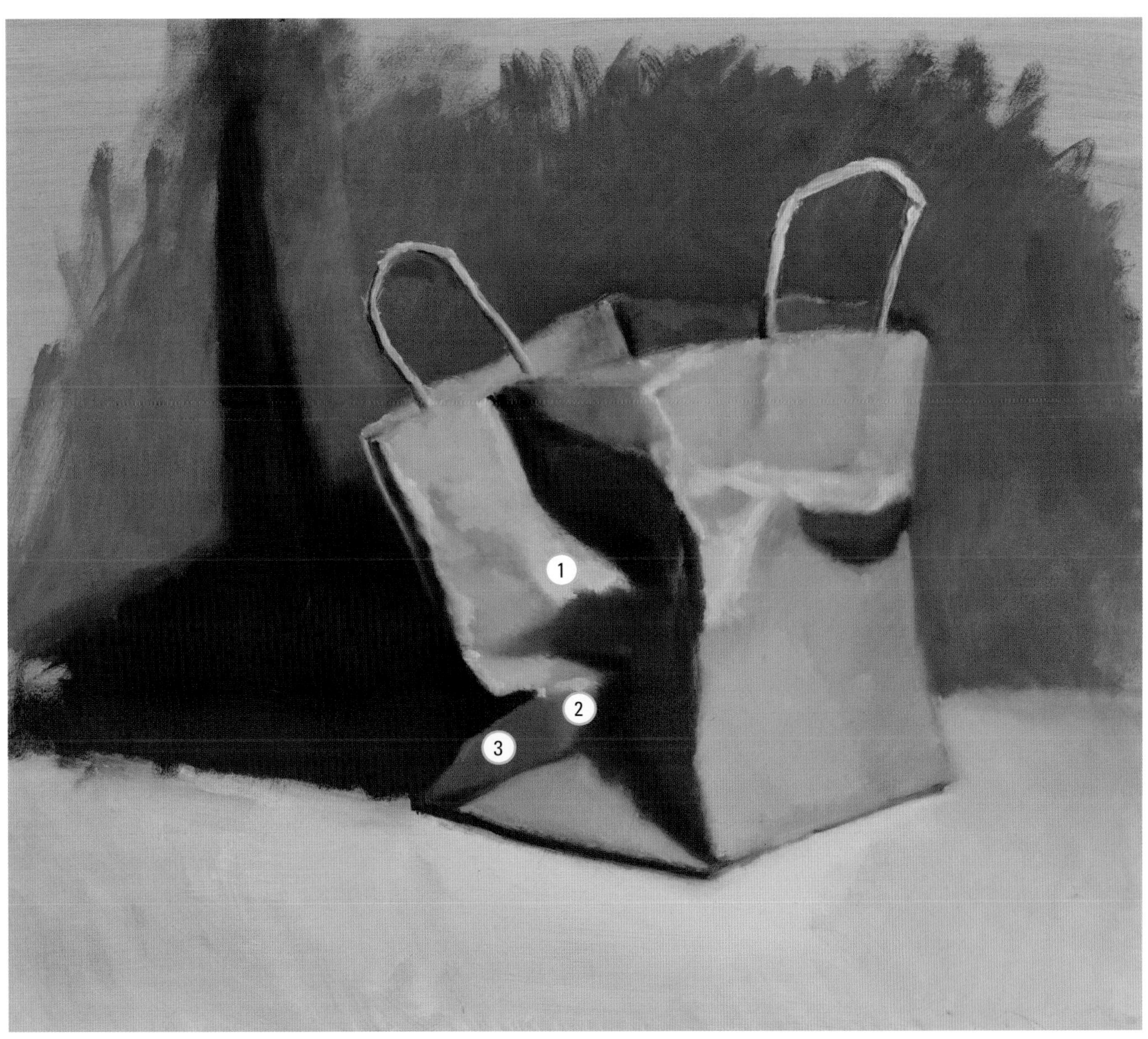


**BREAKING DOWN VALUES**

The value scale on the left shows the divide between values in the light and values in the shadow. You can practice squinting to see the actual separation in the painting.

Remember to set your value range by setting your highlight and dark accent early on. This gives you solid value extremes to help judge. When you paint your own value study your first notes are estimates and your time should be spent adjusting and adding.

1. Highlight; 2. Light; 3. Shadow

# SIMPLIFYING VALUES

When dealing with a complex subject, start with simple value relationships.

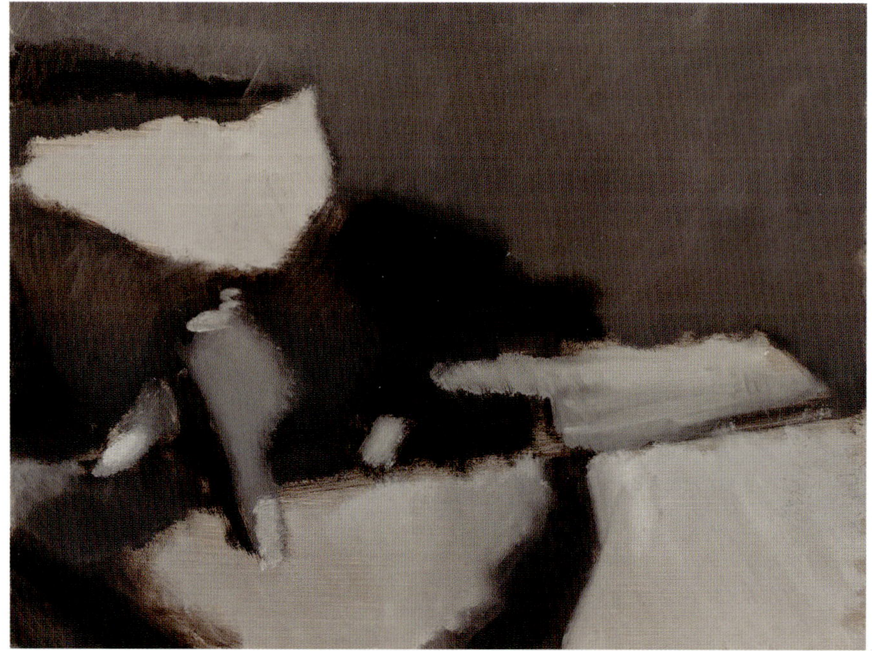

### SQUINT TO SEE SIMPLE MASSES

Squint until you see the simplest masses of light and shadow. Use as few different values as you can reasonably see. Keep an eye on the closest relationship between light and shadow. In this case, it's the wall behind and the pillow in shadow.

### USE THE HIGHLIGHT AND DARK ACCENT AS GUIDES

Continue to find smaller and smaller value differences. Squint especially hard for the closest relationships. Develop these close relationships and immediately compare to the whole. Let your highlight and dark accent guide you.

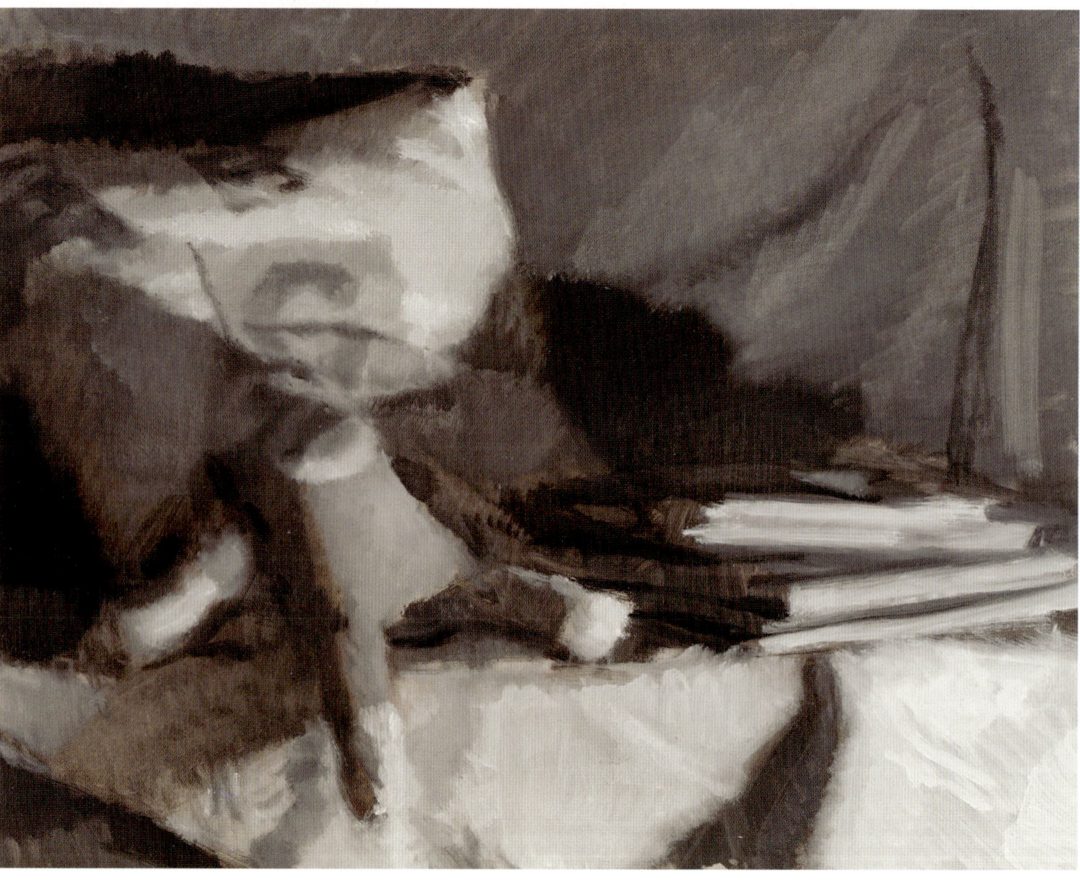

# FABRIC STUDY

This painting illustrates a complex value composition. It is necessary to find the separation between light and shadow during the block-in stage of a painting dealing with so many close values. Squint to confirm the shadow and light separation.

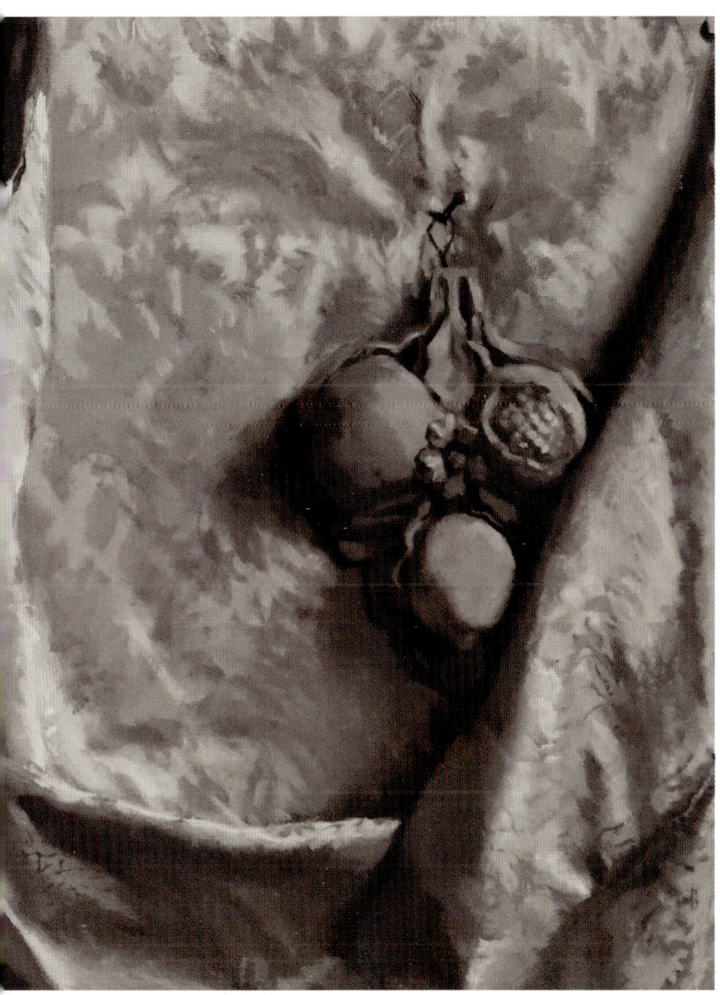

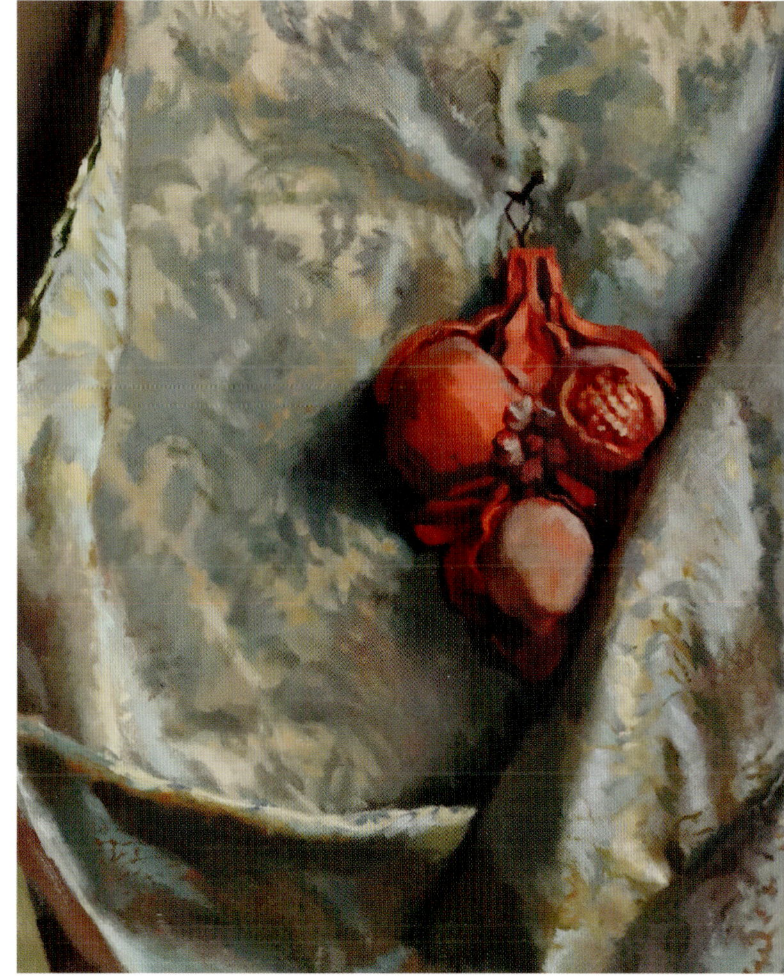

### FINDING SHADOWS

When you're painting the human form or any complex object, it can sometimes be difficult to be certain where your shadow is. One simple way to determine this is to try to cast a shadow on the area in question. No matter how light your shadows are, you will not be able to cast a shadow on a shadow area. Try holding up a brush so that it casts a shadow. Now move it across the area in doubt. The areas where the shadow disappears are your shadow areas in the composition.

## AFTERNOON LIGHT

Complicated subjects like this will be easier if you make sure that your light and shadow separation are locked in first. In this case, the strong shadows present at the end of the day made the values clearer. There is a very close relationship between the bottom lantern in shadow (A) and the box wall behind it (B). Notice the value difference at the bottom of the painting—a cool blue shadow versus warm green light.

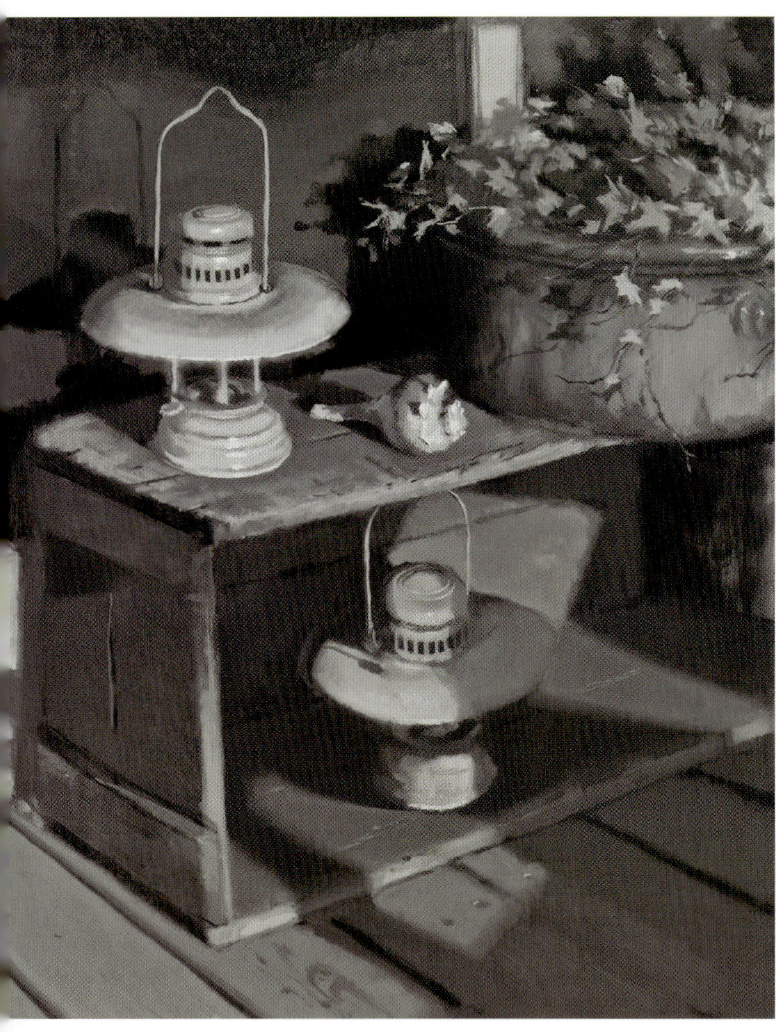

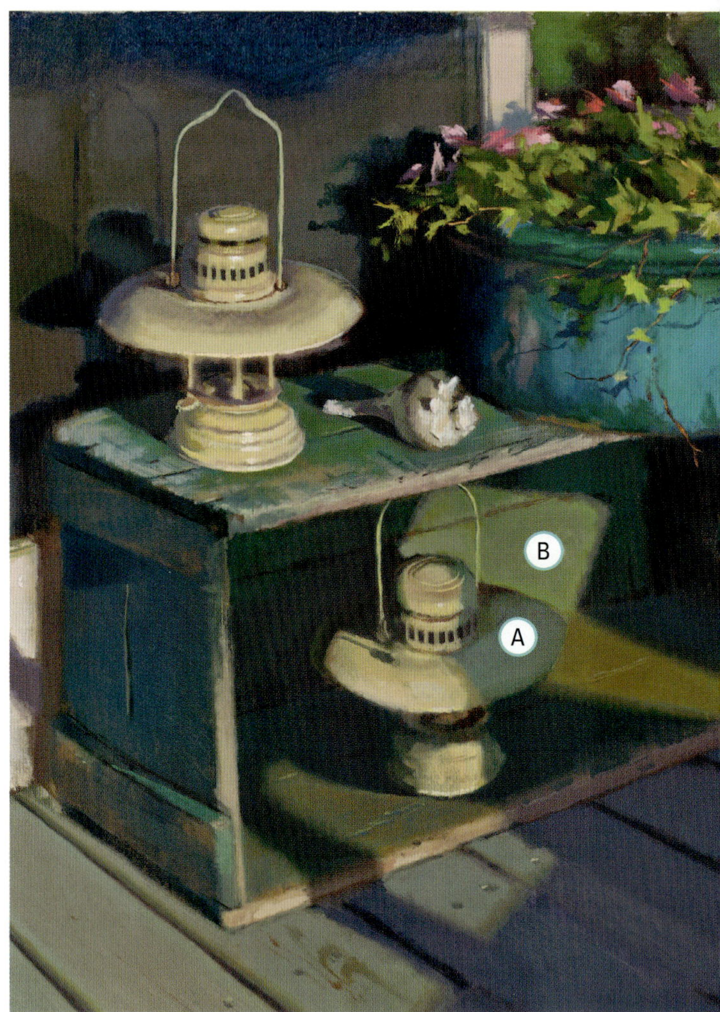


### INTENSE COLOR MAKES SEEING VALUES A CHALLENGE

When you're painting something with intense colors, it can be challenging to see it in value only. Notice how the blue ceramic container and the left side of the box seem closer in value than they actually are. This is because they're so colorful. In shades of gray, however, the difference is clear.

## VALUES AND COLOR COMPARISON

In this comparison of value and color, some extremely close relationships in many spots make it challenging to accurately see the values. The roof of the far building (A) is very close in value to the walkway in shadow (B). Set the lightest and darkest values and the areas closest to the division between light and shadow first.

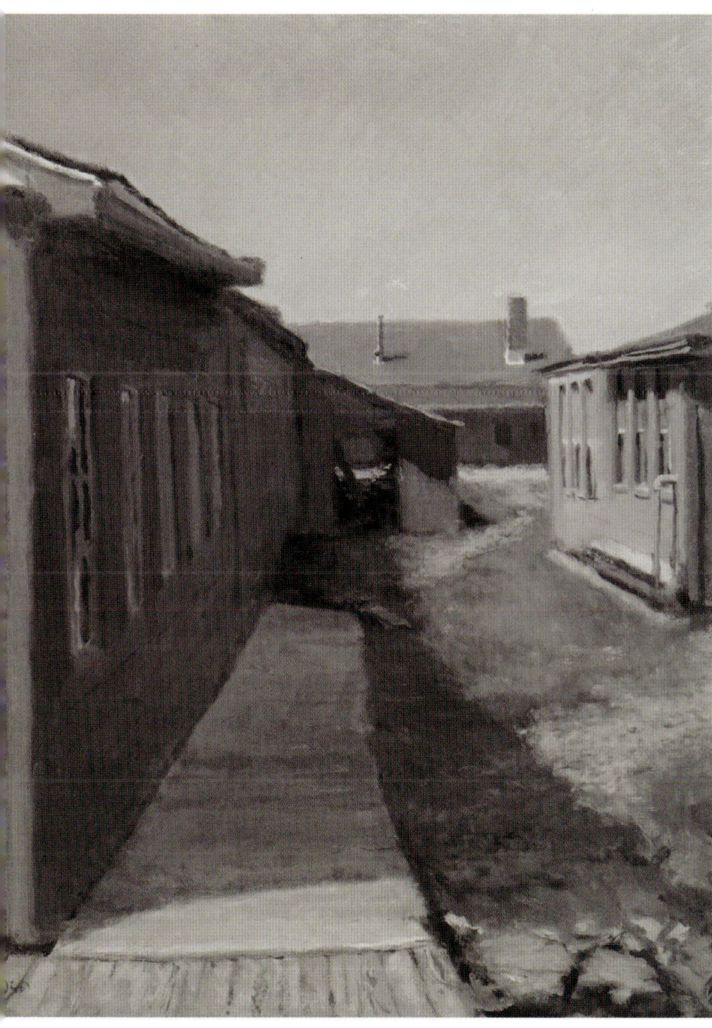

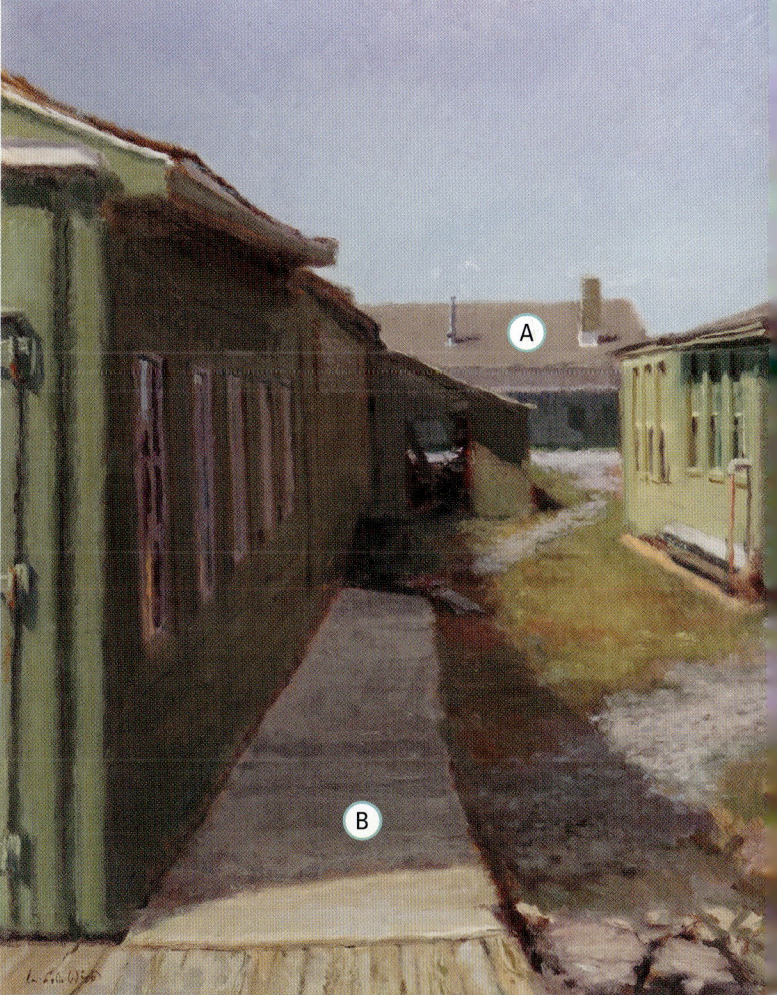


### REFER TO THE DARKEST DARK AND LIGHTEST LIGHT

The closest relationship between light and shadow in your painting is a dividing line. There you will find your darkest light value and your lightest dark value. You can refer back to those two values when you're working on values in other areas of your painting.

## CLOSE VALUE DIFFERENCES

This painting was painted under northern light and has some very close value differences between the light and shadow areas. It is a good example of how important it is to understand your value relationships and be able to paint them correctly. In a subtle setup, if your values are just a little off, it will look odd to the viewer.

First find the area where the shadow and light values are the closest. I see this as the light on the left edge of the second finger from the left. Try squinting at the black-and-white image and you should see that area of light stand out just a bit from the rest of the shadow areas. There is another, clearer area hit by light at the base of the middle finger. Using a strong artificial light would also make the light and shadow stand out clearly.

1. Light; 2. Shadow

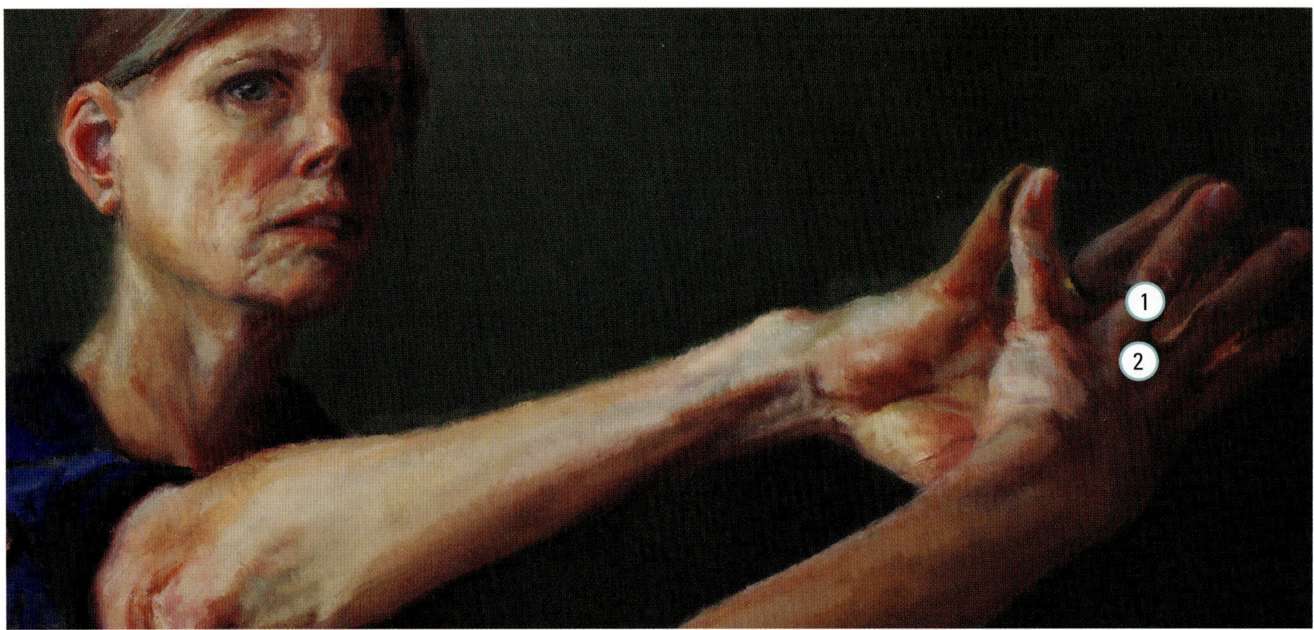


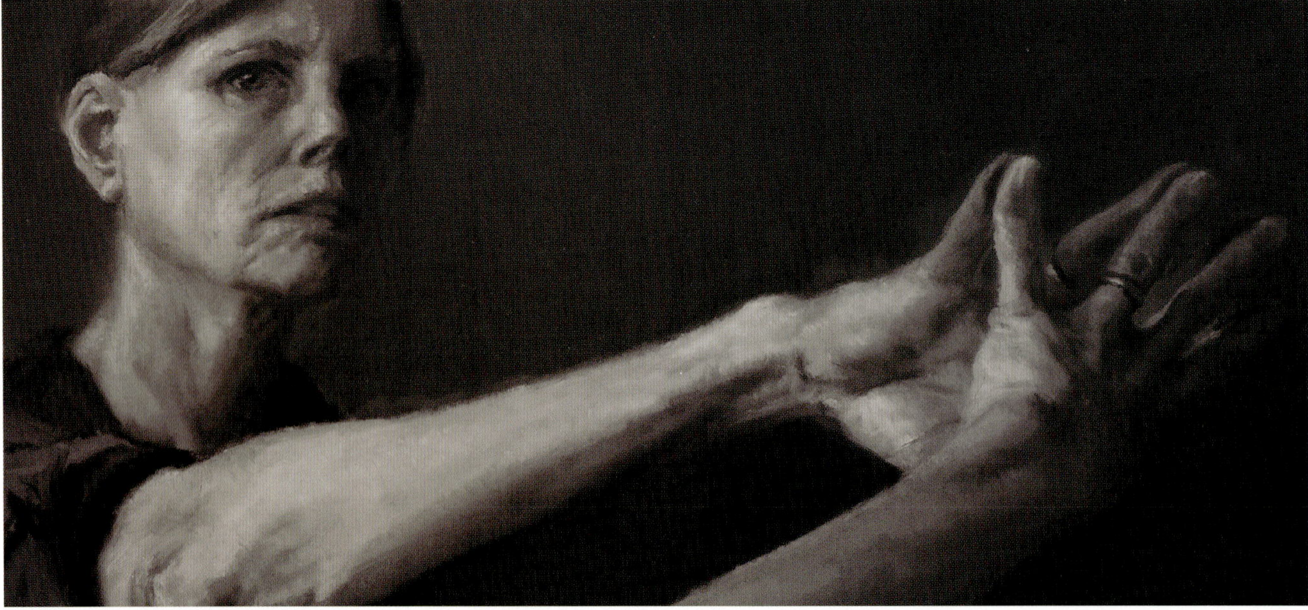

**Push**
Lea Colie Wight
Oil on linen
10" × 20" (25cm × 51cm)

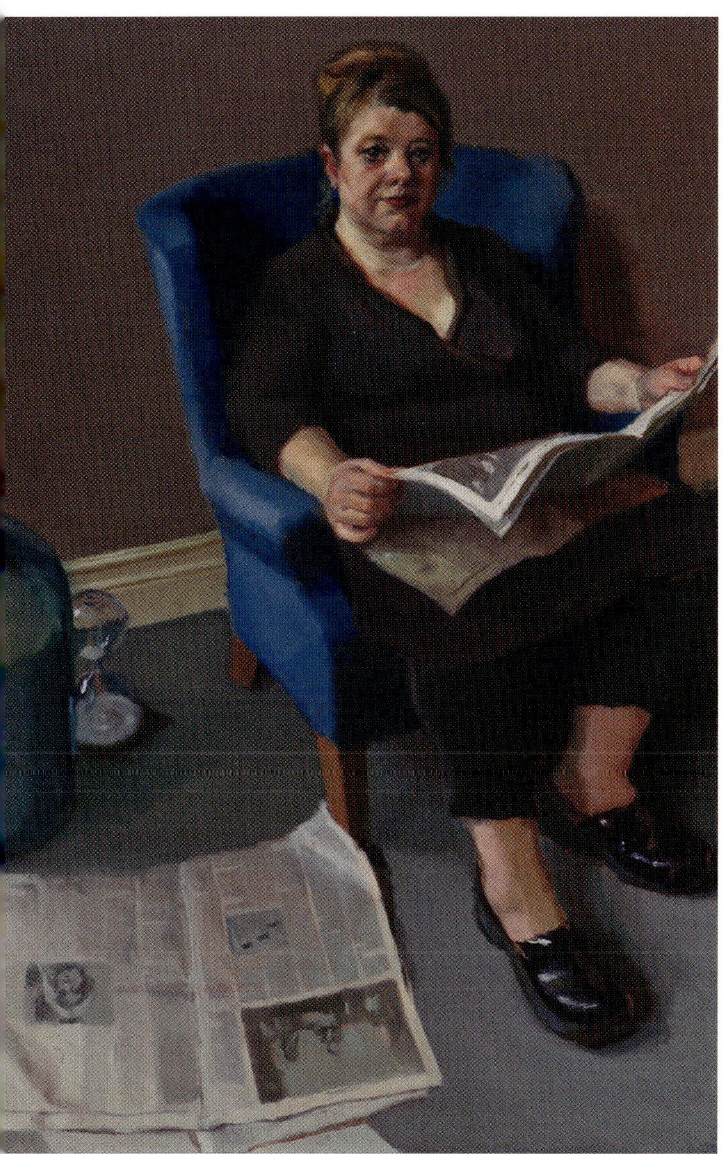

## DOMINANT LIGHT SOURCES AFFECT VALUES

By now you know that there is always a value difference between light and shadow when there is a dominant light source. In this case it is natural light coming from a window on the left. Squint at the subject to find your shadow areas. If there is an area that isn't clear, try moving around your subject and see if there's a view of that area that gives you a sharper difference. Then move back to your easel position, keeping your eye on that area.

Another trick is to cast a shadow on your subject using a thin brush. The brush won't cast a shadow on an area already in shadow.

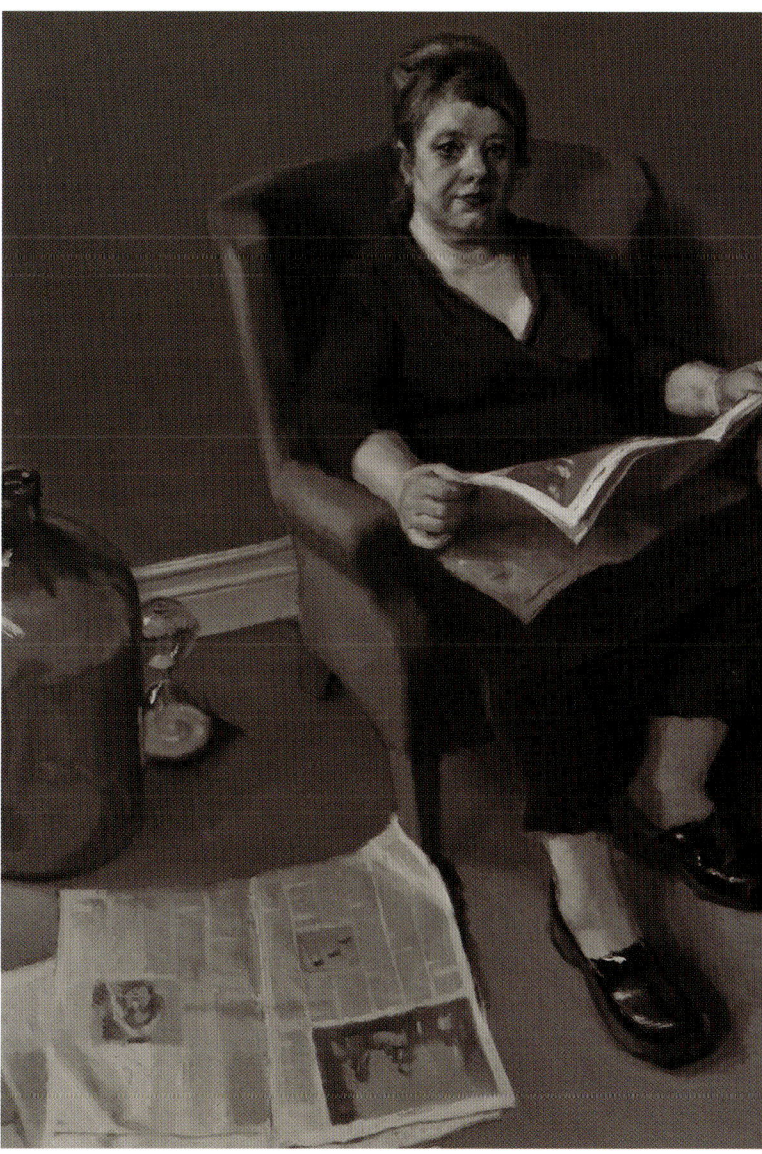

**The News**
Lea Colie Wight
Oil on linen
34" × 24" (86cm × 61cm)

### *It's All About Balance*

For a balanced composition it's important to have areas of quiet set against areas of detail. If there were an equal amount of information across the composition, the viewer most likely wouldn't know where to look.

# COMPOSITION STUDIES

The most effective way to understand composition is to study the compositions of others. Spend some time looking through books of paintings and visiting museums and galleries. Here are some things to consider when composing a painting:

- ***Abstract balance:*** A main element in composition is the balance and clarity of value masses.
- ***Direction:*** The direction of the model's gaze has an influence on the balance of the composition. If your model is placed on the right side of the canvas and her eyes are also looking to the right, the viewer will most likely follow her gaze right out of the canvas without lingering on any other elements in the painting. If, however, the gaze is turned toward the left and into the painting there are opportunities to direct the viewer around the body of the painting.
- ***Rhythm and focal points:*** Consider the balance between areas of detail, increased value, color differences and relative quiet. If a musical composition called for all instruments played at the same volume and tempo, there would be no rhythm. The same is true in painting. You may intend for a high-energy painting or a quiet composition. There are many choices.

By planning out your composition ahead of time, you determine how you want your painting to be balanced. You should always plan your composition, not be surprised by it. All of these elements—rhythm, balance, direction—come together to produce the effect you desire.

Paint sketches of compositions that please you. Use only three to five values in your sketches in order to keep the compositions as clear as possible. Doing composition sketches brings the added benefit of strengthening your simplification skills. Bring your full focus to this exercise and you'll find confidence in your ability to develop strong compositions.

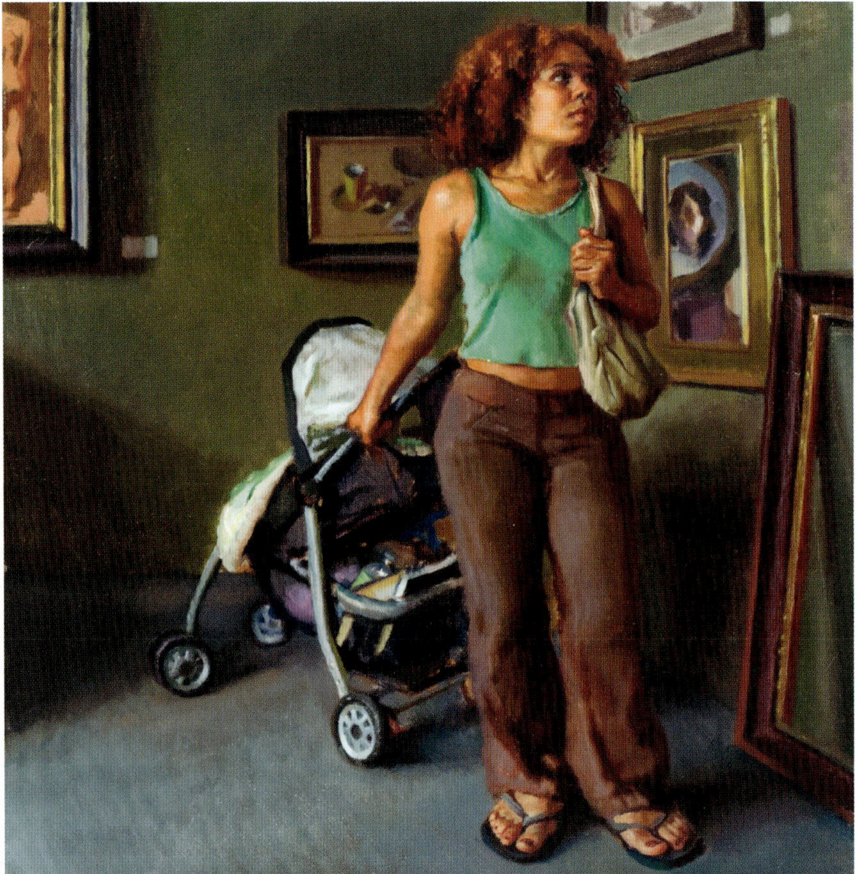

**Motherhood**
Lea Colie Wight
Oil on linen
20" × 20" (51cm × 51cm)

### VISUALIZE YOUR COMPOSITION

Your drawing has set boundaries. A vertical composition (a standing figure, for instance, or head and torso) requires that you decide where the top of the figure is and where the bottom is. You must keep the marks for the top of the head and the bottom of the feet in their set positions and not alter them.

In a horizontal composition such as a reclining figure, the set marks are on the right and left. Identify your focal point and where you want it to occur. If you work your way across without visualizing where you want your subject to end, you could easily wind up with an unintended composition.

In this painting, the head direction was an intentional statement and balanced by the value and detail of the stroller.

# VALUE STUDIES

An excellent way of discovering what makes a strong composition is to make thumbnail value studies of master paintings. The illustrations below are a few studies that I did.

Look at a good, comprehensive book on various painters or search online for museum collections. Execute thumbnail paintings like these studies, keeping them very simple. Spend only about 20 minutes or so on each to avoid getting too mired in detail.

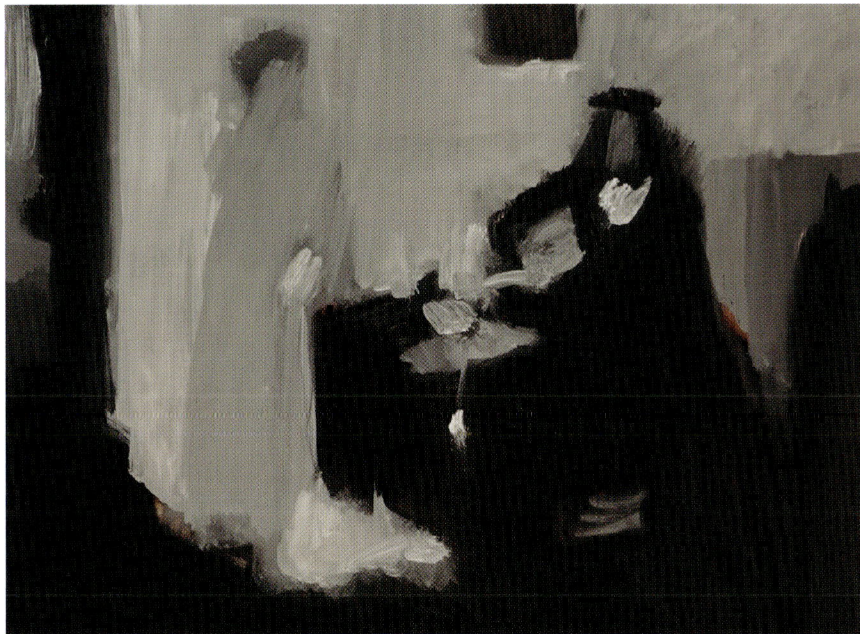

**Illustration for "The Perfect Marriage"**
Dean Cornwell

This is a beautifully balanced composition. There is an area of light and dark small shapes in the spot where the large light and dark masses meet. It's also an interesting composition because of the theme of the painting, which is the marriage between two people. The light area and the dark area combine to form a spiral meeting in the middle.

**Untitled**
Dean Cornwell

Dean Cornwell (1892–1960) was an American illustrator. He was superb at dynamic compositions. Here, the large, simple masses are balanced by areas of smaller detail.

### *Diagnosing Problems*

When you run into trouble with a painting and you're not sure what the problem is, diagnose it. Mentally recheck each stage from the beginning. Is your gesture still correct? If it is, move to your proportions. If you're still happy with your drawing, then check your values and so on. Eventually you'll find the problem.

Get into the habit of periodically taking these steps even if you haven't run into trouble. Quickly recheck your work before you move on and you should progress smoothly.

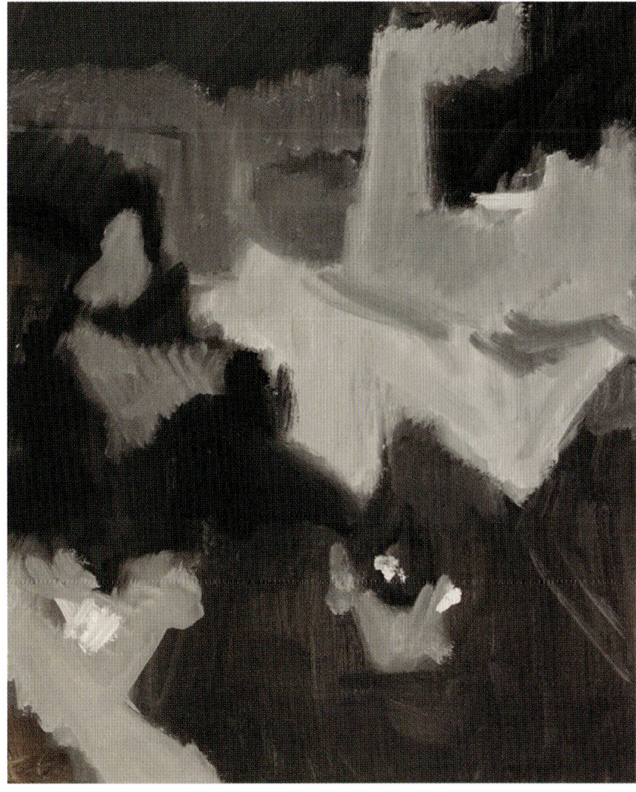

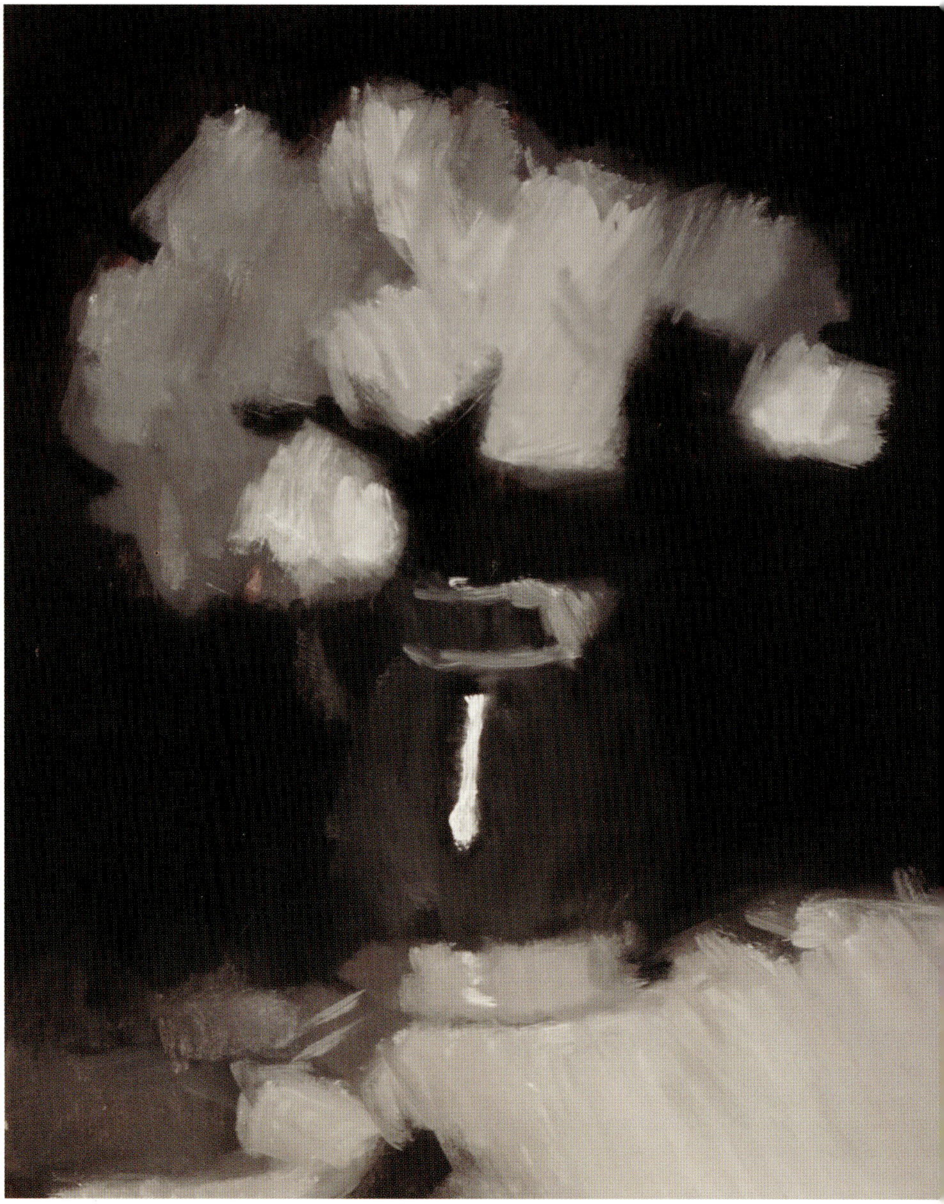

**White Tulips**
William Nicholson

The simple dark area is a good mass to set off the light areas that have more interest. The bright highlight on the vase connects the flowers to the table. The two light areas are also nicely designed with smaller shapes in the flowers and the simpler table top. The only detail on the table snakes from the lower left up to the vase.

**Mauve Primulas on a Table**
William Nicholson

This painting has a larger light mass that brings the eye from the top, sweeping right down to the lower left. The eye then jumps to the darker line of flowers and back up to the top. The large simple light mass is balanced by the detail in the dark areas.

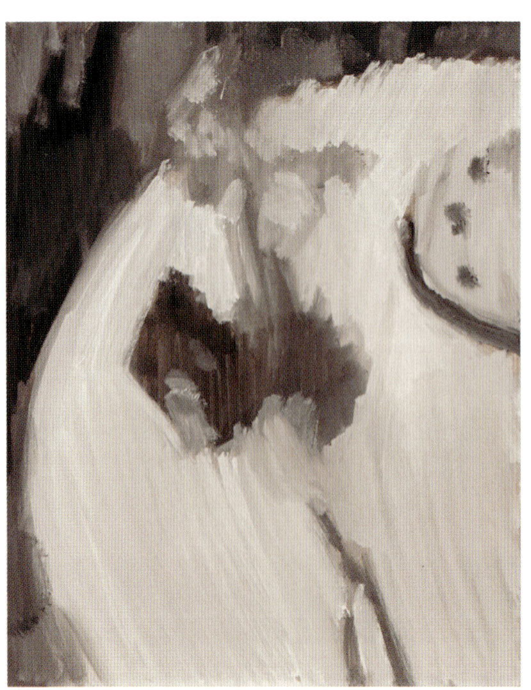

## *Focal Points*

When developing a focal point, think of where you want your viewer to look again and again. Ask yourself why that feature holds your interest. In a portrait it is usually an eye or the hands, which can be very revealing. A technique I use when developing a focal point is to look there and observe, out of the corner of my eye, how the edges surrounding it appear. How out of focus are they? This is what naturally happens when you look at something closely. There can be two or more focal points in a painting and usually are. This can lead the viewer's eye around the canvas. Think of where you want someone to stop and linger and then how their vision will travel to another moment.

## USING GUIDELINES

The second image shows connecting or extended lines that you can use to block in your composition. For example, the model's hand may move up and down along her thigh, and if you're not careful you can start chasing this and compromise your overall drawing. In that area, the primary and generally stationary relationship is from the right arm to the inside of the right leg and from the hairline to the outside of the left arm.

Get in the habit of visually extending lines throughout your painting to guide your drawing. Keep an eye on these lines as your painting progresses. If they no longer line up, then you know something needs correcting.

**Café**
Lea Colie Wight
Oil on linen
48" × 28" (122cm × 71cm)

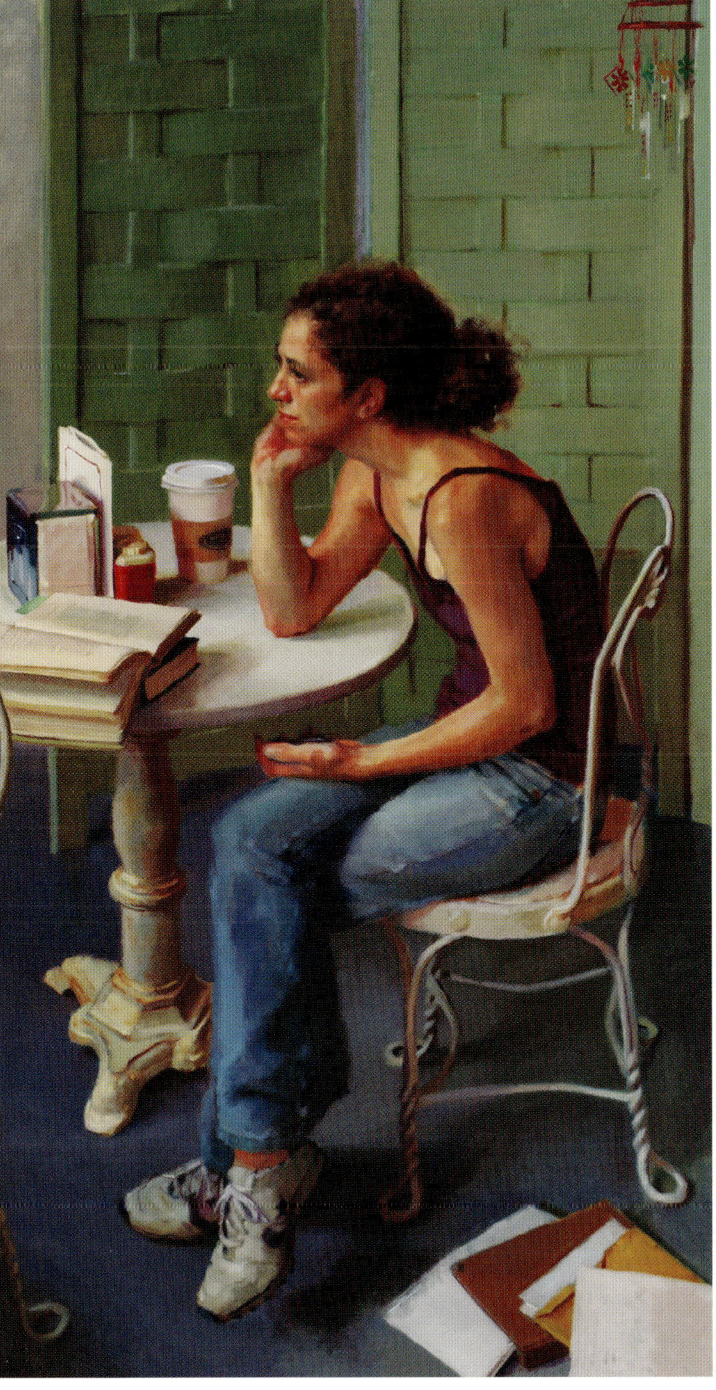

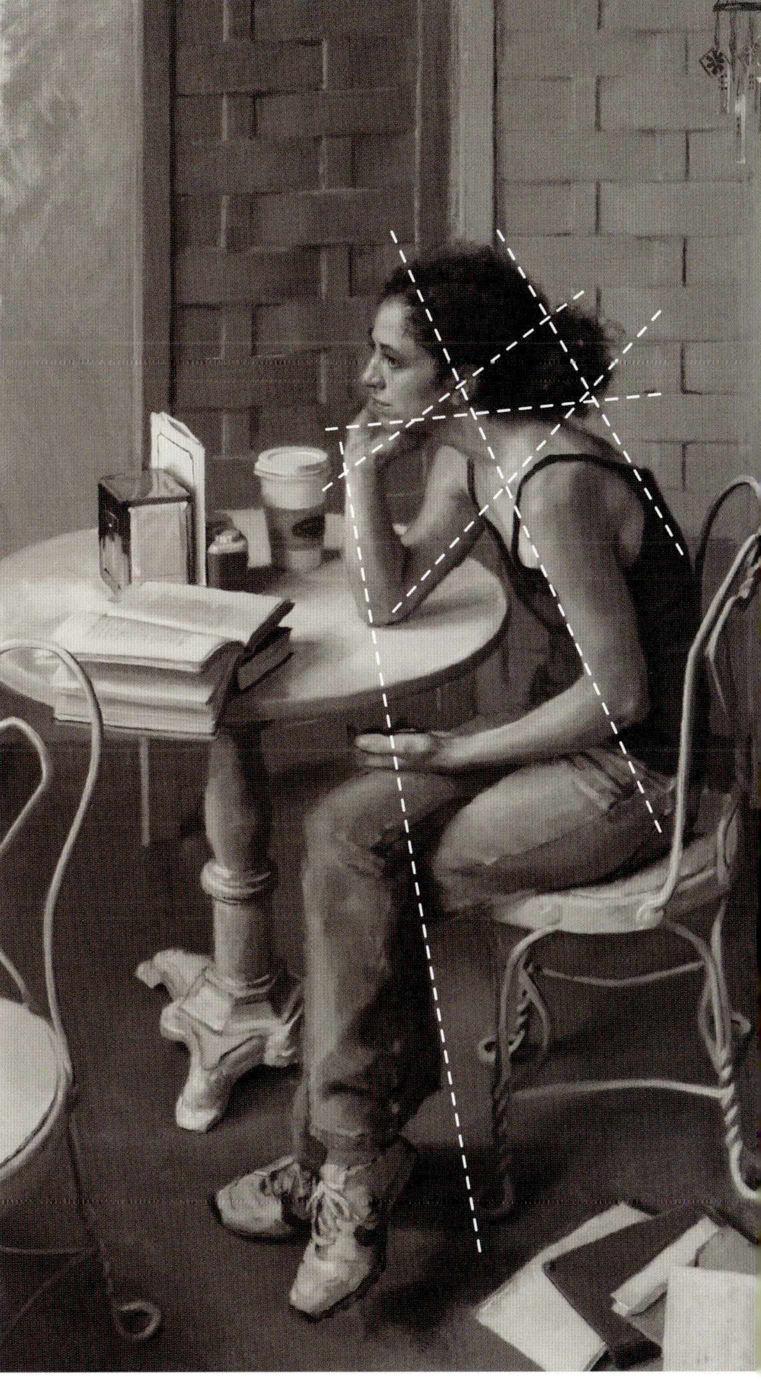

# COMPOSITIONAL STUDIES

Before you actually begin painting, it's best to first visualize the painting on your canvas and do some sketches of possible compositions. After deciding on your general composition, do some quick studies. The following images are all examples of preparatory studies I did for my painting, *Lauren,* on the previous page.

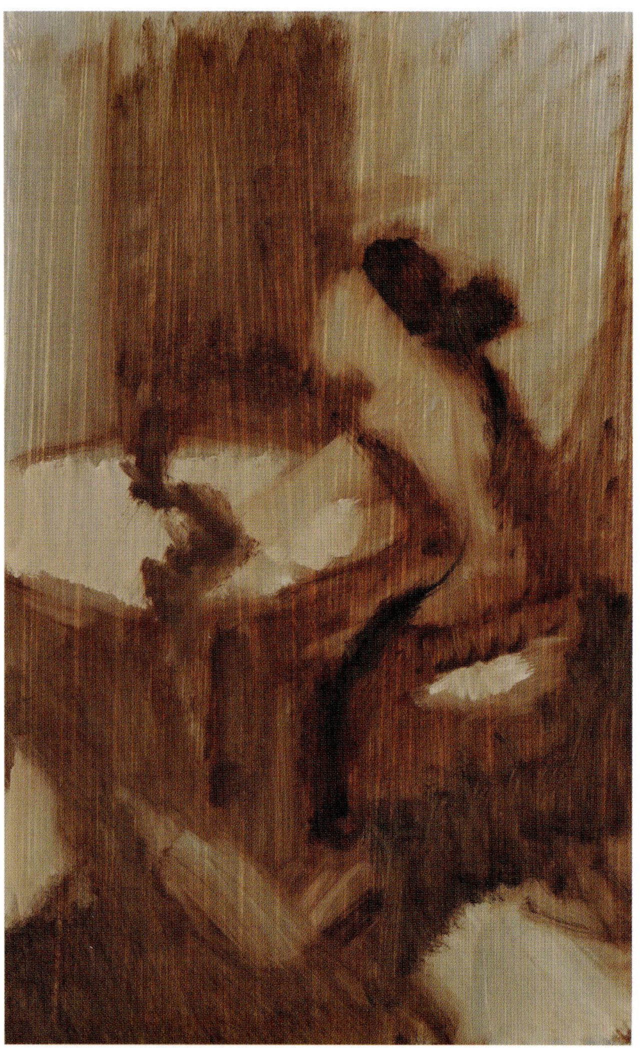

COMPOSITION STUDY

This simple composition study explores the largest light and dark pattern. A study like this will let the you see the balance of your composition and make easy adjustments. Simplify your subject into its largest value shapes, and study the balance of the composition.

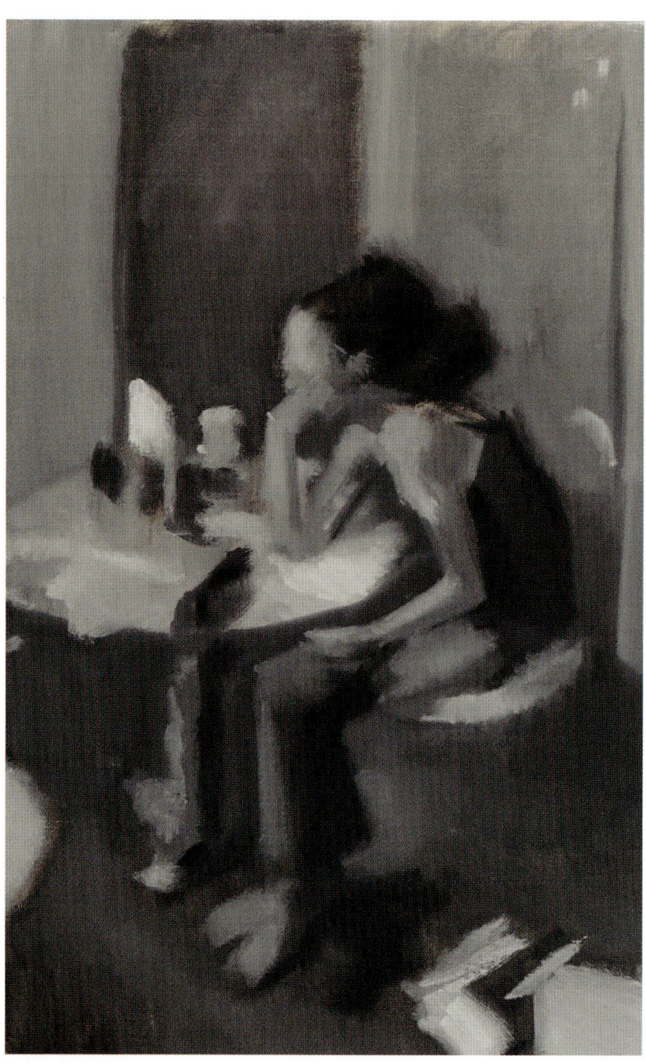

VALUE STUDY

This value study is more specific than the composition study. The goal of this study is to find the correct value relationships.

## *Where to Begin?*

When you start to work on your painting, begin with an area that isn't detailed—maybe the background or a large mass of color. This gets you warmed up and back in sync with the colors and values of the painting. Avoid jumping right into a detailed area. It's not a good idea to have to mix and test in a small area.

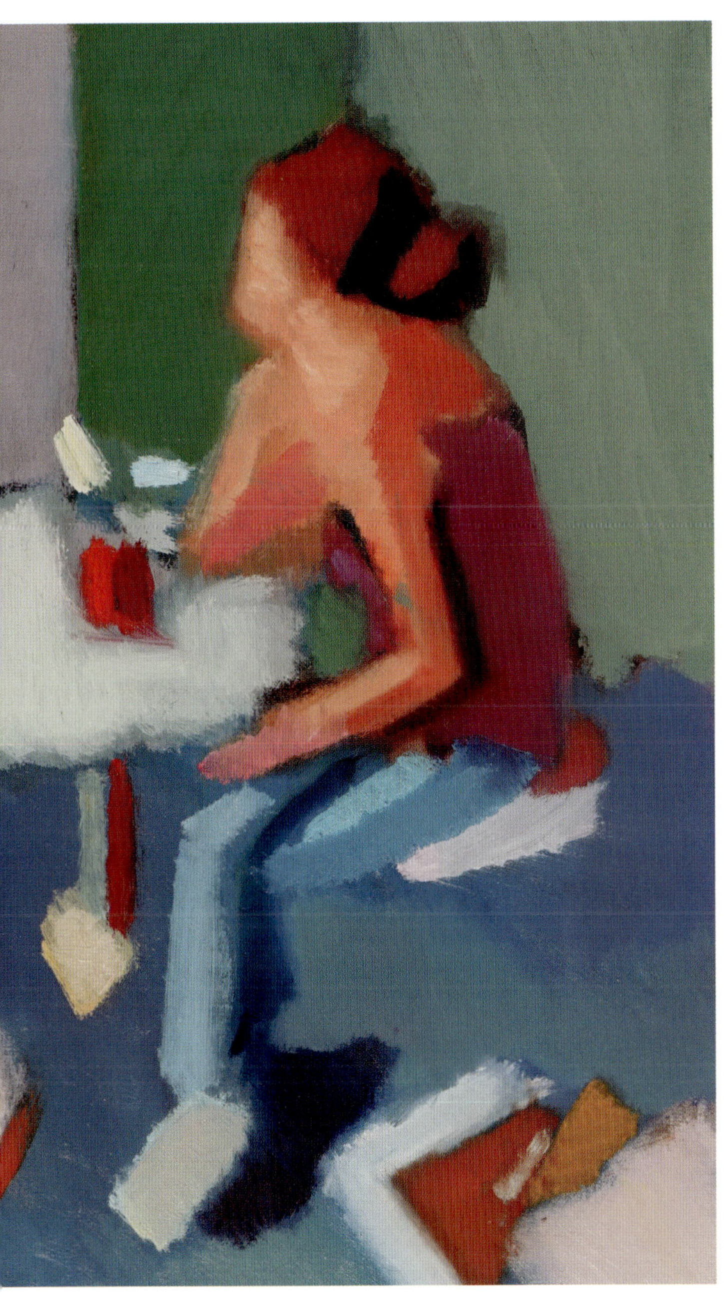

COLOR STUDY
A color study will allow you the opportunity to explore the basic, simple color relationships of the composition so that you may better see the more complex and subtle colors in the final painting.

## *Working from Photographs*

It's likely that you will find yourself needing to work from photographs for some paintings. Some compositions just can't be executed working strictly with live models. If you're knowledgeable about working from life, you'll know what a good reference photograph is and how to get the information you need from it.

However, if you don't have solid groundwork laid after working from life, it will show in your paintings. I've seen many paintings in which there is no understanding of structure, how forms overlap, what is going on in the shadows or a sense of dimension. They are simply the transferring of one flat surface to another, much like a high-quality print. I'll hear people say, admiringly, that it looks just like a photograph. Well, it does! If that is the artist's intention, that's completely valid and obviously successful. If, however, the artist's intention is to create a lifelike painting, it hasn't succeeded.

# 2 ANATOMY

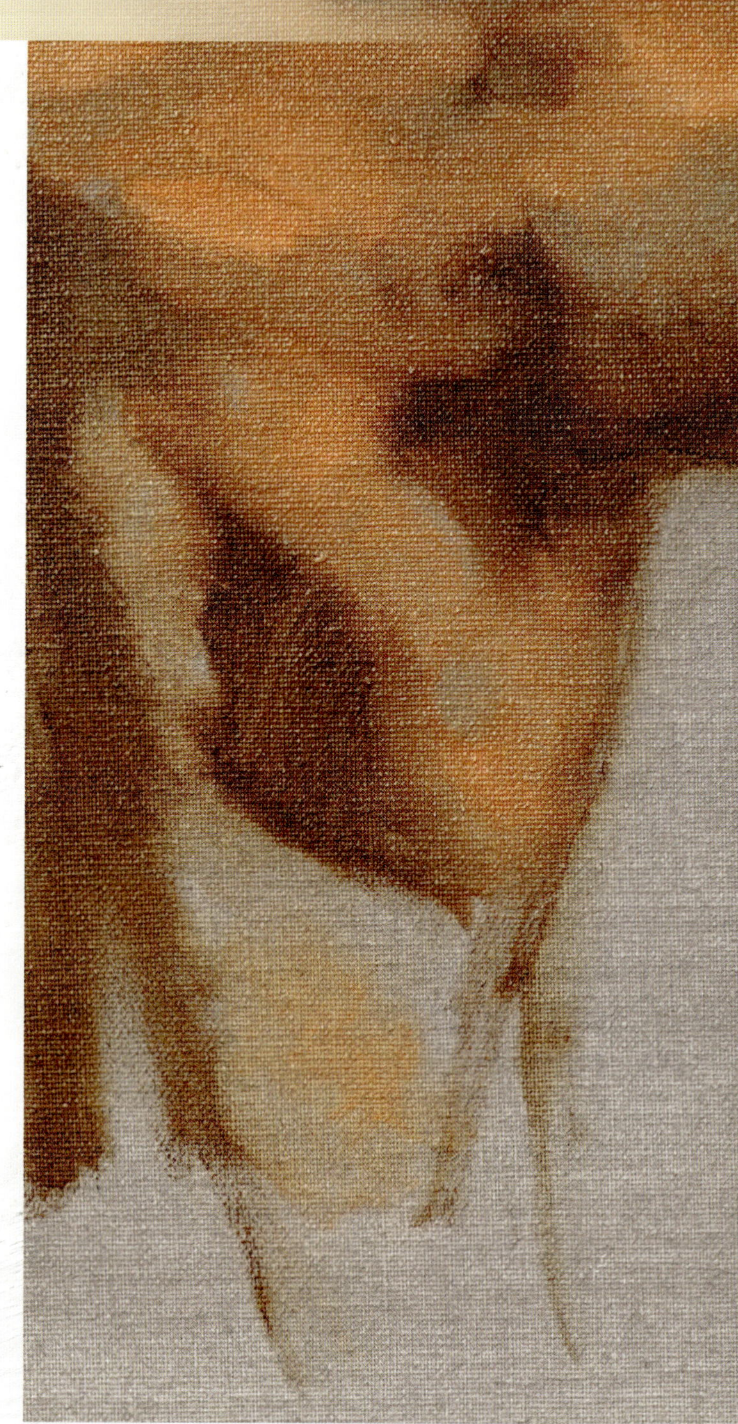

A familiarity with human anatomy is essential for any artist who's interested in painting or drawing people. This is equally important whether you're working with a nude or with a clothed subject, whether a cropped portrait or a full figure.

This chapter will give you some basic anatomical information, but it really just scratches the surface. There are many excellent books and videos dedicated solely to the study of anatomy, and I strongly recommend using them. I also suggest taking an écorché sculpture workshop, which focuses on the study of the human form from the skeleton through the muscles.

In addition to these resources, you have one right at hand—your own body! Feel your bones and joints to see how they work. Move, stretch and bend to identify your muscles. Then use this knowledge to relate to what you're seeing when you are with your model. Without this basic knowledge and understanding of anatomy, it's easy to make a blunder that will compromise an entire painting.

**Study of Arm Muscles**
Lea Colie Wight
Oil on canvas
16" × 20" (41cm × 51cm)

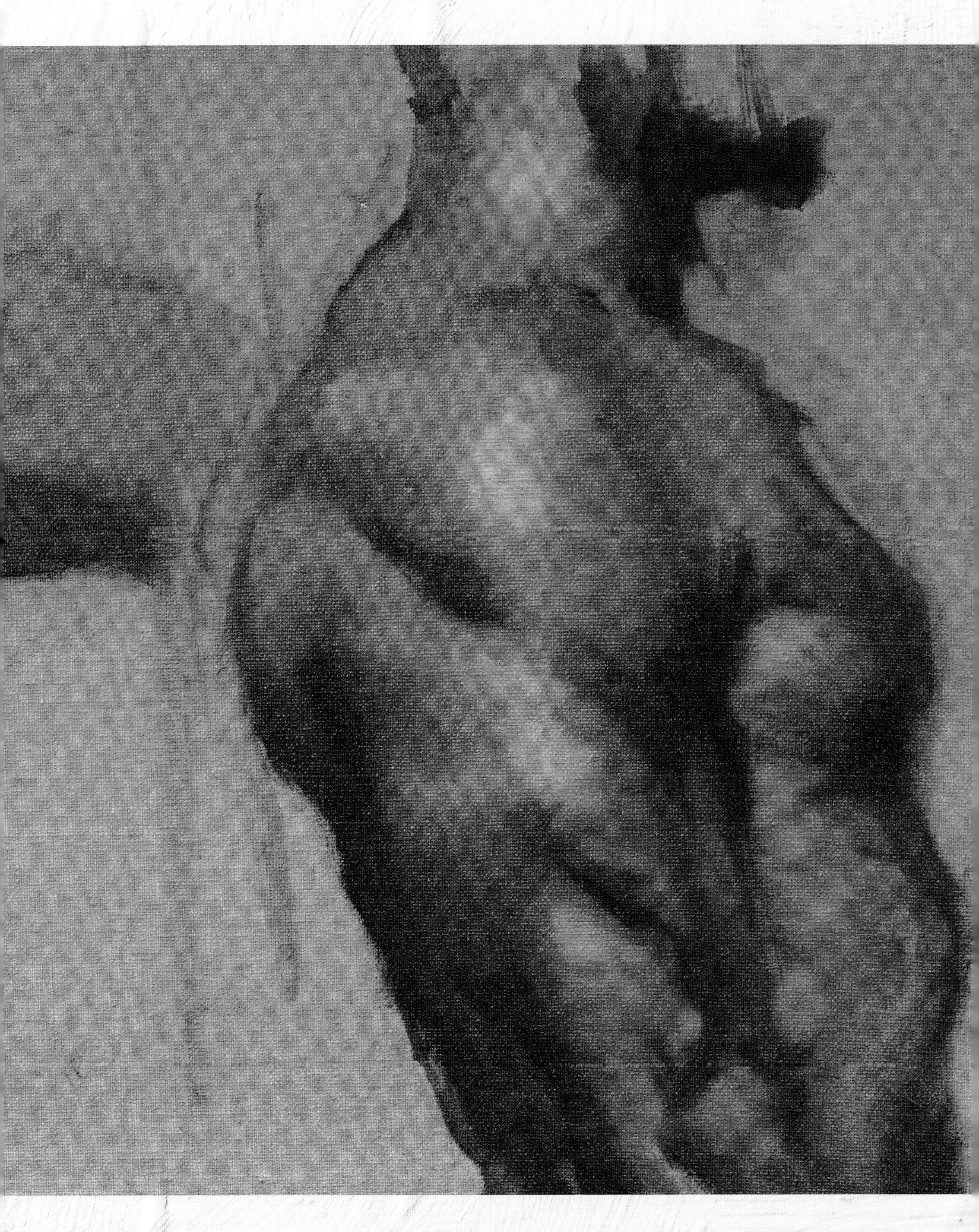

# ANATOMY & PLANES OF THE HEAD

An understanding of the skull is essential to a good portrait. All of the beautiful rendering of the features won't correct it. Without a good understanding of the shoulder girdle and that the neck is an extension of the spine, it's pretty hard to pull off a good portrait.

It's important to know, too, that what happens on one side of the body affects the other. When a person bends to the side, that side is compressed and you will see folds. The other side is extended and stretched. The body works in unison. When a neck is turned, the muscle running from the base of the skull to the clavicle stretches and shows clearly, while the same muscle on the compressed side is hidden.

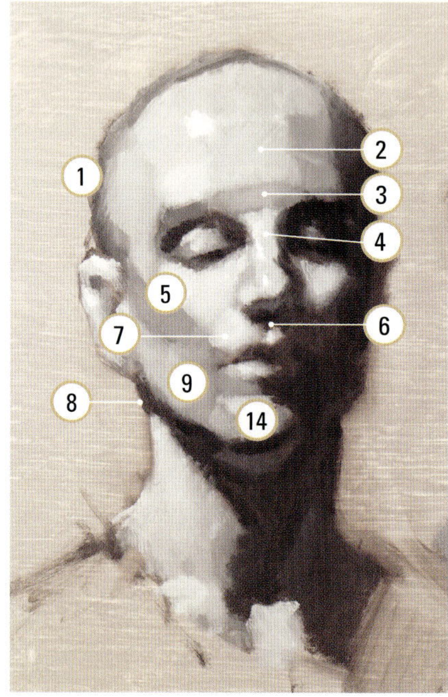


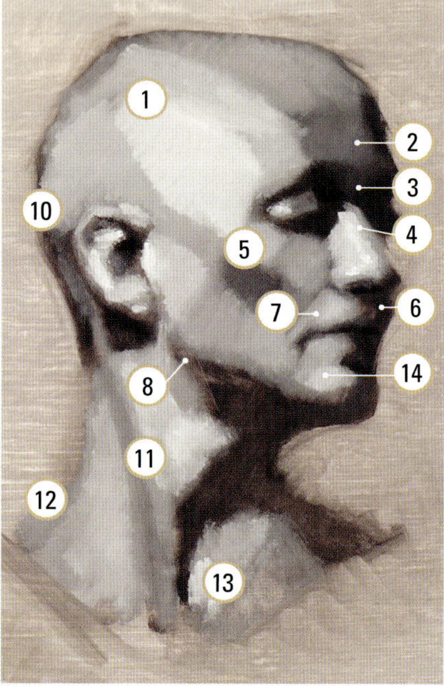


PLANES OF THE HEAD AND NECK
1. Peak of convexity; 2. Brow ridge; 3. Glabella (keystone); 4. Nasal bone; 5. Zygomatic arch; 6. Base of the nose; 7. Maxilla; 8. Angle of the jaw; 9. Mandible; 10. Occipital notch; 11. Sternocleido-mastoid muscle; 12. Trapezius muscle; 13. Sternal notch; 14: Mental protuberance or Tubercle

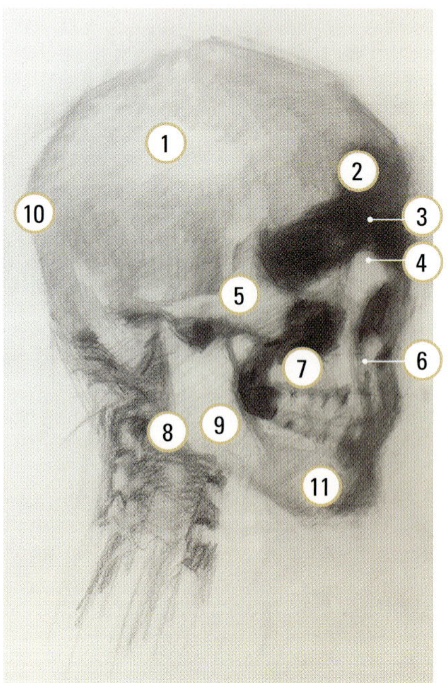


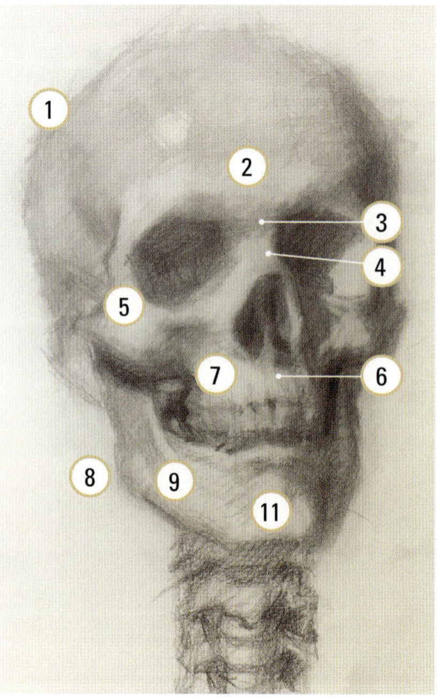


SKELETAL LANDMARKS OF THE SKULL
1. Peak of convexity; 2. Brow ridge; 3. Glabella (keystone); 4. Nasal bone; 5. Zygomatic arch; 6. Base of the nose; 7. Maxilla; 8. Angle of the jaw; 9. Mandible; 10. Occipital Notch; 11. Mental protuberance or Tubercle

# ANATOMY & PLANES OF THE BODY

I've seen many portraits where the shoulders extend out to oblivion or simply aren't there at all. A believable painting of a person should show, for instance, the correct point at which the leg joins the torso. If the artist isn't sure of this, the result could easily be that the leg joins sort of somewhere at the bottom of the torso rather than at the hip joint. Lack of knowledge about the human skeleton and muscles will show in a clothed figure as clearly as in a painting where form is exposed. It's easy to see whether there are shoulders under the shirt and whether the clavicles meet in the middle.

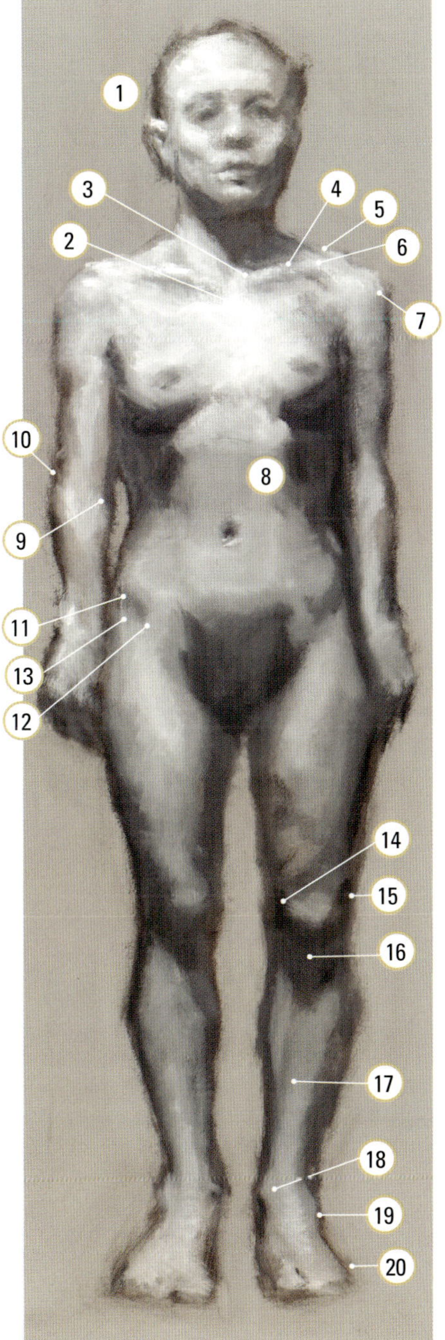


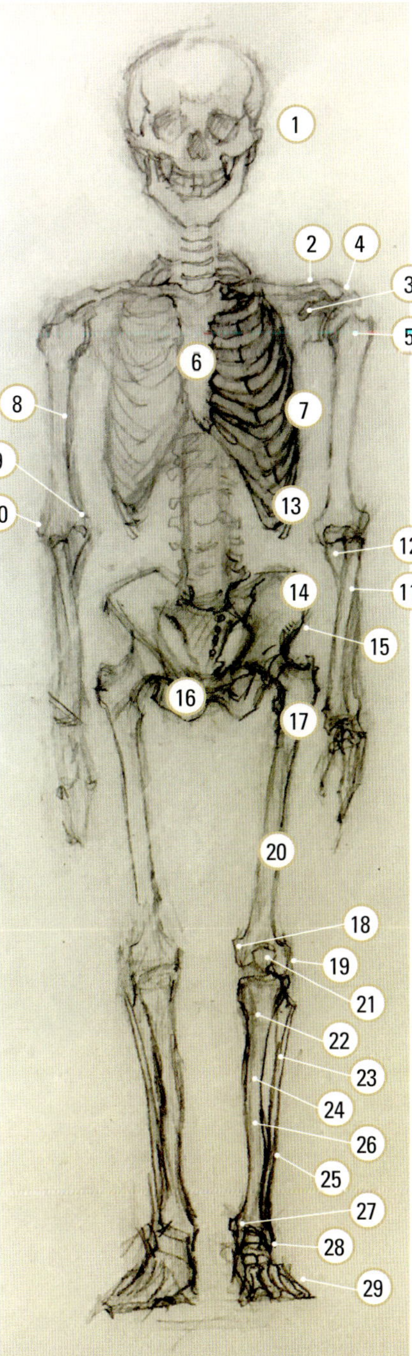


PLANES OF THE BODY, FRONT VIEW

1. Skull; 2. Sternum; 3. Sternal notch; 4. Clavicle; 5. Acromion process (top of the scapula); 6. Coracoid process (end of the clavicle); 7. Greater tubercle of the humerus; 8. Rib cage; 9. Medial epicondyle of the humerus; 10. Lateral epicondyle of the humerus; 11. Iliac crest; 12. ASIS; 13. Great trochanter; 14. Medial epicondyle of the femur; 15. Lateral epcondyle of the femur; 16. Patella; 17. Curve of the tibia (shin bone); 18. Medial epicondyle of the tibia (inner ankle bone); 19. Lateral epicondyle of the tibia (outer ankle bone); 20. Phalanges (toes)

SKELETAL LANDMARKS OF THE BODY, FRONT VIEW

1. Skull; 2. Clavicle; 3. Coracoid process; 4. Acromion process; 5. Greater tubercle of the humerus; 6. Sternum; 7. Rib cage; 8. Humerus; 9. Medial epicondyle of the humerus; 10. Lateral epicondyle of the humerus; 11. Radius; 12. Ulna; 13. 10th rib; 14. Iliac crest; 15. ASIS; 16. Pubic bone; 17. Great trochanter; 18. Medial epicondyle of the femur; 19. Lateral epicondyle of the femur; 20. Femur; 21. Patella; 22. Medial epicondyle of the tibia; 23. Lateral epicondyle of the tibia; 24. Tibia; 25. Fibula; 26. Curve of the tibia (shin bone); 27. Medial malleolus; 28. Lateral malleolus; 29. Phalanges (toes)

## PLANES OF THE BODY, SIDE VIEW

1. Skull; 2. 7th cervical vertebrae; 3. Clavicle; 4. Acromion process; 5. Greater tubercle of the humerus; 6. Spine of the scapula; 7. Medial border of the scapula; 8. Humerus; 9. Medical epicondyle of the humerus; 10. Lateral epicondyle of the humerus; 11. Iliac crest; 12. PSIS; 13. Great trochanter; 14. Lateral epicondyle of the femur; 15. Patella; 16. Tibia; 17. Lateral malleolus; 18. Calcaneus (heel); 19. Phalanges (toes)

## SKELETAL LANDMARKS OF THE BODY, SIDE VIEW

1. Skull; 2. Clavicle; 3. Coracoid process of the clavicle; 4. Acromion process; 5. Head of the humerus; 6. 7th cervical vertebrae; 7. Spine of the scapula; 8. Scapula (wing bone); 9. Spine; 10. Rib cage; 11. ASIS; 12. Iliac crest; 13. PSIS; 14. Coccyx (tail bone); 15. Pubic bone; 16. Great trochanter; 17. Femur; 18. Lateral epicondyle of the femur; 19. Patella head of the fibula; 20. Lateral epicondyle of the tibia; 21. Fibula; 22. Fibia; 23. Tibial tuberosity; 24. Curve of the tibia (shin bone); 25. Lateral malleolus; 26. Calcaneus (heel); 27. Phalanges (toes)

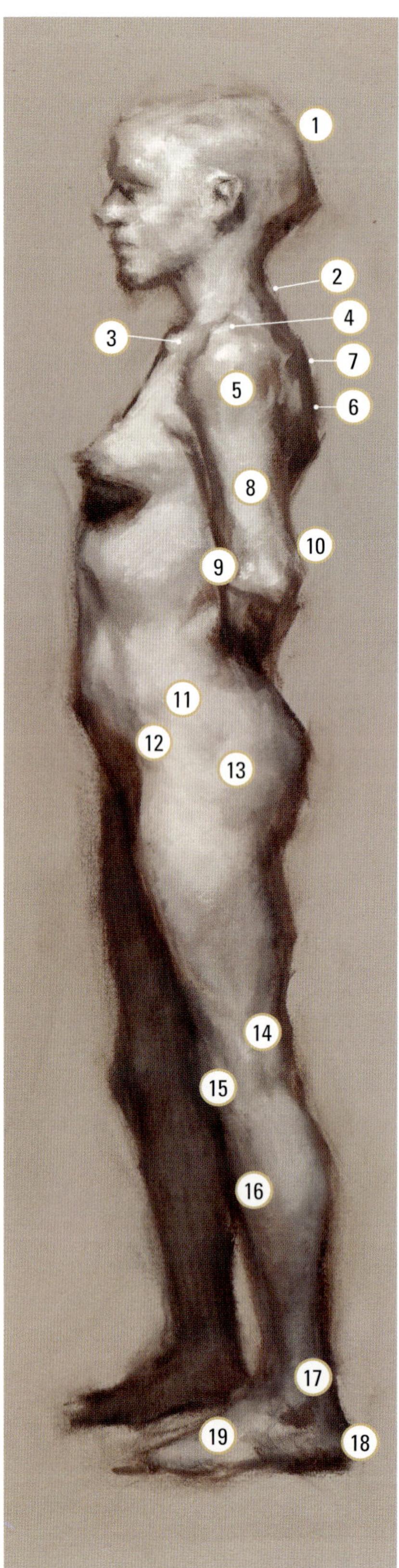


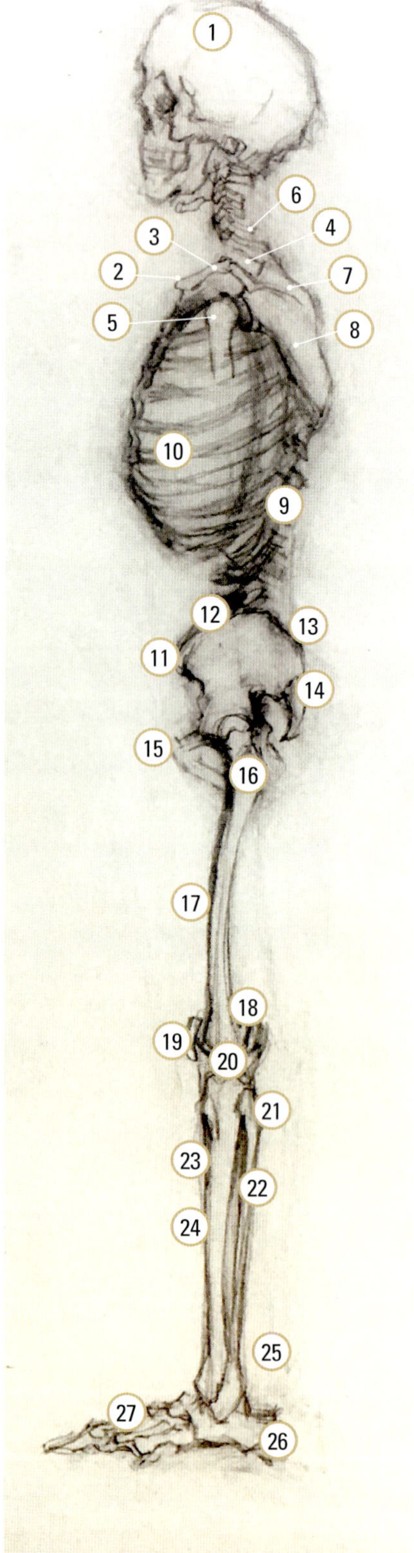

# MUSCLES

If you're worried about remembering the technical names of each landmark or muscle, don't worry. The most important thing is to recognize them for what they are and how they work—to know a muscle from a fatty area, and to know the difference between what a flexed muscle looks like compared to one at rest.

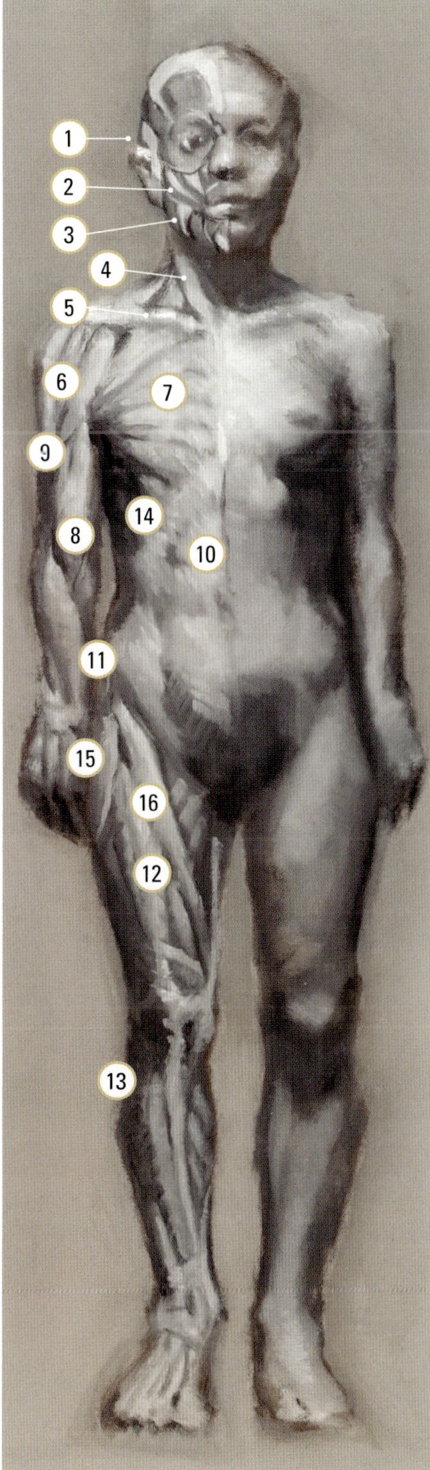


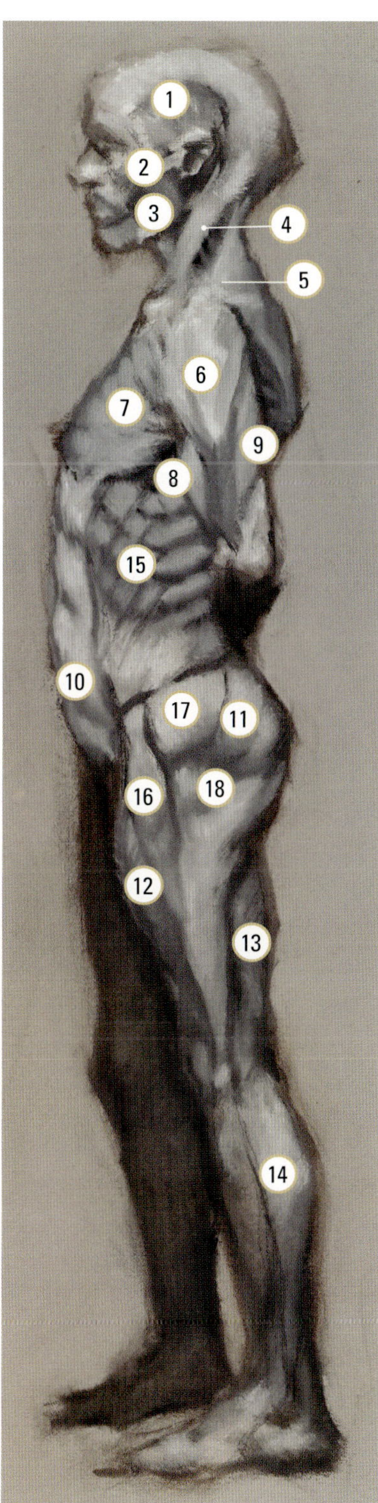


MUSCLES, FRONT VIEW

1. Temporalis; 2. Zygomaticus; 3. Masseter; 4. Sternocleidomastoid; 5. Trapezius; 6. Deltoid; 7. Pectoralis; 8. Biceps; 9. Triceps; 10. Rectus abdominis; 11. Gluteus maximus; 12. Quadriceps; 13. Gastrocnemius; 14. External obliques; 15. Tensor fasciae latae; 16. Sartorius

MUSCLES, SIDE VIEW

1. Temporalis; 2. Zygomaticus; 3. Masseter; 4. Sternocleidomastoid; 5. Trapezius; 6. Deltoid; 7. Pectoralis; 8. Biceps; 9. Triceps; 10. Rectus abdominis; 11. Gluteus maximus; 12. Quadriceps; 13. Hamstrings; 14. Gastrocnemius; 15. External obliques; 16. Tensor fasciae latae; 17. Sartorius; 18. Great trochanter (landmark)

# BONY LANDMARKS

As an artist, it's necessary to understand what you're seeing and to be able to simplify the complex form into clear structure. There is a lot of important information hidden under the skin, and there are universal landmarks on each human body. These landmarks occur at fixed skeletal points where bone is close to the surface.

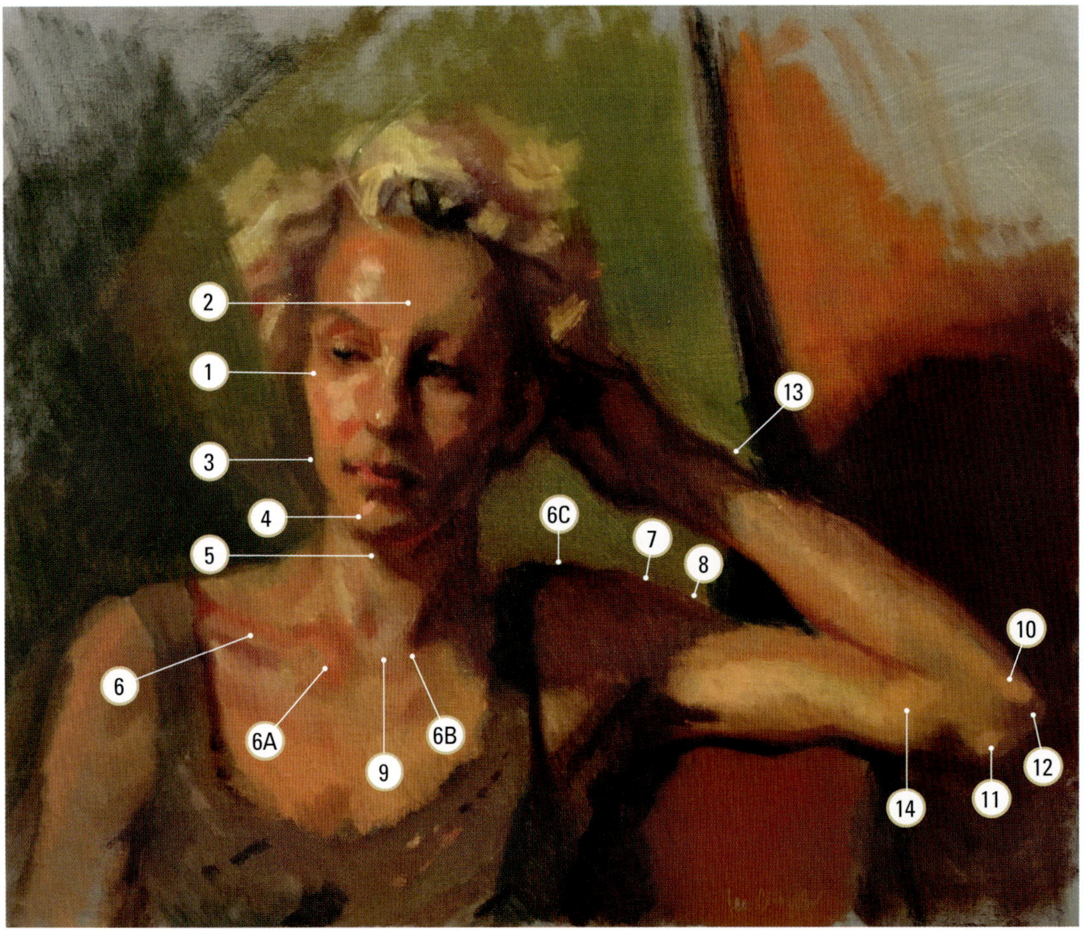


**Three-Hour Portrait Study**
Lea Colie Wight
Oil on canvas
18" × 20" (46cm × 51cm)

### IDENTIFYING BONY LANDMARKS

Here you can see the bony landmarks as they appear in a painted figure. These are spots where the bone comes closest to the surface, which let you know the structure underneath the form you are painting is accurate. Knowledge of the skeletal framework is essential to understanding form. If you look at number 14, you will see that it is not a bony landmark but simply a fat pad that appears when the arm is bent. These forms can often be misleading.

1: Zygomatic Bone; 2: Glabella; 3: Angle of the ramus or mandible; 4: Tubercle; 5: Sternocleidomastoid muscle (muscle running from the clavicle and sternum to the skull); 6: Clavicle (collar bone); 6A: Clavicle (sternal head); 6B: Clavicle (sternal head hidden by shoulder position); 6C: Clavicle (acromial end); Scapula (acromion); Humerus (greater tubercle, hidden in this position); 9: Pit of the neck (sternal notch); 10: Ulna (olecranon); 11: Humerus (medial epicondyle); 12: Humerus (lateral epicondyle); 13: Radius (styloid process); 14: Compressed fat mass (not a bony landmark!). Note that 6B, 7 and 8 make up the acromion process.

# HANDS & FEET

The only way to become accomplished at painting hands and feet is to set it as a goal. Just do it! You'll get tired of always painting hands in pockets and people at the beach in boots.

The best way to approach hands is to look at their overall shape as mittens. Don't think about the individual fingers. Remember that the hand is an extension of the arm and look for the long lines from the wrist to the tips of the fingers. From there, build your hand by looking for the next most obvious thing you notice when you squint. Eliminate any information you don't see, even if you know it's there. Only put in what you see at a glance.

Approach feet in the same way.

## THE EARLY STAGES OF PAINTING HANDS

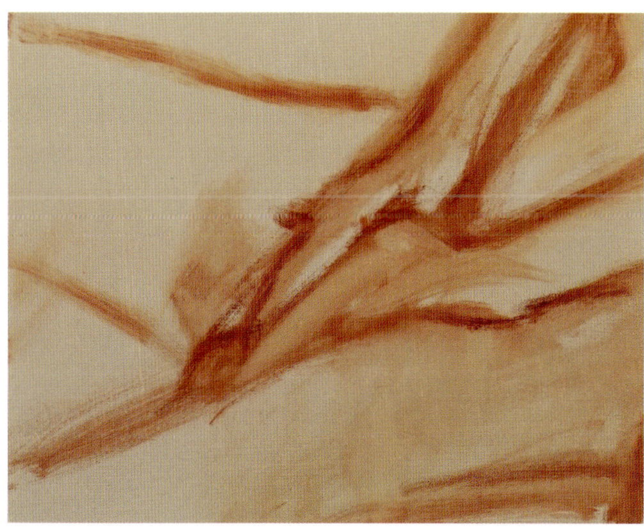

1. The gesture—simple shapes with the hands painted as a mitten shape.

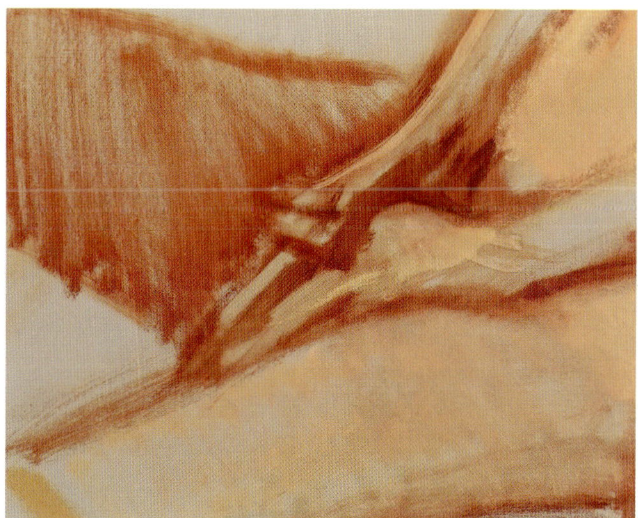

2. A bit of color is added for shaping.

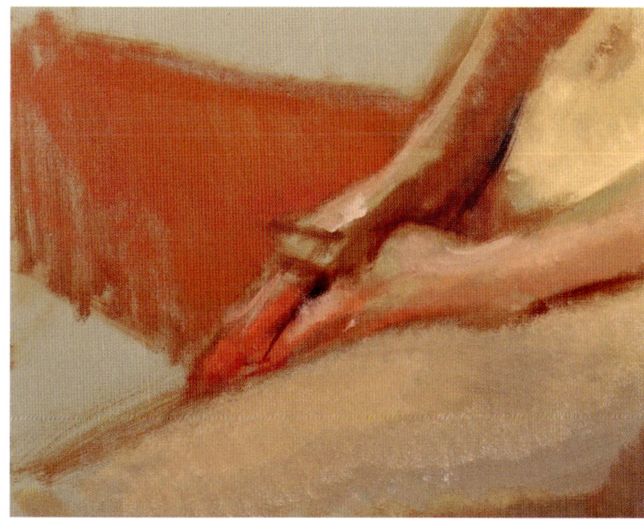

3. The first real color notes are placed for color comparison.

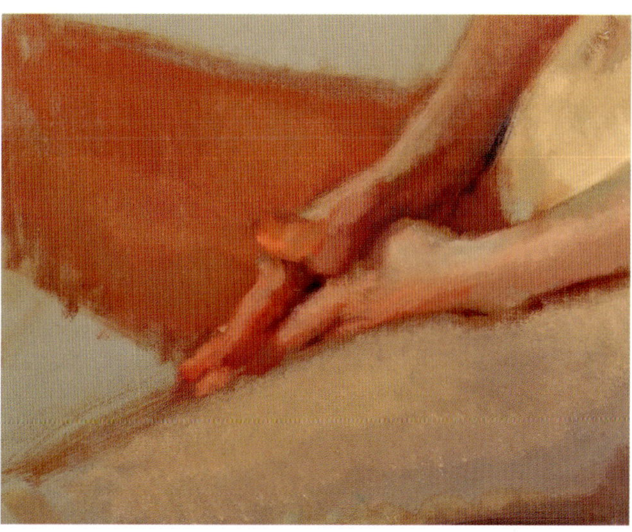

4. Now you're on the way to developing the hands as the rest of the painting progresses.

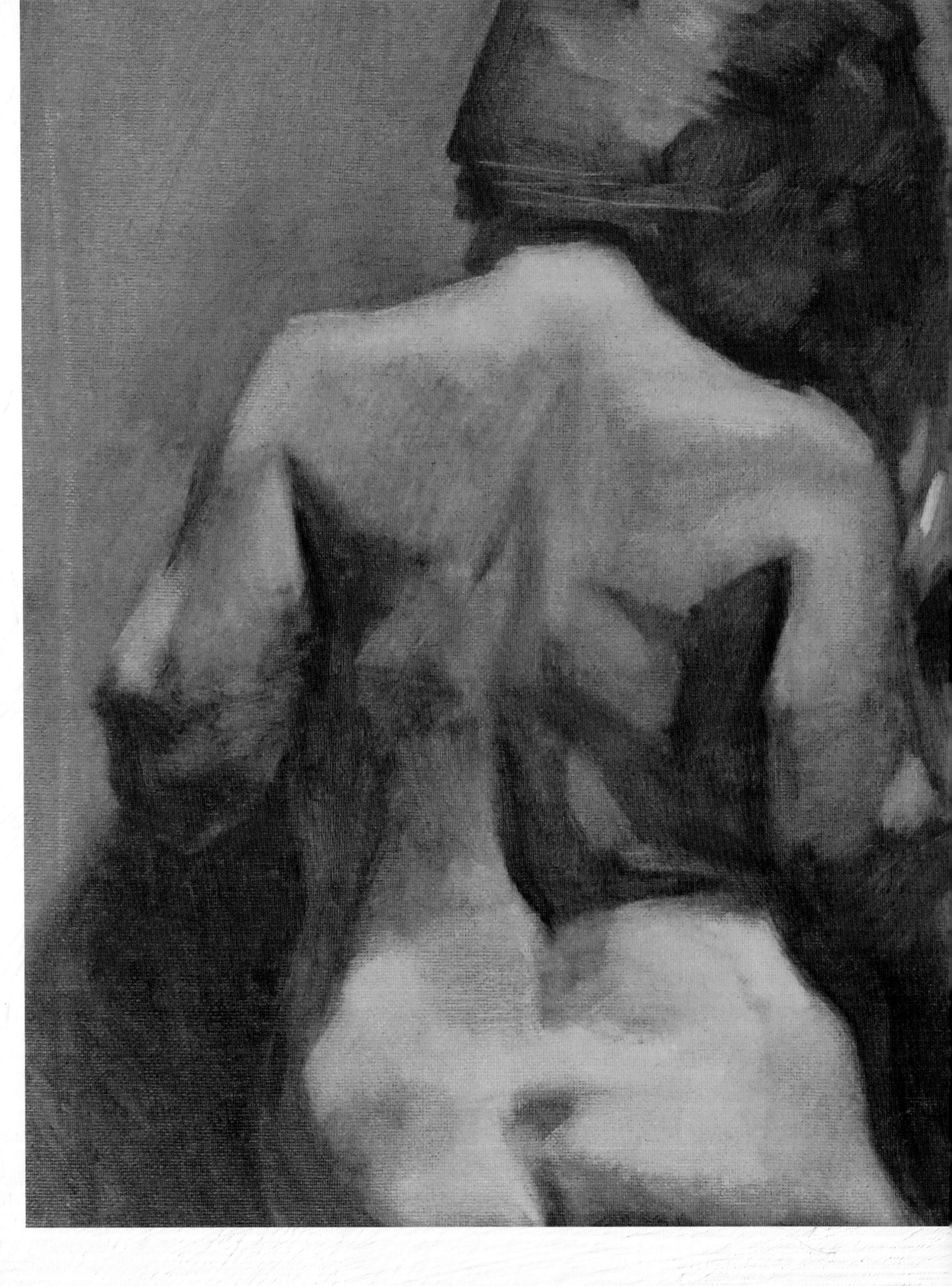

# 3 GESTURE *and* GRISAILLE

This chapter deals with the building stages that are critical to a successful realistic painting. These stages form a natural progression and are the same regardless of the subject matter or your timeline.

- ***The Gesture:*** This is where you make your first marks—a few swift lines that capture the very basic shape or movement of the subject.
- ***Open Grisaille:*** In this stage you begin massing in shadows and adjusting light areas.
- ***Closed Grisaille:*** Here you are working with just enough paint to shape the forms, and you will begin developing the values.

Becoming skilled at the individual stages takes practice and repetition, but in time, you'll see marked improvement. The more time you spend building a painting, the less time you'll spend correcting it later on.

**Figure Study, Open Grisaille**
Lea Colie Wight
Oil on linen
16" × 20" (41cm × 51cm)

# GESTURE

The first step in building any painting or drawing should be a strong gesture taking in the entire subject. This should be few quick action lines taking no more than 10 seconds—too fast for indecision.

If your subject is living, a human or animal, an energetic gesture captures their movement and essence. Imagine that you're a choreographer and you're taking notes of movements to recall later on. Your goal is to capture the essence of the dancer's motion, not his eyebrows.

If your subject is a still life or landscape, do a very fast compositional gesture. Don't worry about the exact measurements or detail. All that will come as the paining is developed. Have confidence in your ability and try to build up from the simplest things you see.

KEEP IT SIMPLE

Don't make things difficult for yourself by starting out with a complicated, exaggerated pose. As your painting develops it will undoubtedly become stiffer and less energetic, and it will likely no longer capture the movement. Keep the initial gesture in place all through your painting. Keep checking back to see if you can still see it. Maintain a balance between correctness and energy.

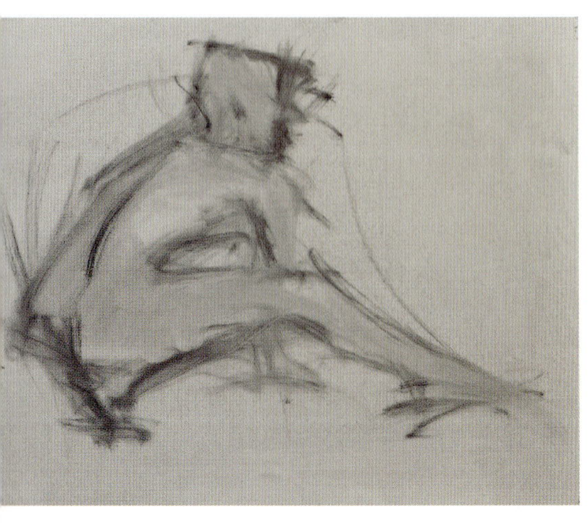

***Demonstration***

# CAPTURE GESTURE

Follow the steps to practice capturing gesture. Try several variations of poses. Have your model change poses every 30 seconds. Keeping the poses short can feel really nerve-wracking at first, but the idea is to work so quickly that you don't second guess yourself. When the model changes poses, wipe the gesture off and start the new one. When the model takes a break, use the time to give your canvas a really good wipe down. Keep only the gestures you're happy with and think are good examples.

## *Materials*

SURFACE
stretched canvas

OIL PAINTS
Burnt Umber or black

BRUSHES
Silver Brush #1034 size 3 or 4 long bristle filbert

OTHER
odorless mineral spirits or Gamsol
paper towels

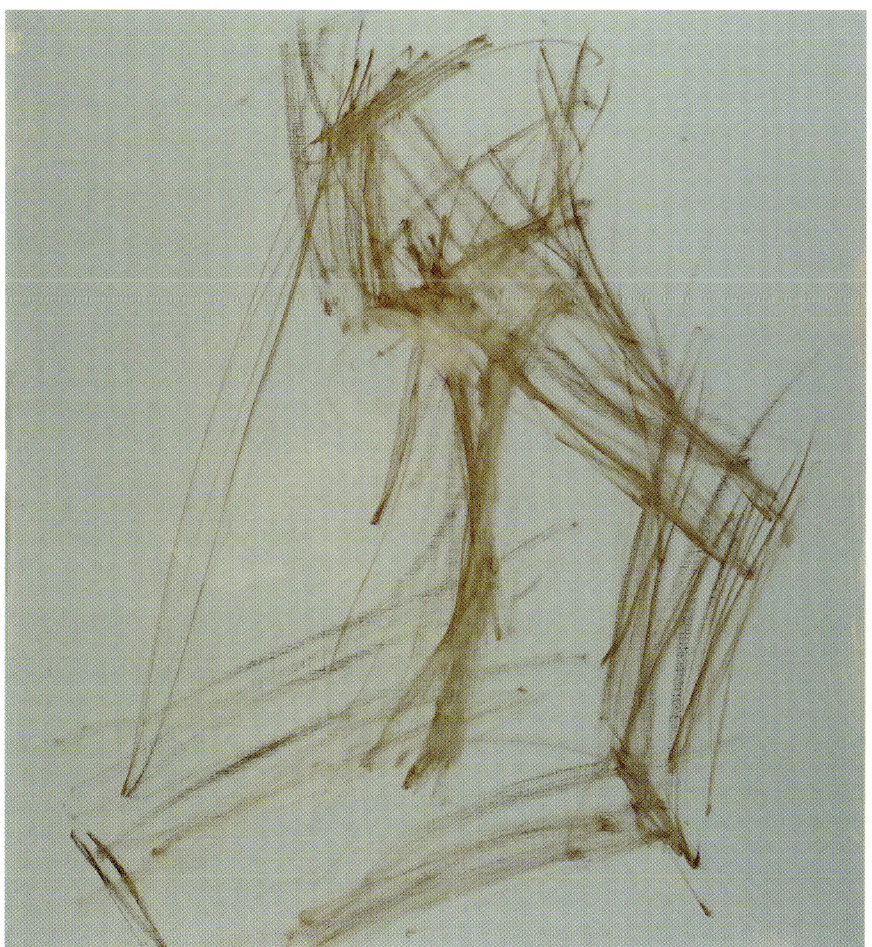

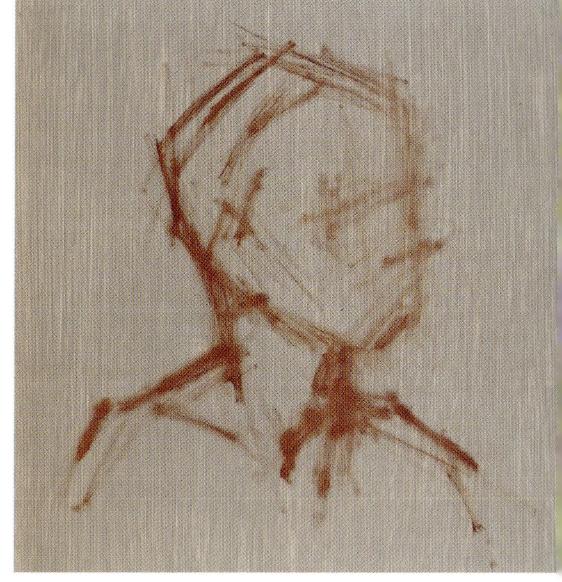

### 1 BLOCK IN THE MAIN GESTURE LINES

Dip your brush in your solvent and wipe it well to take off most of the moisture. Pick up a little Burnt Umber or black with the tip of the brush and move it around on your palette until it's not thin enough to be runny and not thick enough to be clumpy. The amount of paint you need on your brush will change as you paint because of repeated cleaning, so keep an eye on it.

Avoid completed shapes where the lines end at a specific point and new lines begin. The idea of open lines crossing each other gives the artist the feeling of freely adjusting rather than deciding an exact spot. Straight lines, curvy lines or arcs—experiment to see which approach feels the most natural to you. The important thing is to be loose and energetic, and to find the simplest interpretation of the pose from top to bottom.

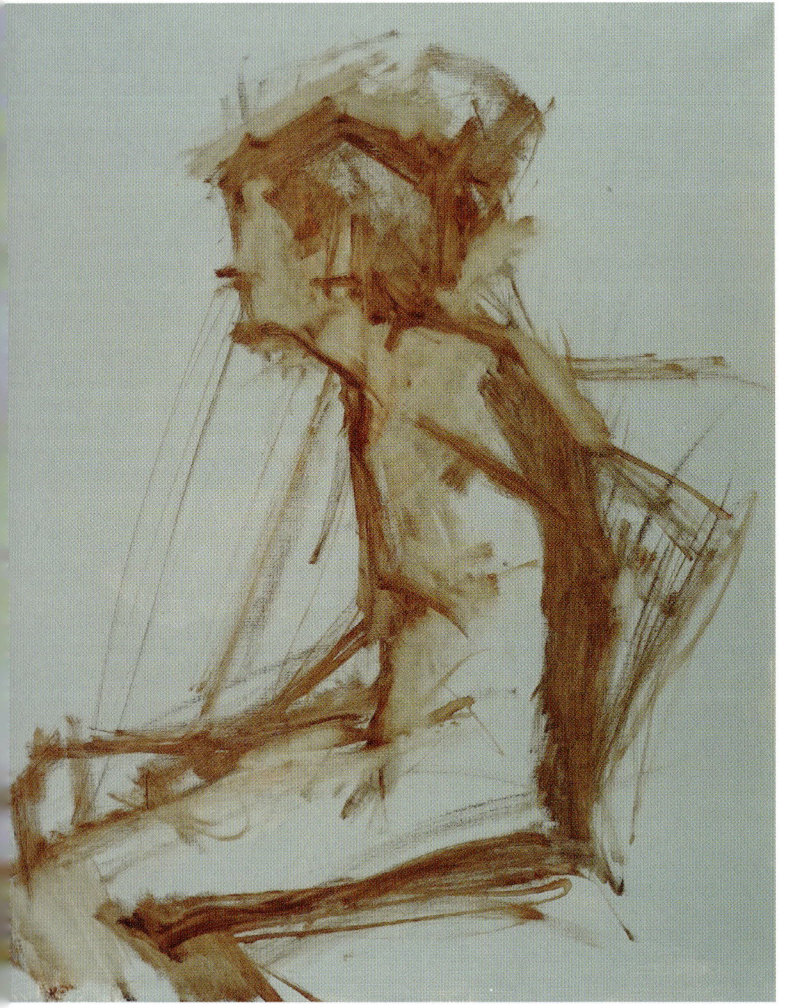

## *Paint Consistency*

Always brush your paint around on the palette first so that it has the consistency you desire when you apply it to the canvas.

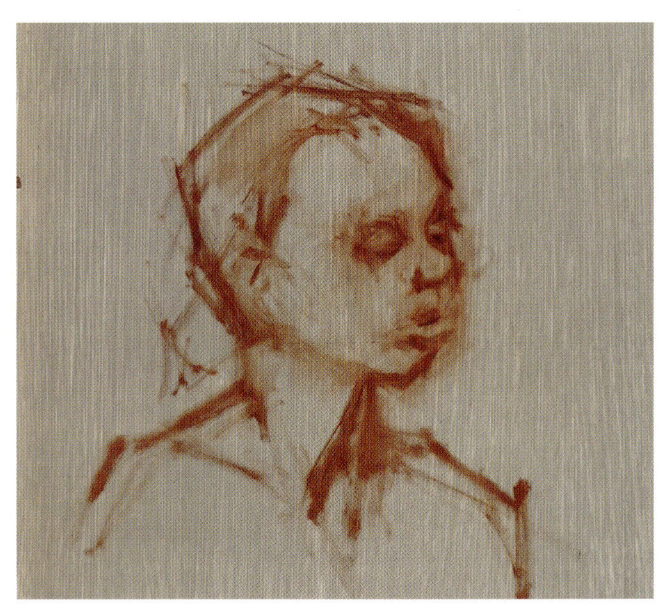

### 2 DEVELOP AND CORRECT THE GESTURE

Once you have a good strong energetic gesture, stand back and study the subject and your canvas. Carry your vision back and forth and make a judgement as to the largest division you see. In a standing pose it may be the waist, but remember that every pose is different. Let your eyes calmly, without rush, look back and forth, back and forth. Soon you will see the areas where adjustment and development are needed.

Keep moving forward in this way, building up and refining the gesture until you have the basic shape and proportions of the figure in place.

## SUGGESTED EXERCISE

Head outside and do some quick sketches of people going about their day. Grab their gestures as quickly as you can because they could move at any moment.

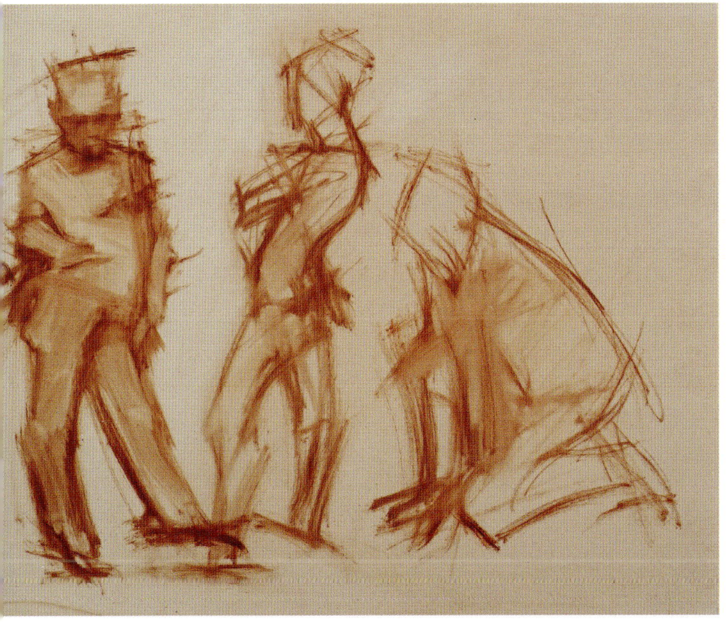

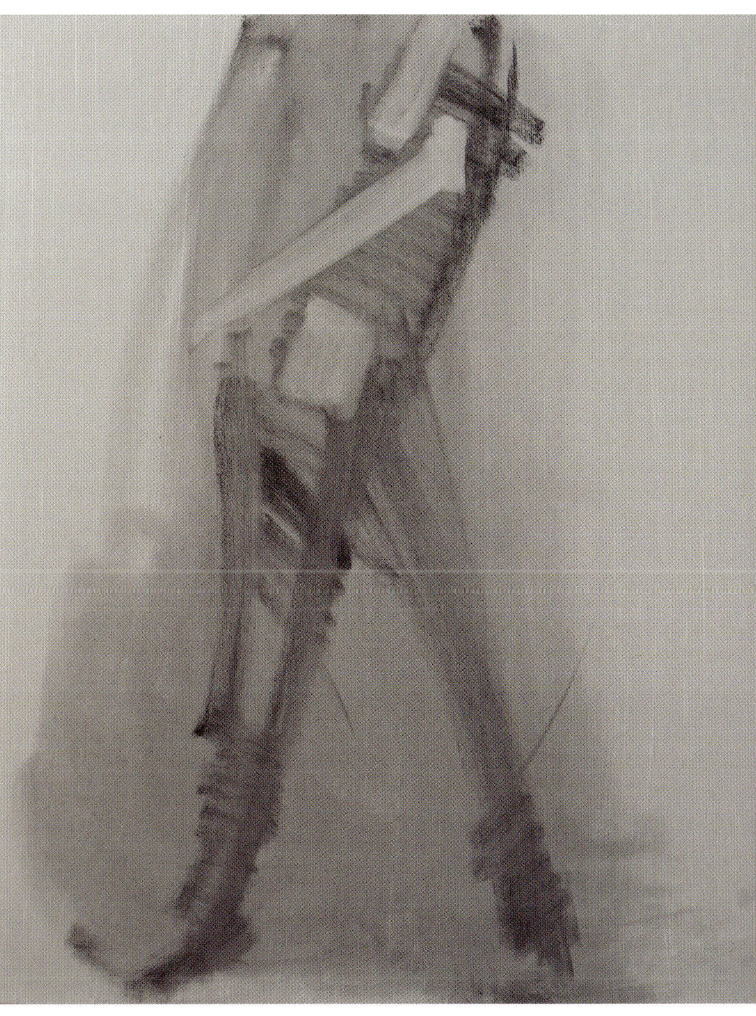

**Gesture**
JaFang Lu
20" × 16" (51cm × 41cm)

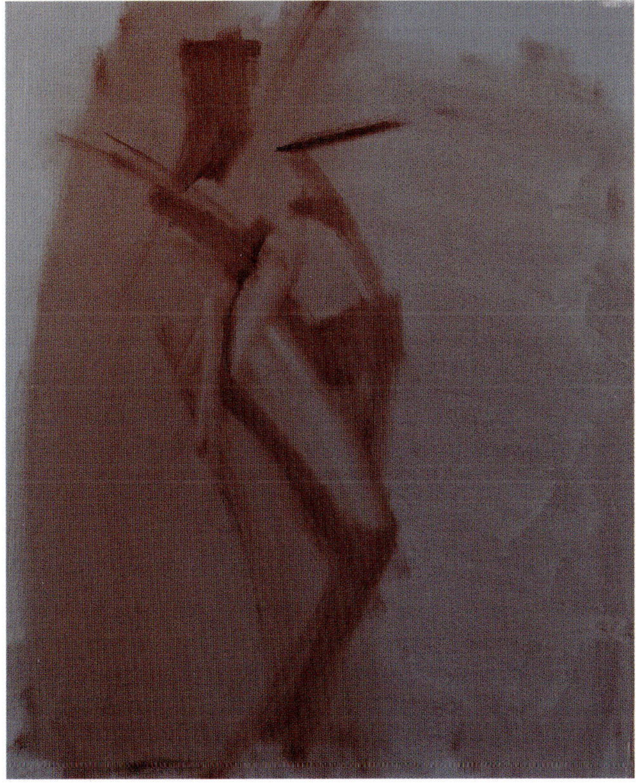

**Gesture**
JaFang Lu
20" × 16" (51cm × 41cm)

### *Check Your Brush Length*

Gesture exercises really wear down brushes. You can check your brush length by comparing it with an unused brush.

## DIFFERENT SUBJECTS, SAME PROCESS

Whether you are painting a figure, a portrait, a still life or a landscape, your approach for capturing the gesture should be the same regardless of the subject. When you're beginning a still life or landscape, envision your composition on the canvas before you pick up your brush. Try to see the largest gesture. No amount of detail will correct your painting if the biggest statement is wrong.

Start with big shapes, taking in the entire composition. It is very important to stand back and judge these lines and shapes. As with a portrait or figure painting, look for the most apparent adjustment you see and make that correction. Keep working this way until you don't see anything to correct.

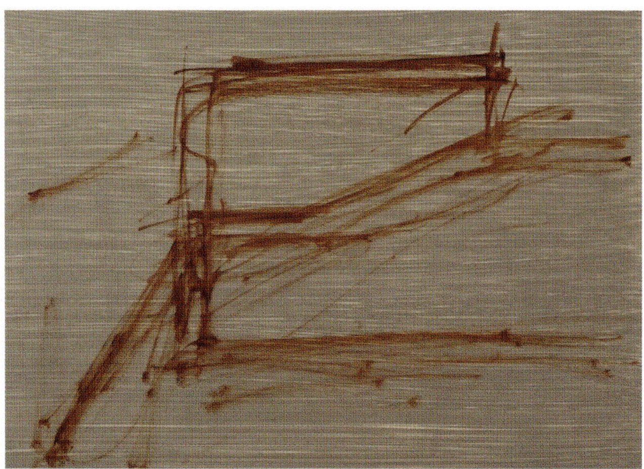

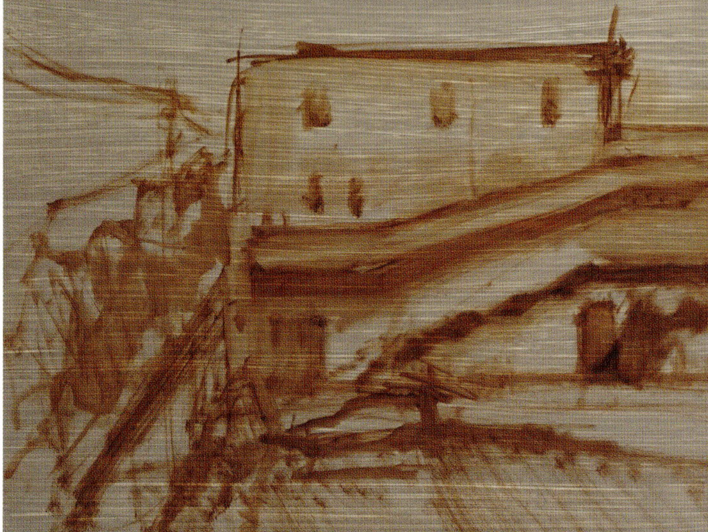

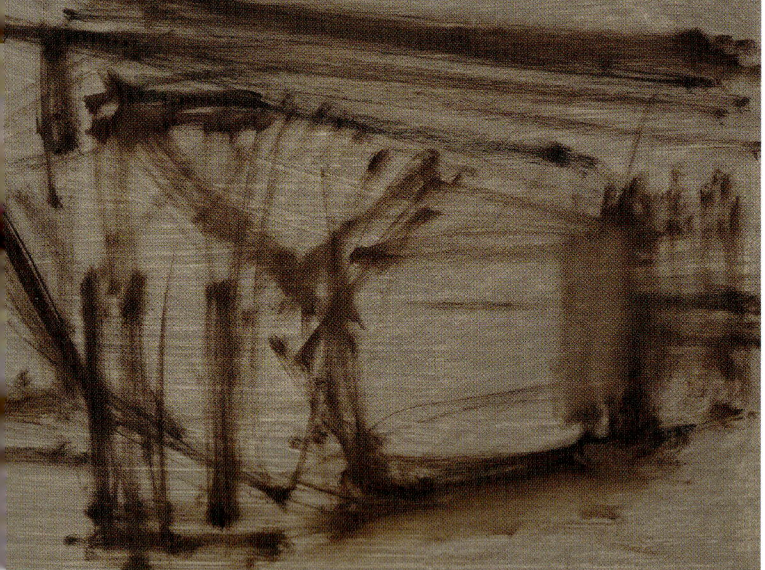

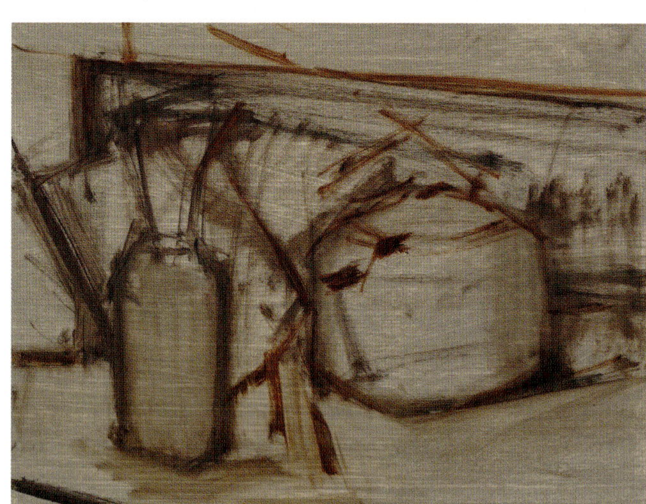

CHECK PROPORTIONS BEFORE MASSING SHADOWS

Many artists make the common mistake of painting objects more equal in size to each other than they are in reality, so be sure to look for the differences. Only move forward to massing your shadows once you are confident in your foundational drawing.

### *Remember to Practice*

Try to complete ten examples of still life and ten of landscape. Keep a sketchbook specifically dedicated to these, or use a pad of canvas sheets.

# OPEN GRISAILLE

Now let's explore the open grisaille stage as a further step in a developed painting. Open grisaille is the process of massing in your shadow areas. It is called "open" because you leave the areas in light clear, without paint.

Continue to work simply and generally, just as you did in the gesture and adjustment stages. The longer you work on this stage, the more precise your painting will become.

The goal is to simplify your composition into a dark and light pattern. This is the beginning of your value stage. This process makes it easier to see proportions and sets your painting up for the next stage in development.

Following are examples of open grisaille at various levels of development because of the different goals and amount of time each one took.

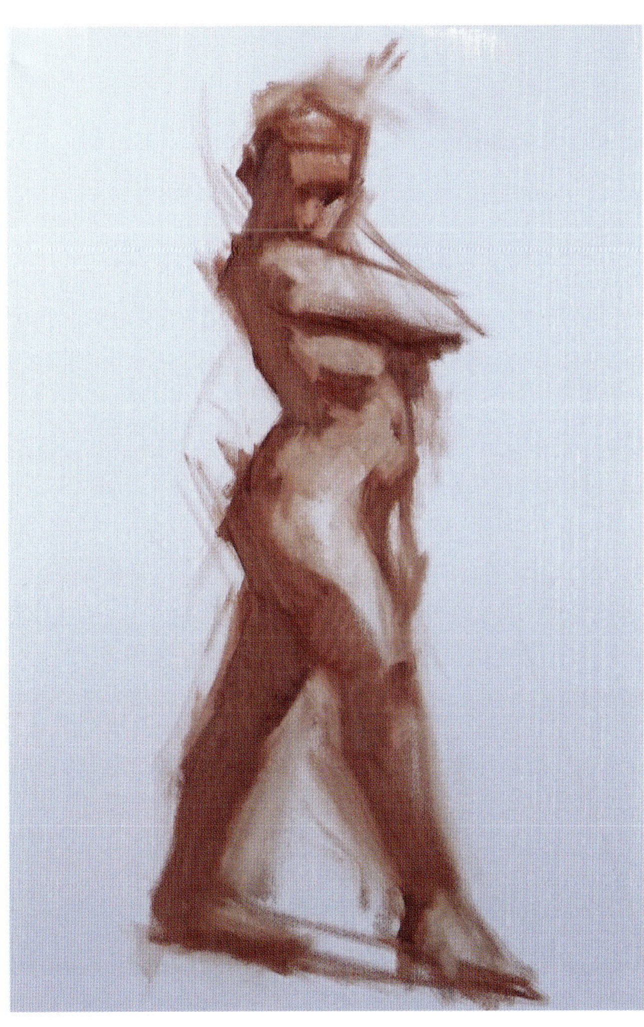

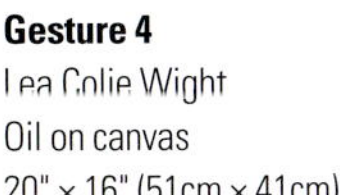

**Gesture 4**
Lea Colie Wight
Oil on canvas
20" × 16" (51cm × 41cm)

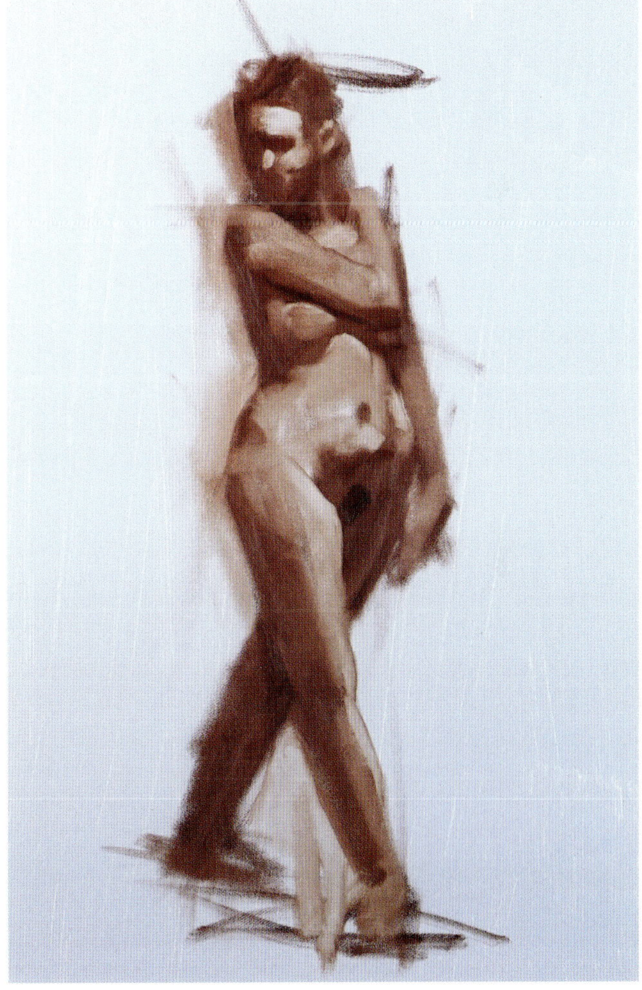

**Gesture 25**
Stephen Early
Oil on canvas
20" × 16" (51cm × 41cm)

10 MINUTE OPEN GRISAILLE

These two examples were painted at the same time, by different artists and from different easel locations. Even at this stage, you can see differences between the two. These were painted specifically to show examples of open grisaille. The painting on the right shows more variation in the light areas and additional dark accents in the shadows. Either one could easily be taken to the next stage of closed grisaille.

# THE PROCESS

In the two examples below, you see another variation of open grisaille painting. They were not intended to be developed further, but to be only open grisailles. This method involves spreading a light layer of grisaille mixture over the canvas first, then building the gesture on top of that and massing in the shadows. The leftover paint that is in the light areas is shaped and wiped with a paper towel, cloth or brush to show the light planes.

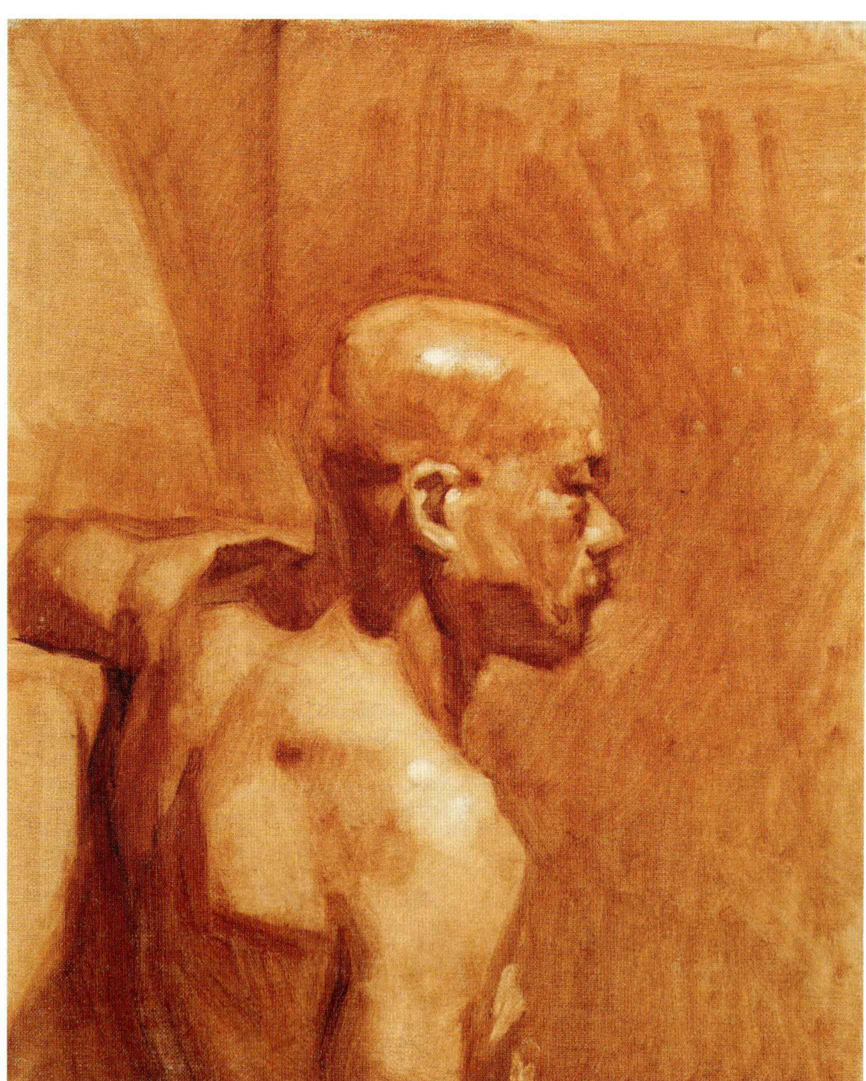

**Open Grisaille (Detail), 1 Hour**
Lea Colie Wight
Oil on linen
20" × 16" (51cm × 41cm)

**Open Grisaille, 2 Hours**
Lea Colie Wight
Oil on linen
20" × 20" (51cm × 51cm)

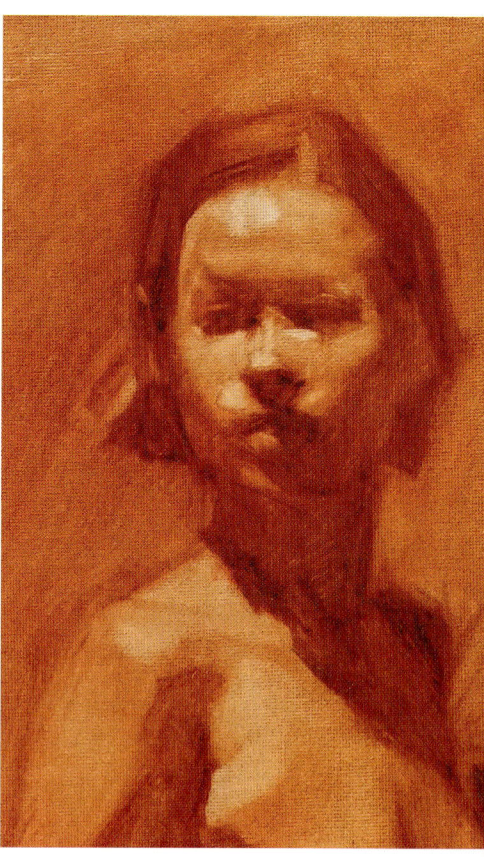

*Demonstration*

# OPEN GRISAILLE—MASSING SHADOWS

Follow the steps to practice massing shadows in the open grisaille stage of a painting.

## *Materials*

SURFACE

stretched canvas

OIL PIGMENTS

Burnt Umber

BRUSHES

Silver Brush #1034 size 3 or 4 long bristle filbert

OTHER

odorless mineral spirits or Gamsol

nitrile or vinyl gloves

paper towels

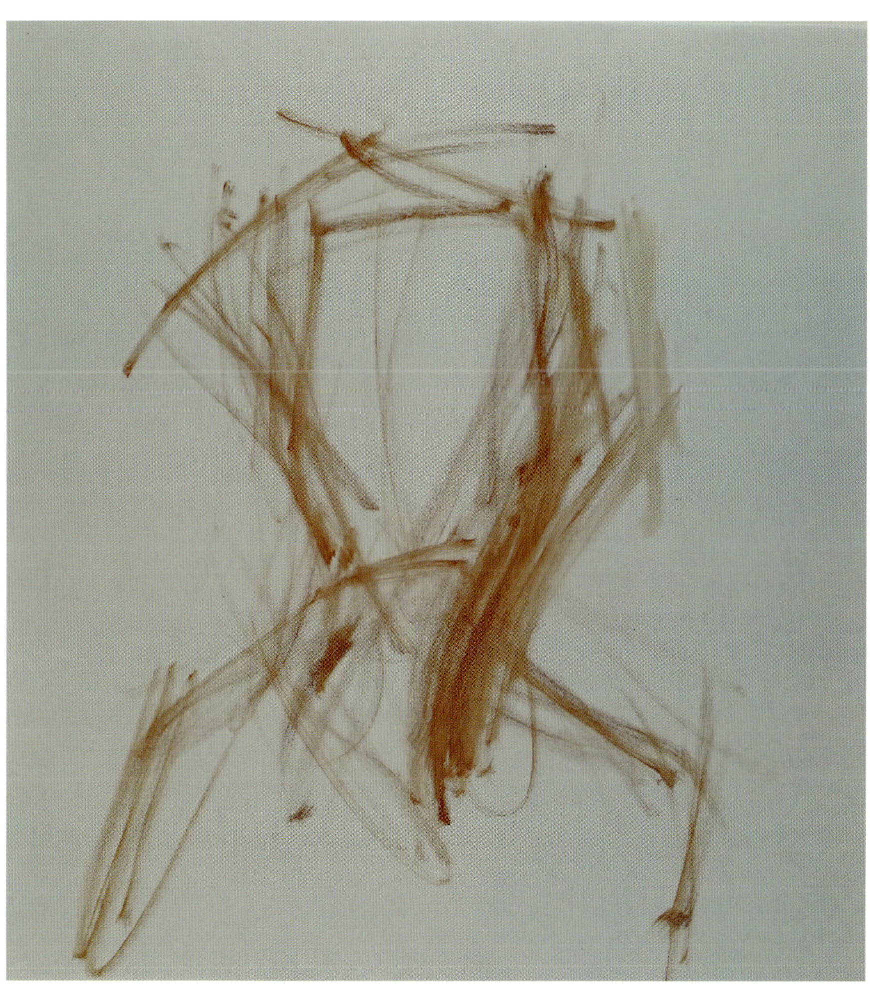

1 BEGIN THE GESTURE

Squint to identify your dark values using just one neutral color. By using only one color you are able to build and shape without the additional task of deciding color relationships. Once again you are building from the simple to the complex.

In some compositions the dark and light patterns do not involve shadows. A landscape on an overcast day may involve "local" values like a dark building against a light field instead of strong shadows caused by sunlight.

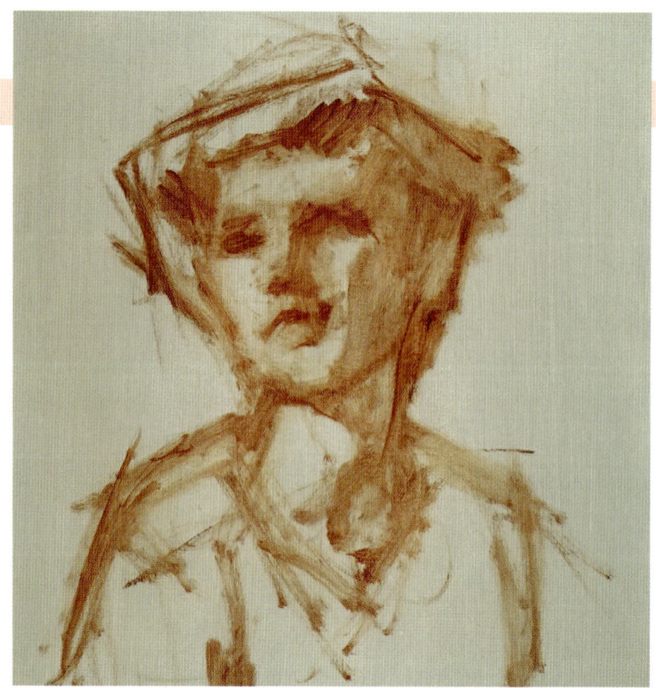

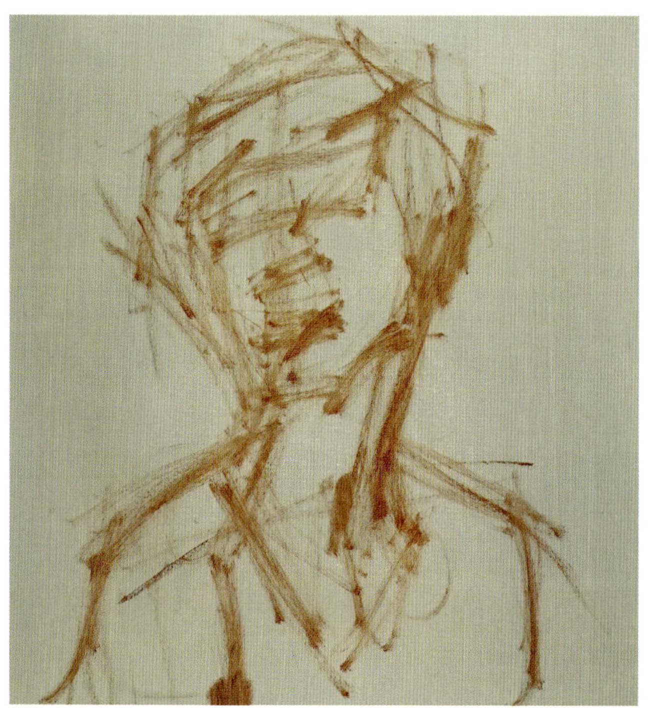

## 2 ADJUST AND DEVELOP

Dip your brush in your solvent and wipe it well to take off most of the moisture. Grab a little Burnt Umber, or a simple, neutral color to your liking, and move it around on your palette until it is the correct consistency. It should brush out on your canvas, allowing it to be controlled. The amount of paint you need on your brush will change as you paint because of repeated cleaning so keep an eye on it.

## 3 MASS IN SHADOWS

Block in the general shape of your dark value with your grisaille mixture. Use either your brush or a paper towel to adjust the shapes. Add a dark accent to show different shapes in the shadows using a darker concentration of your grisaille paint.

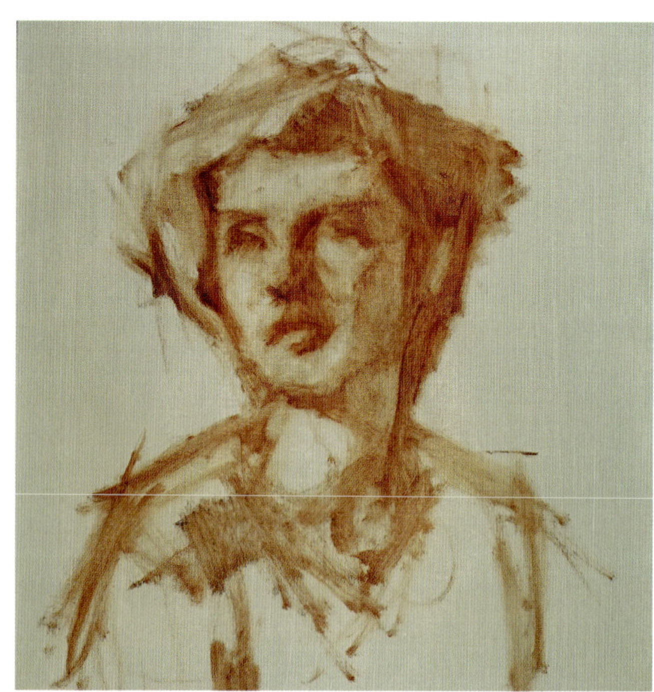

## 4 BEGIN DEVELOPING PLANES

If you choose to and have residual paint in your light area, you can begin to develop your planes and form using your paper towel. Remember, though, that in the following stage you'll be adding light value paint to this area so don't get too detailed.

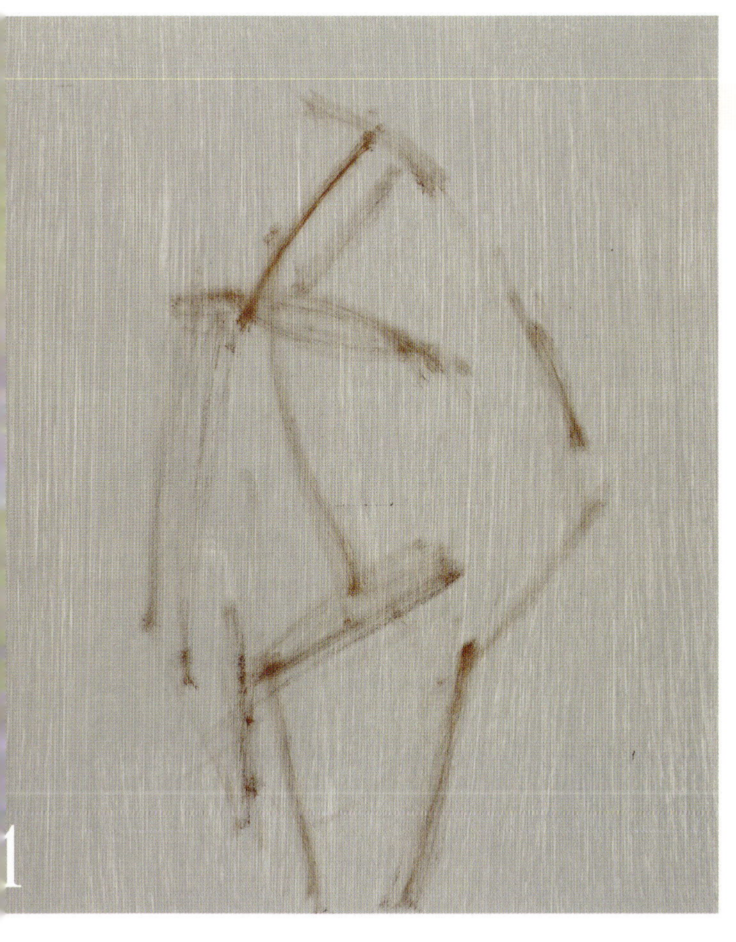
1

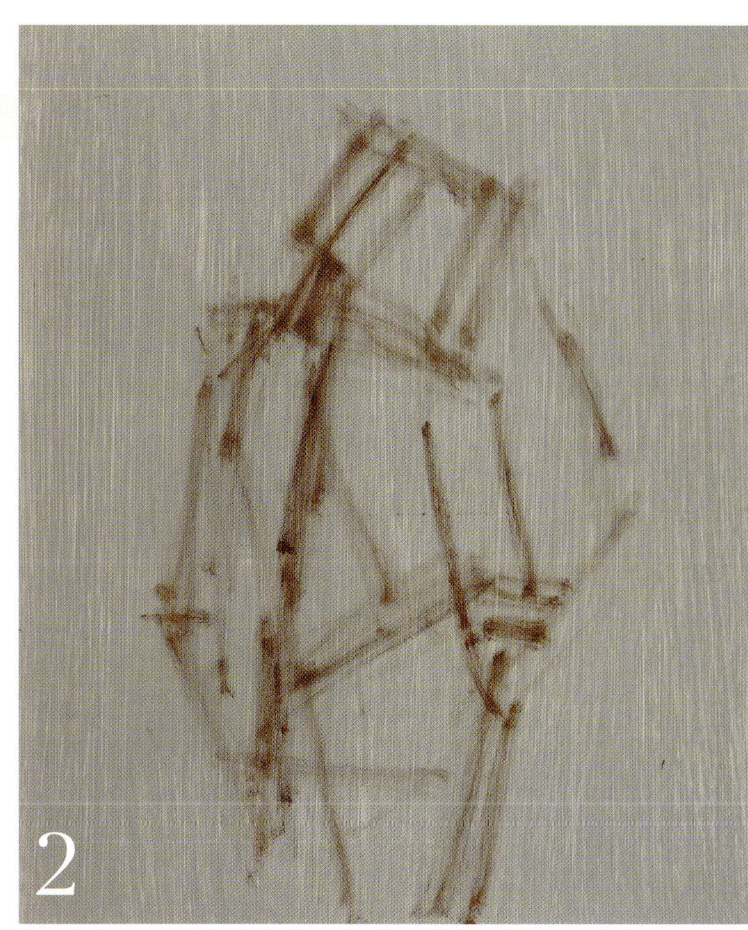
2

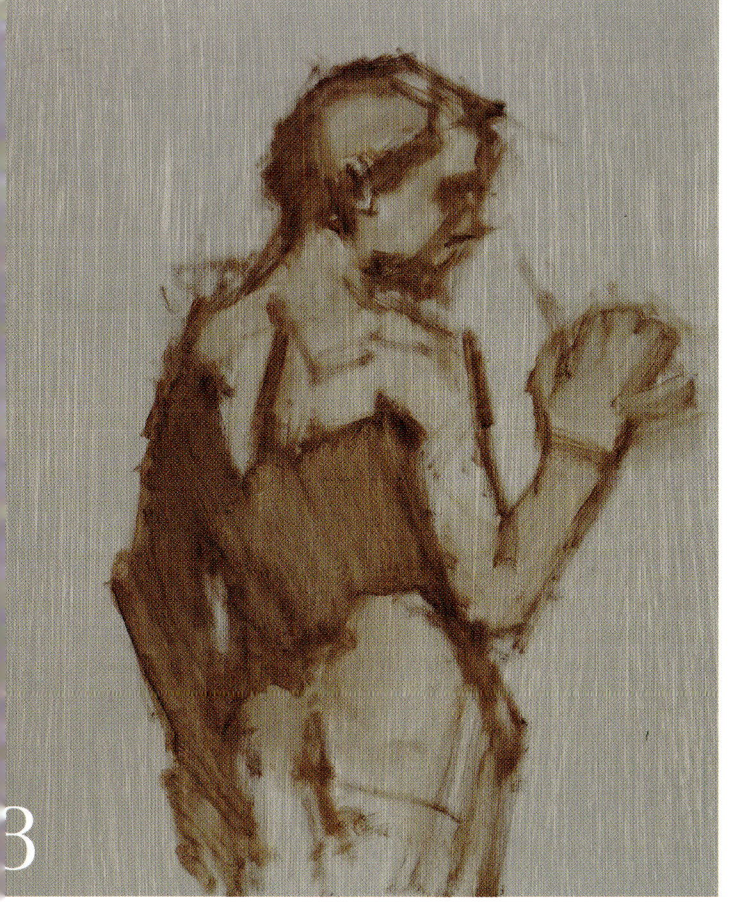
3

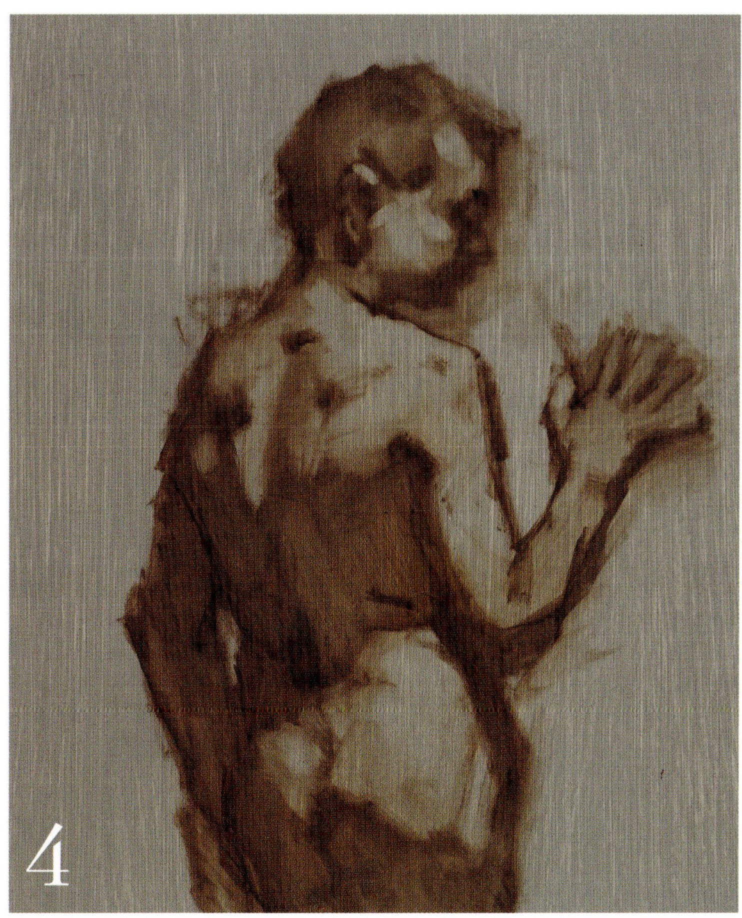
4

# CLOSED GRISAILLE

Once you are happy with the gesture and proportions, and you have massed in your shadow shapes, you can proceed to blocking in a light value. This is known as the closed grisaille stage.

In figure and portraiture, this would be the area where the light hits the model. The color you use for the skin in light should cover two bases. It should represent the general color of your model, which should not be so different as to be distracting. It should also represent the main value of the skin in light, not the darkest light or the highest light.

Test out your paint mixture on the side of your canvas and add a dark accent and a highlight next to it. This will tell you if you're in the general range. If you were allowed only one value to represent the light, this would generally be it.

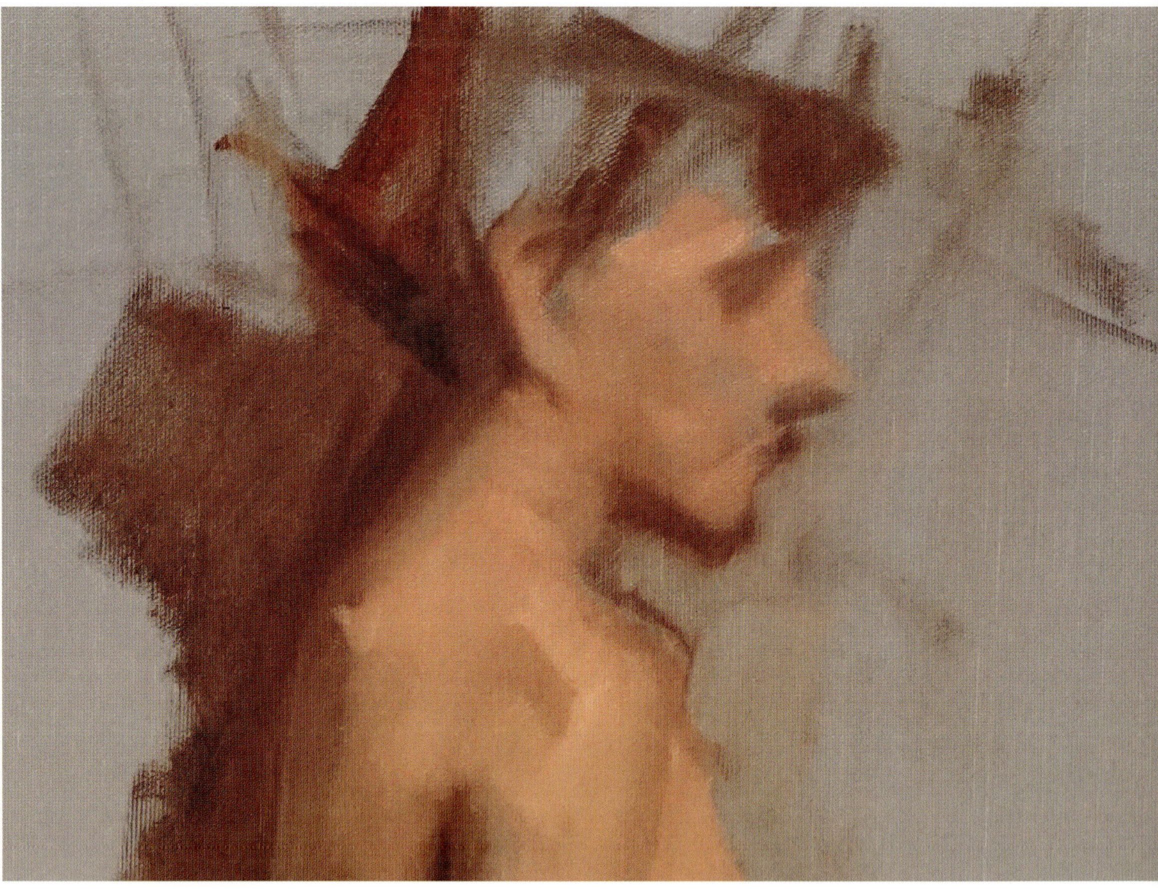

MIXING SKIN TONES

For the sake of simplicity, you can create a paint mixture for a skin tone in light with Burnt Sienna, Ultramarine Blue and white. However, there are many other possible color combinations when mixing skin tones, and I encourage you to experiment with the colors on your palette. Regardless of the color combinations you choose, be sure to keep your shadow color separate from your skin mixture. This will keep your shadows clearly defined.

## *Various Methods, Same Result*

There are several variations on these closed grisaille exercises and all of them are valid. I have chosen to present the process I use most often, as I have found that it best suits the goal of the exercise. My preference is to start with a middle value and work up and down from there. Another closed grisaille method would be to pick one of the darker values found in the light, and then build up the lighter values.

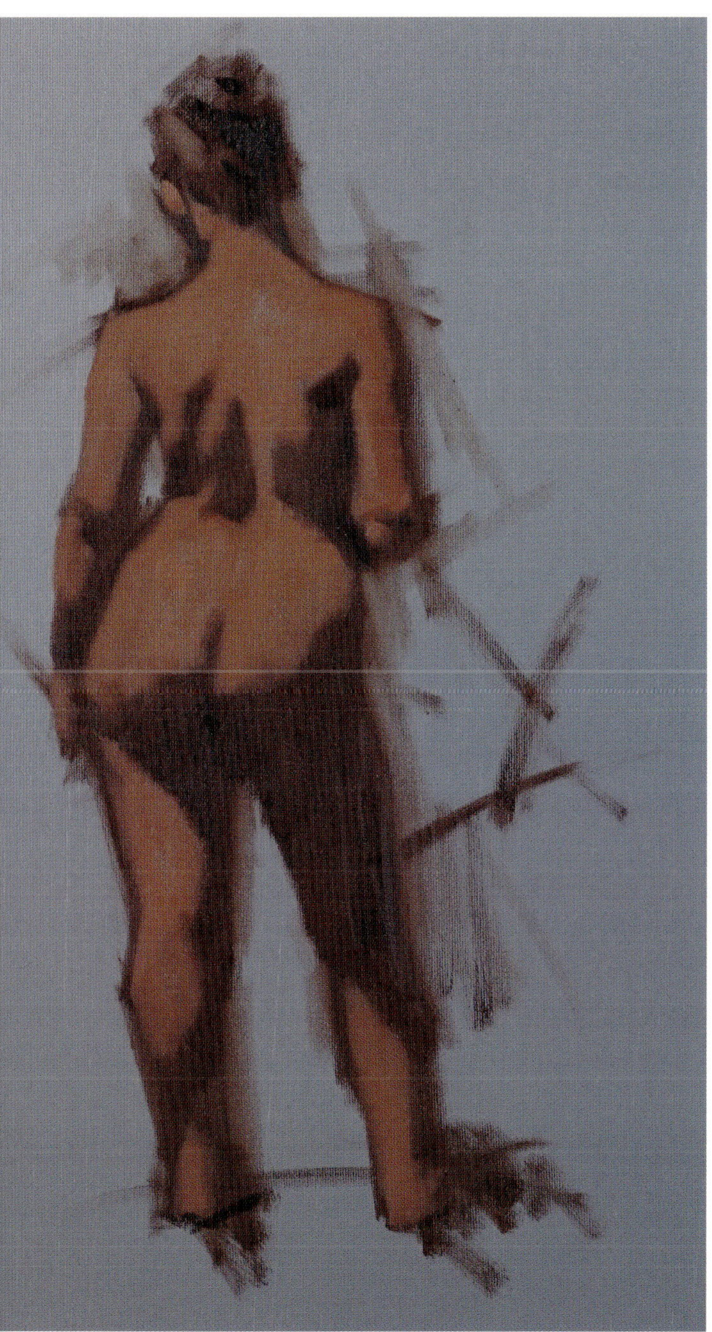

## ADDING LIGHT TONES

As you paint the light areas you are not simply filling in the space, you are still squinting and adjusting your shadow masses along with your light masses. Scan the whole figure and try to see proportional adjustments you can make.

Just like your grisaille mixture, your light color should be worked around with your brush on your palette until thoroughly mixed and pliable. Begin by applying your paint according to the major planes of the form you're looking at.

**Closed Grisaille**
Darren Kingsley
Oil on linen
20" × 16" (51cm × 41cm)

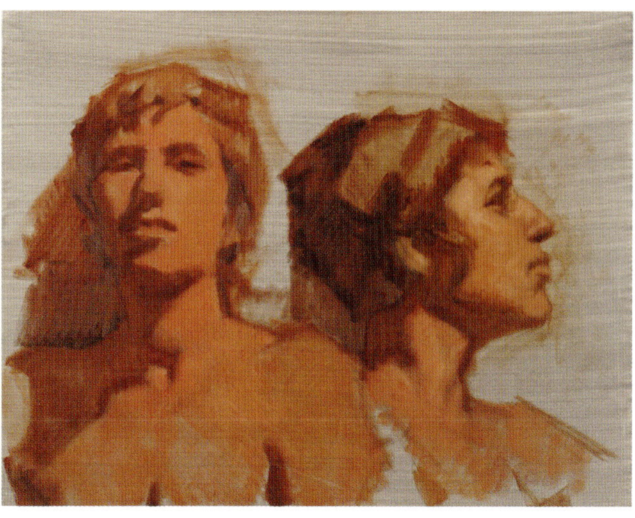

## BUILDING VALUE THROUGH THIN PAINT LAYERS

Here, the thinness of the paint is apparent since you can see the tone of the canvas through the paint. The head on the right, the profile, shows the very beginning of laying in another value. This can be seen on the top planes of the model's face, among the temple, bridge of the nose and cheek bone.

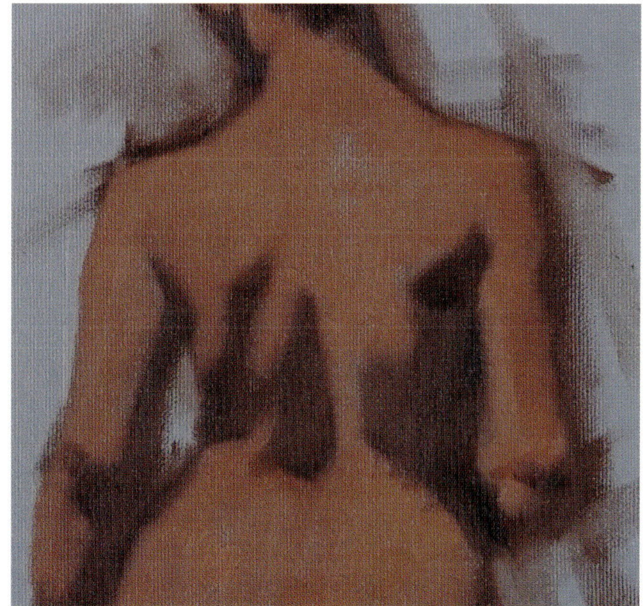

## DETAIL TO SHOW APPLICATION

The enlarged detail shows how thin the layer of paint is. You want to avoid a thick layer of paint. Notice how the edges are not sharp but they are clear and shaped.

*Demonstration*

# THE CLOSED GRISAILLE STAGE

Follow the steps to practice adding light values in the closed grisaille stage of a painting.

## *Materials*

SURFACE
stretched canvas

OIL PIGMENTS
Burnt Sienna, Burnt Umber, Ultramarine Blue, Titanium White

BRUSHES
Silver Brush #1034 size 3 or 4 long bristle filbert

OTHER
paper towels

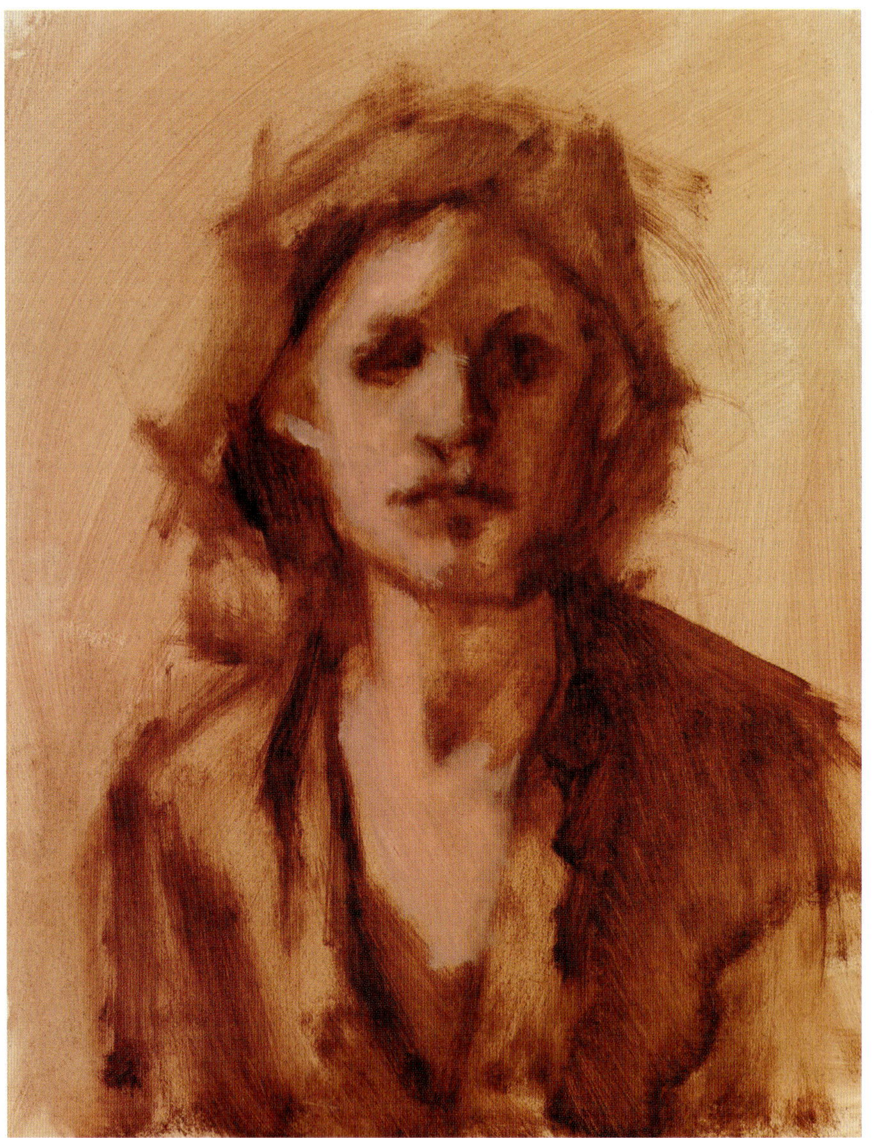

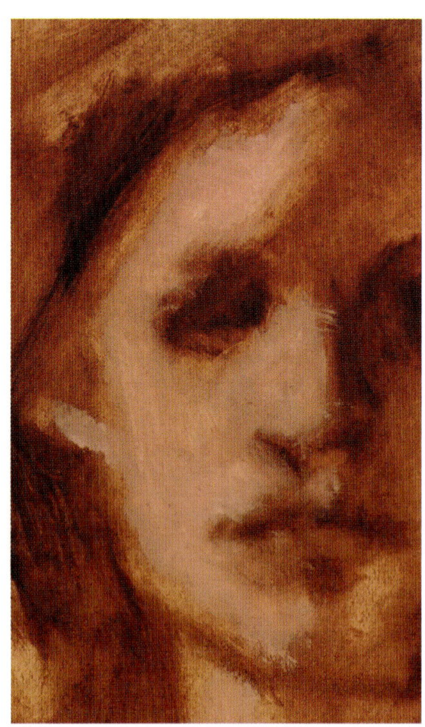

Notice how little paint is actually used at this stage.

### 1 BEGIN ADDING AND SHAPING COLOR IN THE LIGHT AREAS

Once you have refined your gesture and completed the open grisaille, you are ready to begin the closed grisaille stage of the process.

Use a no. 3 or 4 long bristle filbert to begin adding color for the light areas and shaping it.

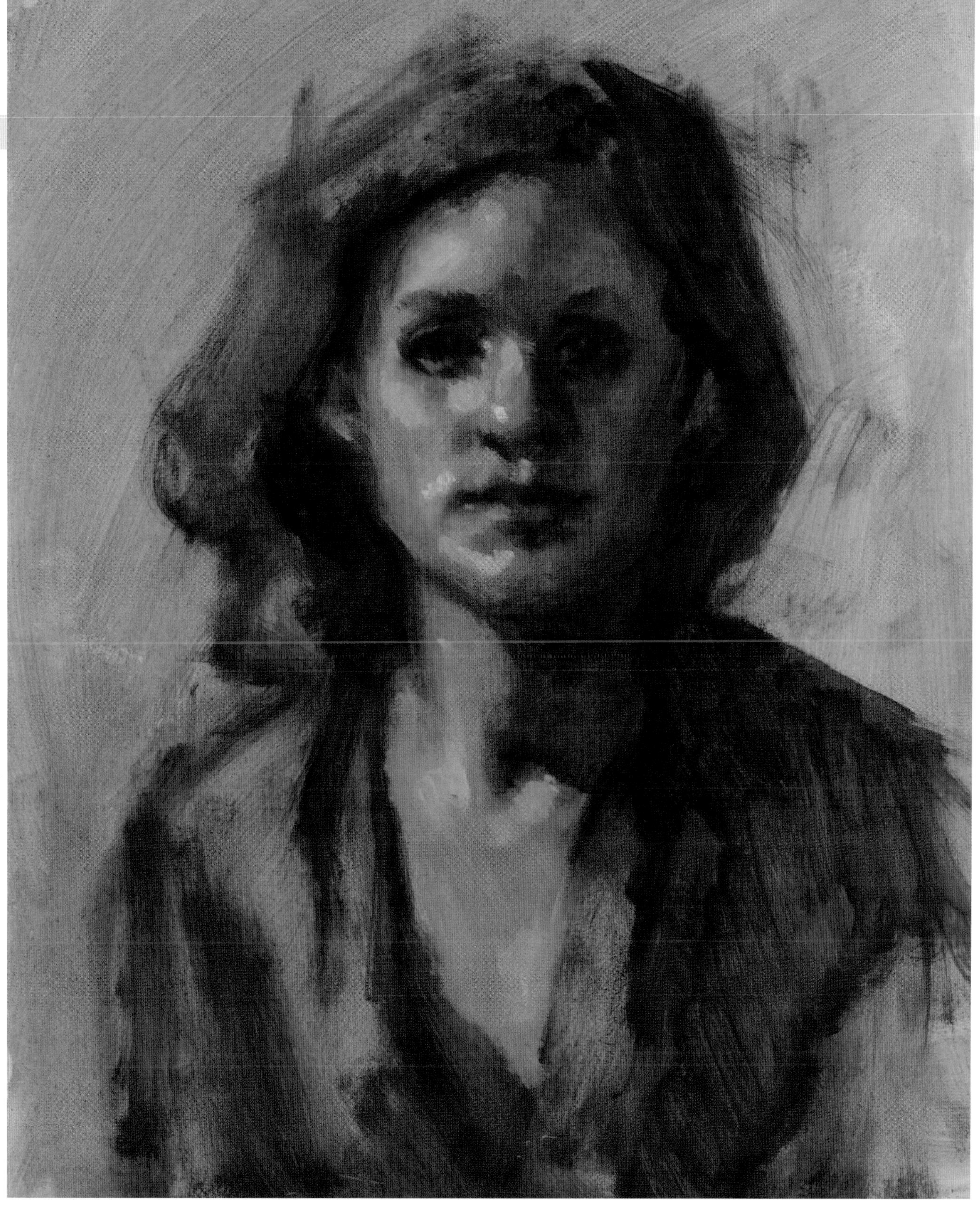

## 2 ADD MORE VALUES

Next add two more values to her face. Now the painting is really taking shape! Continue to build on your single-tone closed grisaille by adding more values.

The purpose of this exercise is to develop your form into gradually smaller and smaller value differences, but keeping them in their correct relationship. What you learn through this will be used when you're painting in full color.

# LIGHT VALUES

After completing the single-tone closed grisaille, continue developing your painting in an organized way. Add additional values to the areas in light, and add one or two more values to the shadow areas.

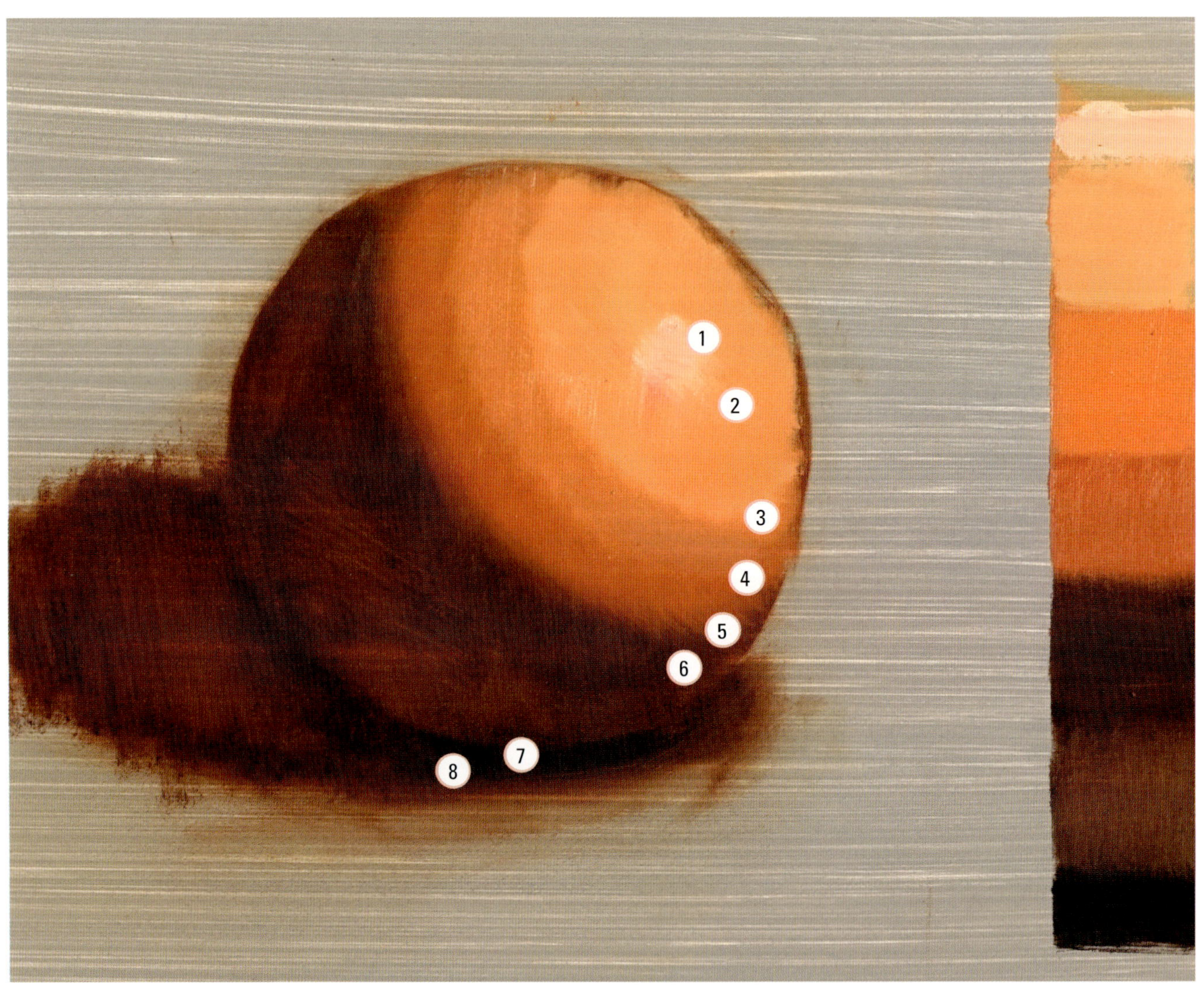


**LIGHT SOURCE AFFECTS COLOR**

This ball shows some flesh colors broken into values. People possess many distinct skin colors, all of which are dependent on the color of the light source.

Light Values: 1. Highlight; 2. Light light; 3. Middle light; 4. Darkest light; 5. Terminator

Shadow Values: 6. Middle dark; 7. Reflected light; 8. Dark accent

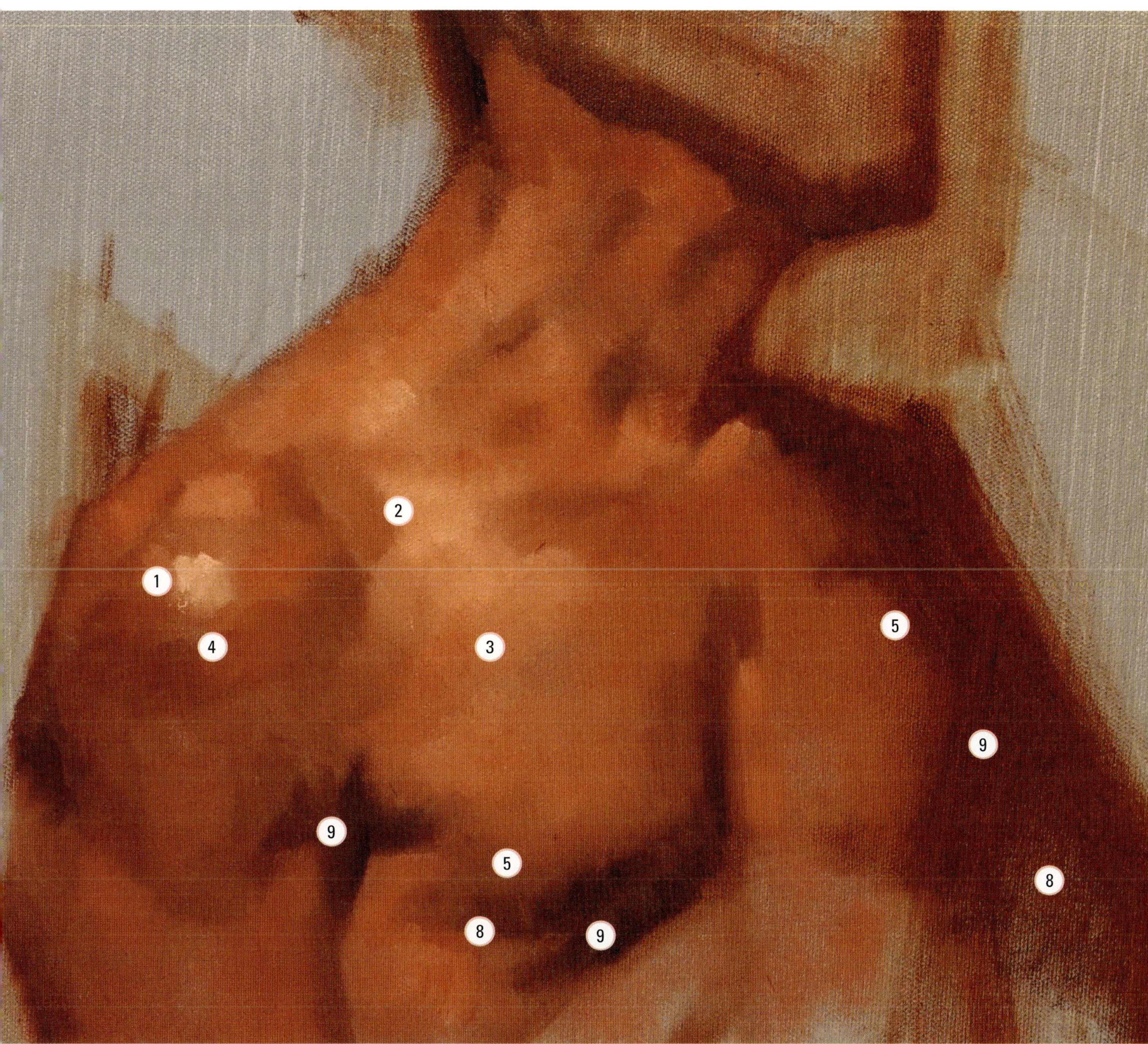


**Study**
JaFang Lu
Oil on linen
16" × 20" (41cm × 51cm)

HIGHLIGHT AND DARK ACCENTS

This painting shows the same value scale as the ball. Highlights and dark accents are the two value extremes. Additional values were then related to those two notes. An overall body color was added to shape the form. Finally, a lighter value for the lighter planes and a darker value for the darker planes was added.

Light Values: 1. Highlight; 2. Light light; 3. Middle light; 4. Darkest light; 5. Terminator

Shadow Values: 6. Middle dark; 7. Dark dark; 8. Reflected light; 9. Dark accent

## Go Easy on Yourself

If you're new to this, it can be difficult. There are many plane changes on the human form, and sorting them into three or four values is challenging. It's like learning a sport. Each time you practice you improve.

# COLOR SHIFTS

In the following examples, some color shifts are introduced as the plane/value changes. Patience here really pays off. Keep your planes clear and make sure you're happy with the figure when you step back to evaluate. Add smaller changes in an area, but keep stepping back and judging whether your big planes are still clear. This is how a painting is built.

### *Fixing Mistakes*

It is inevitable that, at some point, you will make a mistake. However, mistakes in this stage are simple to fix. Just restate the big plane and then try again.

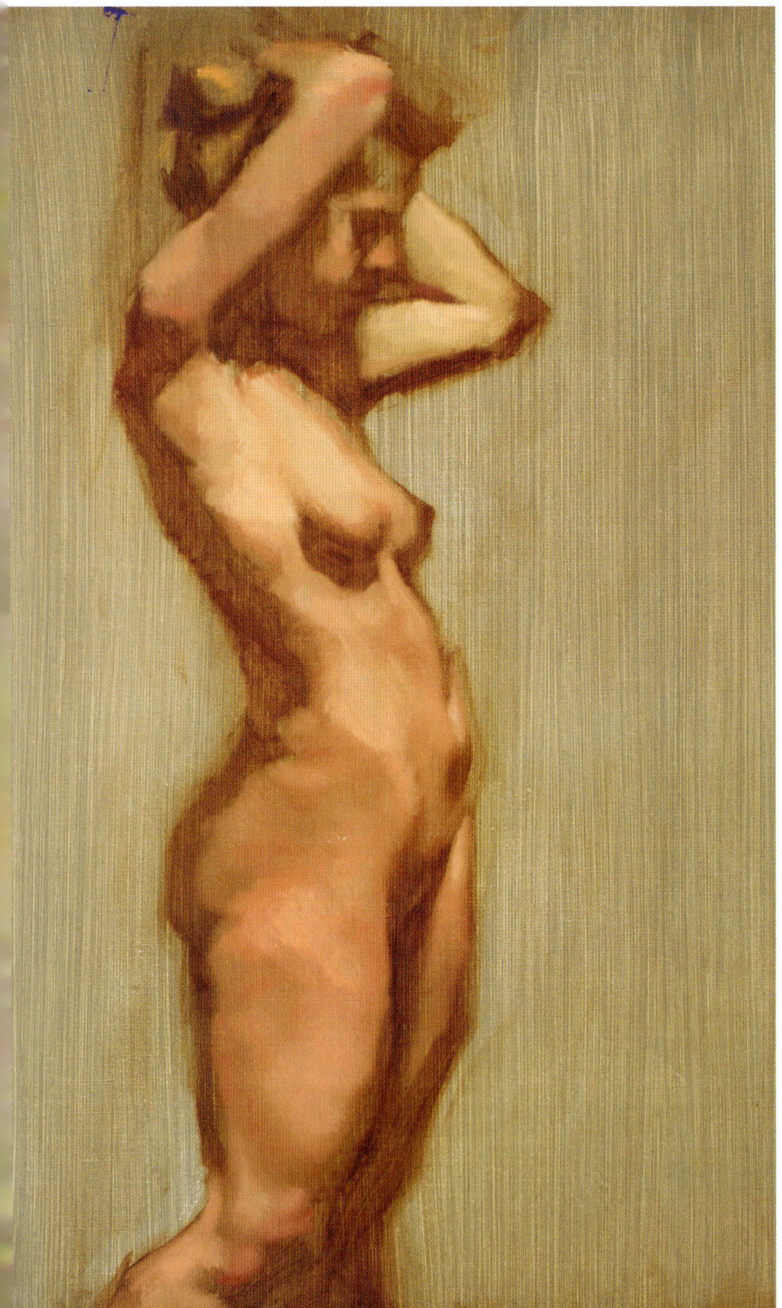

**Standing Figure**
Lea Colie Wight
Oil on linen
20" × 16" (51cm × 41cm)

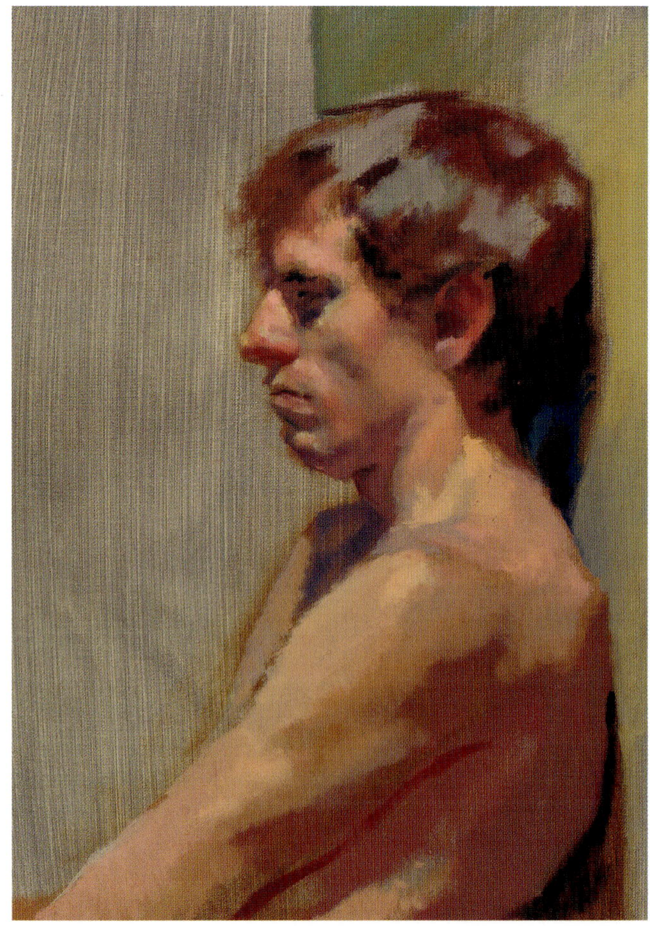

**Russell**
Lea Colie Wight
Oil on canvas
18" × 16" (48cm × 41cm)

**Resting Model**
Lea Colie Wight
Oil on linen
20" × 16" (51cm × 41cm)

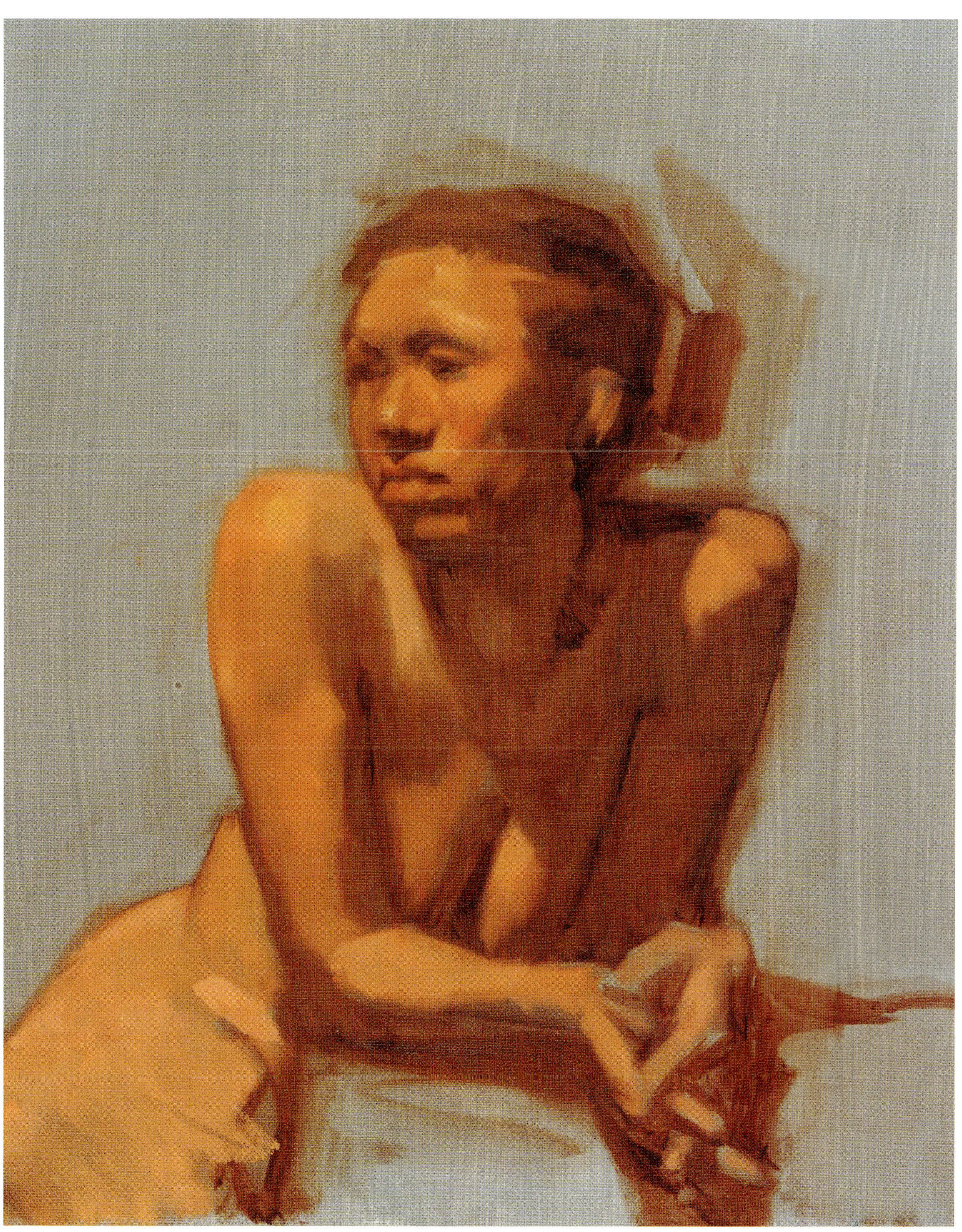

*Demonstration*

# THE ADVANCED CLOSED GRISAILLE STAGE

Follow the steps to practice blocking in shadows during the advanced closed grisaille stage of a painting.

### *Materials*

SURFACE
stretched canvas

OIL PIGMENTS
Burnt Sienna, Burnt Umber, Ultramarine Blue, Titanium White

BRUSHES
Silver Brush #1034 size 3 or 4 long bristle filbert

OTHER
paper towels

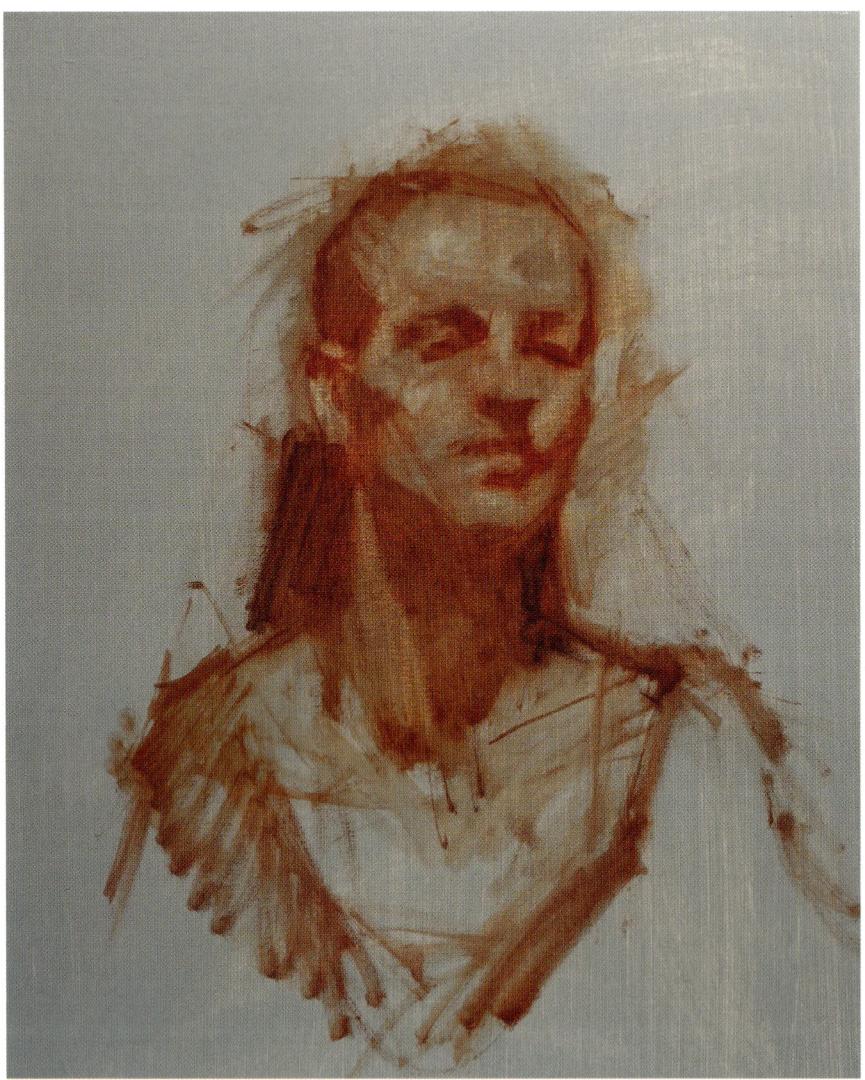

1 BLOCK IN THE MAIN SHADOWS
Begin to block in the shadows.

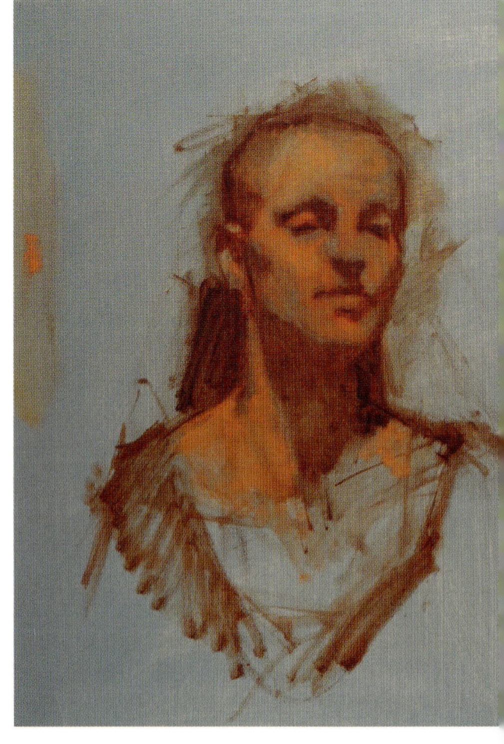

2 ADD COLOR
Apply a layer of color. You can see how just this one color can be shaped using the gray canvas.

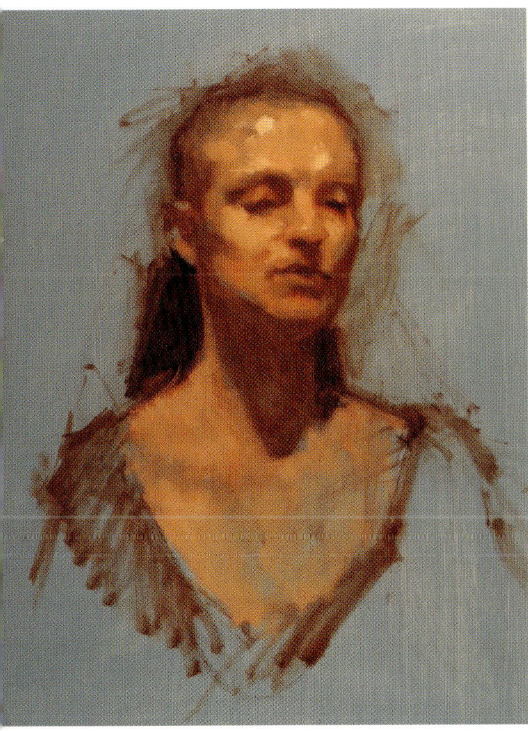

## 3 APPLY VALUE CHANGES

Apply the first additional value changes. Build them gradually.

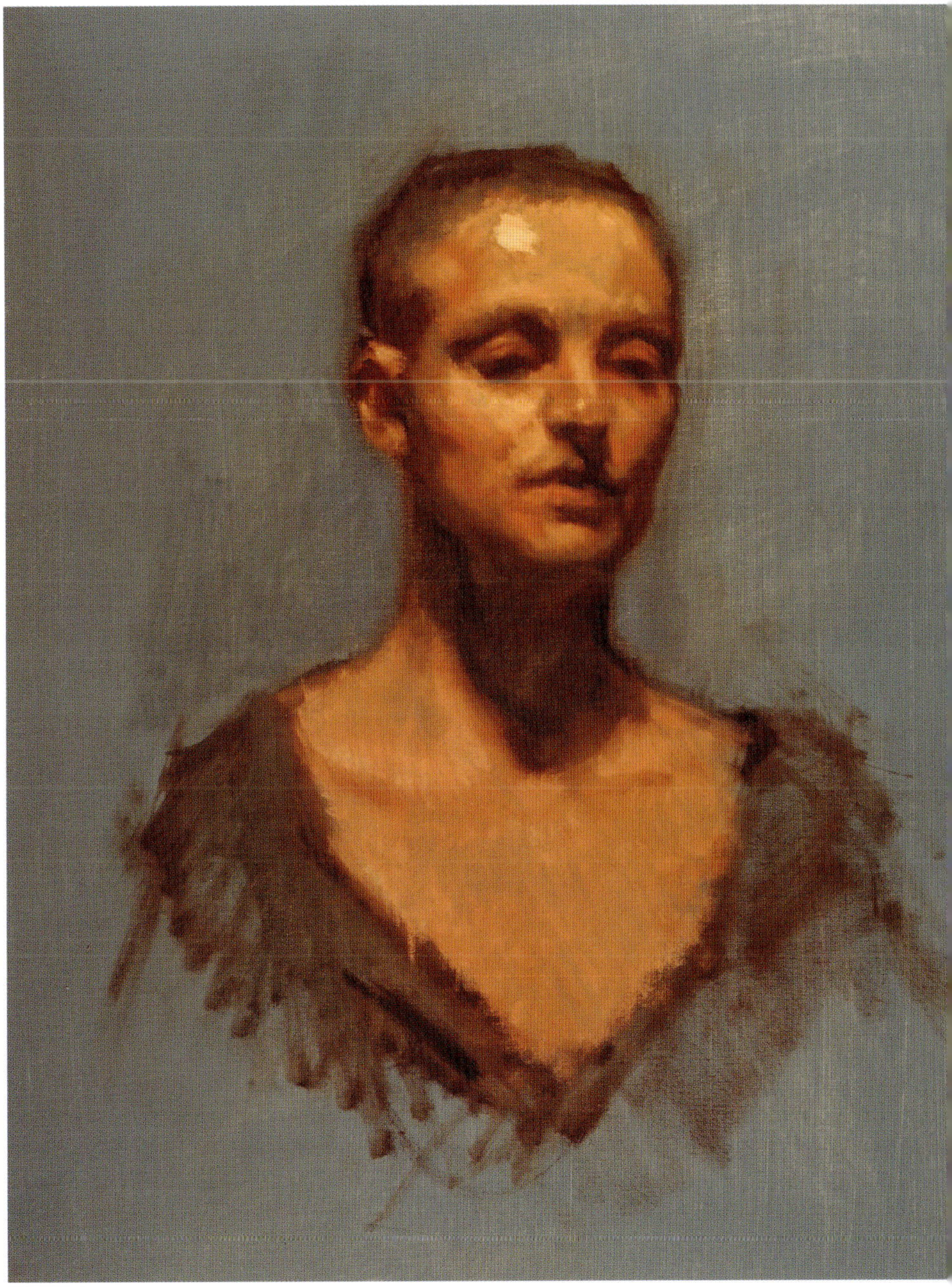

## 4 SHAPE AND ADJUST

Continue shaping your color and make final adjustments. Here, I decided to get rid of the shadow behind her.

The difference between closed grisaille and a full-color painting is pretty clear here. There's not any color in the shadows, and even in the light, the colors are mostly just value changes instead of color changes. You can choose.

# THREE-HOUR PAINTING

Here's another variation on closed grisaille. You can add a few more color changes as your values change. It's completely up to you. You could leave it here or start building color.

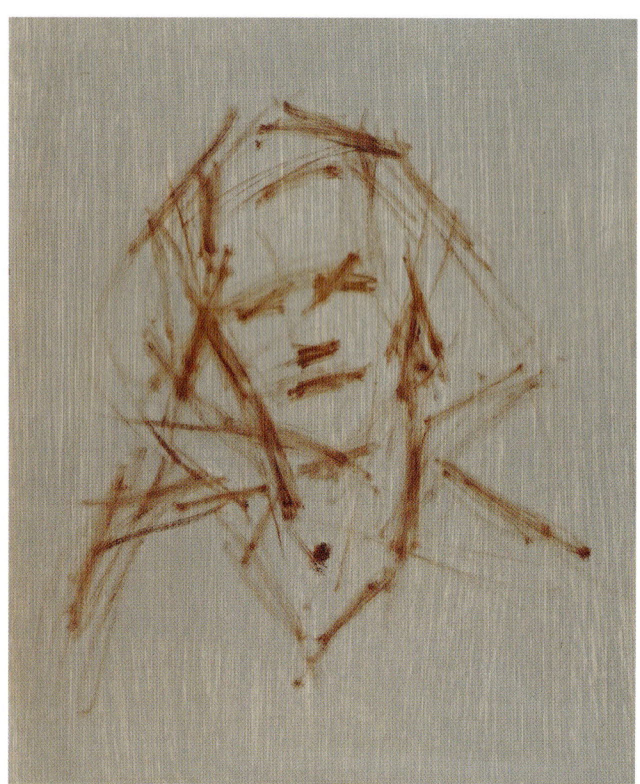

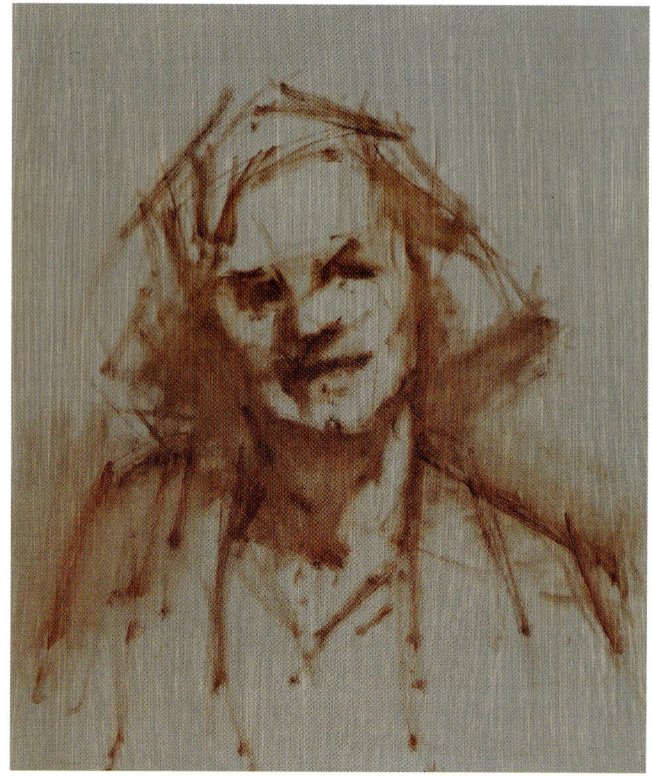

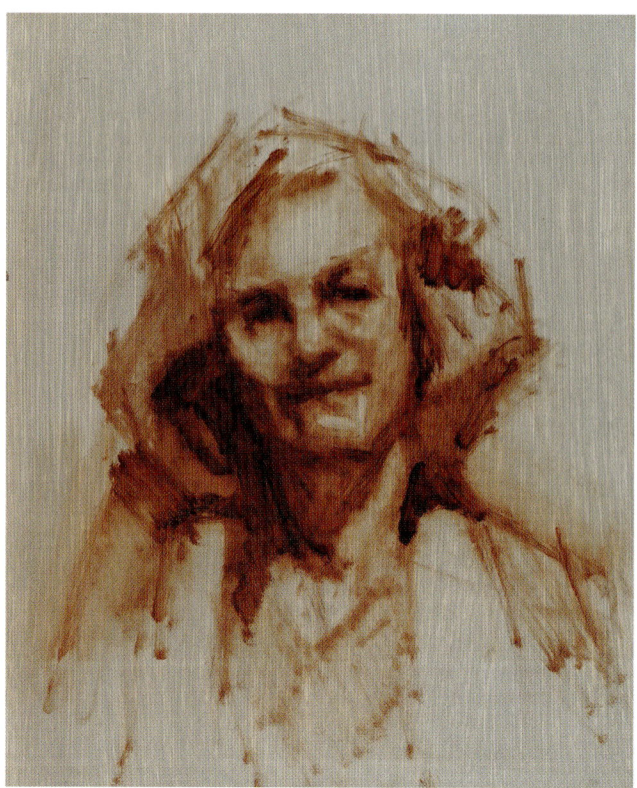

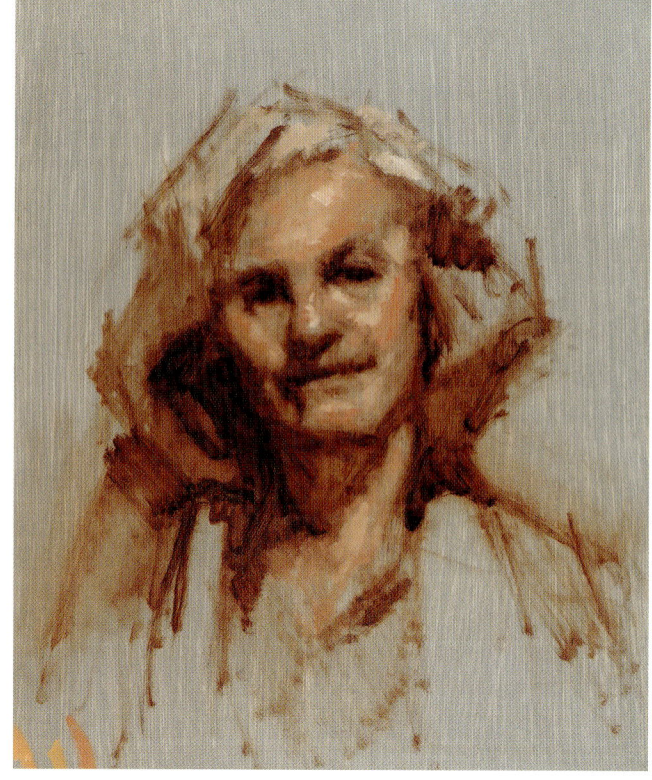

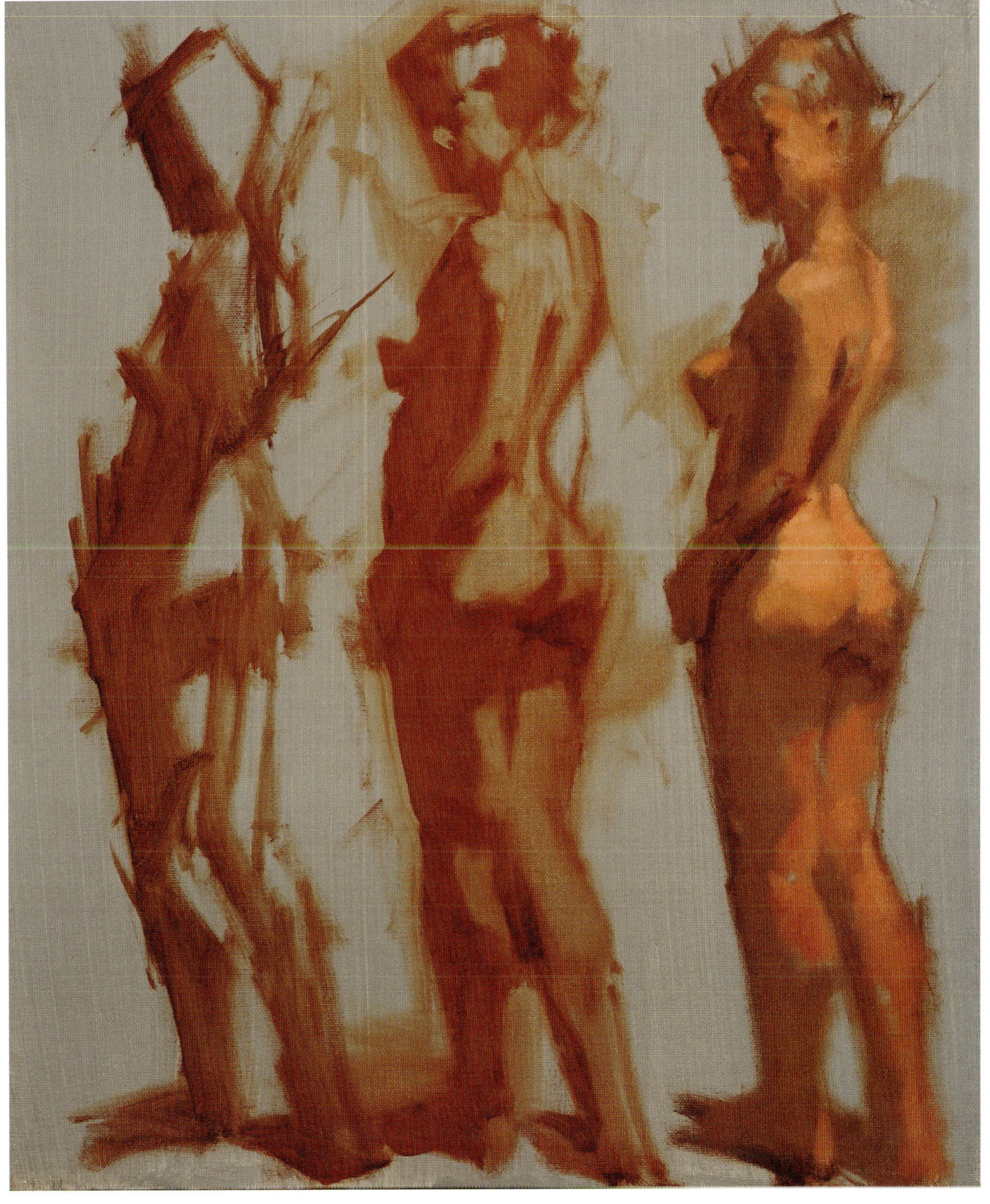

GESTURE OPEN GRISAILLE CLOSED GRISAILLE

# 4 COLOR *and* LIGHT

We are one of the few fortunate species able to see in vivid color. Why is this so important? Color can lead you to the cool shade of a tree on a hot day or a spot in the sun on a chilly day. It can help you pick out a friend in a crowd. It can lead you to safety in a burning building. And it can also show you the beauty surrounding us every day. The ability to paint color as it really is gives the artist the ability to share this beauty.

Studying color made a profound difference on my awareness of the world around me and the potential to express this through color. I vividly remember driving home in the late afternoon and noticing beautiful colors I'd never seen before. The road was a warm gold, and the shadows under the car in front of me a deep purple. Now instead of seeing colors in isolation, I was seeing them as they related to each other.

I will be forever indebted to Nelson Shanks for opening the world of color to me. Through his teaching I learned how to see color and use that knowledge in all my paintings. I hope this book helps you in this same way.

**Yellow Runner, Morning**
Lea Colie Wight
Oil on linen
18" × 26" (46cm × 66cm)

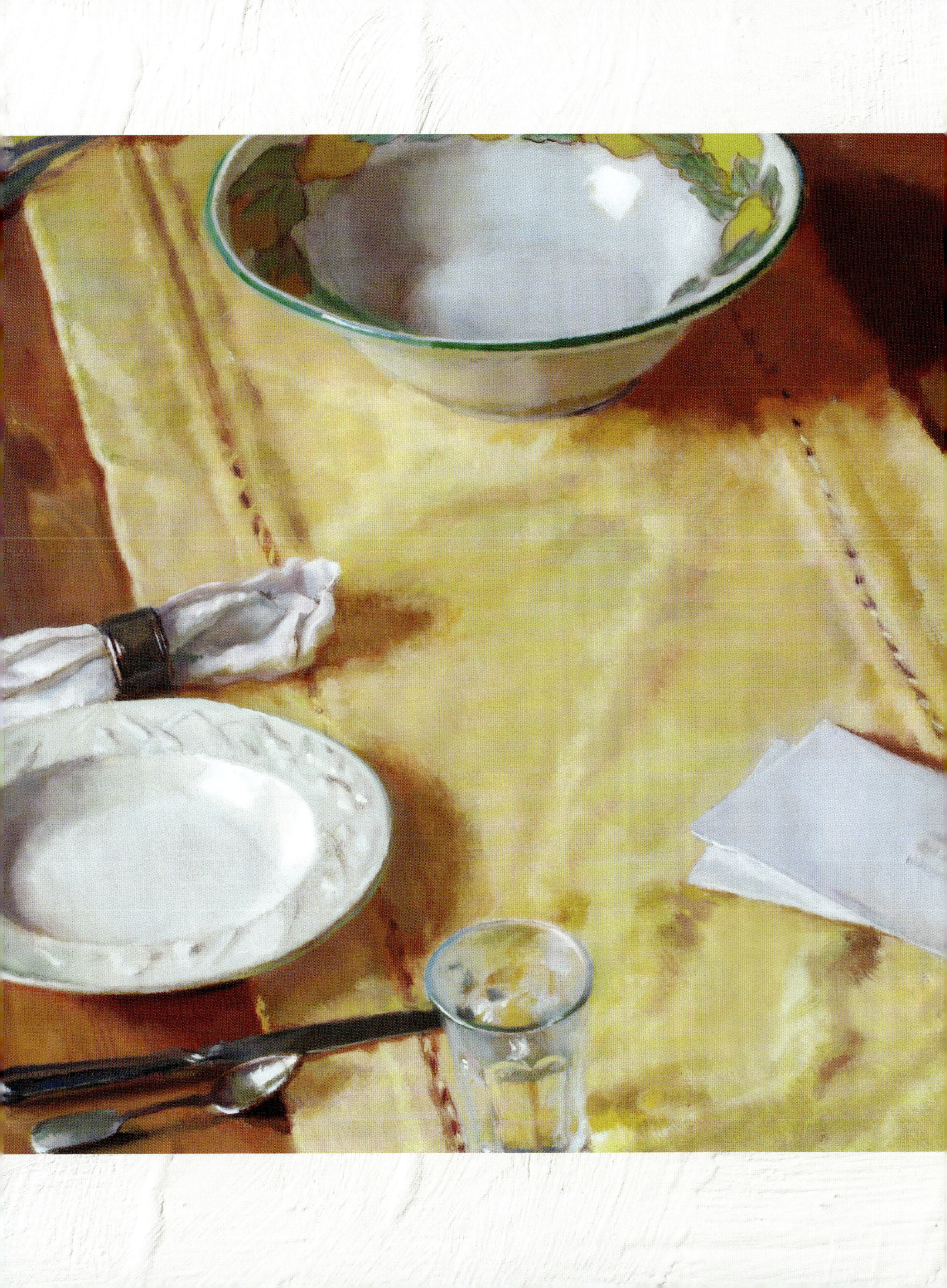

# THE COLOR OF LIGHT

All light has a color and there is a power in understanding color relationships: the power to show a viewer the glory of color as it really appears. This can be the warm beauty of the end of a day or the cool blue light at midday or it can be sunlight shining through stained glass. An artist can develop the power to accurately show this or to twist reality and control the painting, emphasizing focal points through color relationships and letting other areas merge together in the background through use of a more subdued color range. No matter what your aesthetic is, it is important to study color because it gives you the freedom to handle color as you choose, through knowledge not lack of ability.

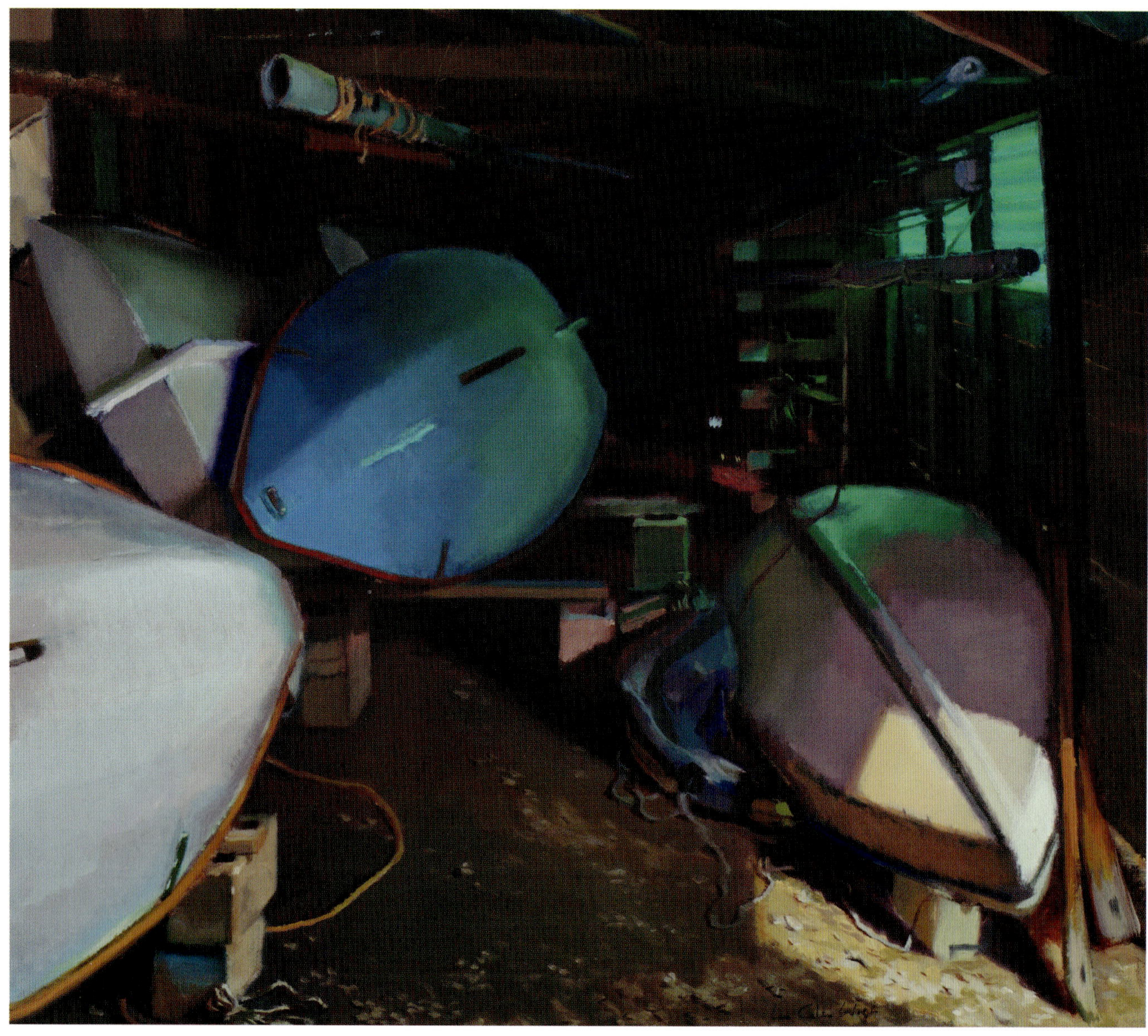

**Boat Shed**
Lea Colie Wight
Oil on canvas
40" × 30" (102cm × 76cm)

# COLOR SHIFTS

Not all color is high keyed. The ability to show very subtle color differences is an important strength that comes from studying color relationships. The best way to train yourself to recognize these differences is to practice by doing color studies. The easiest way to go about this is to set up strong yet simple compositions, then learn how to see—and paint—the differences between them. As you master the simple setups, your strength will continue to build, and you'll be able to progress to more and more subtle setups.

If you are new to color study exercises, you may find that you just can't see the subtle differences in color yet. In fact, you may not be able to see any differences at all. For example, many people have trouble seeing color variations in deep shadows because it all looks so dark. Just keep practicing with color studies and don't be too hard on yourself. The longer you study color, the stronger your color vision will become.

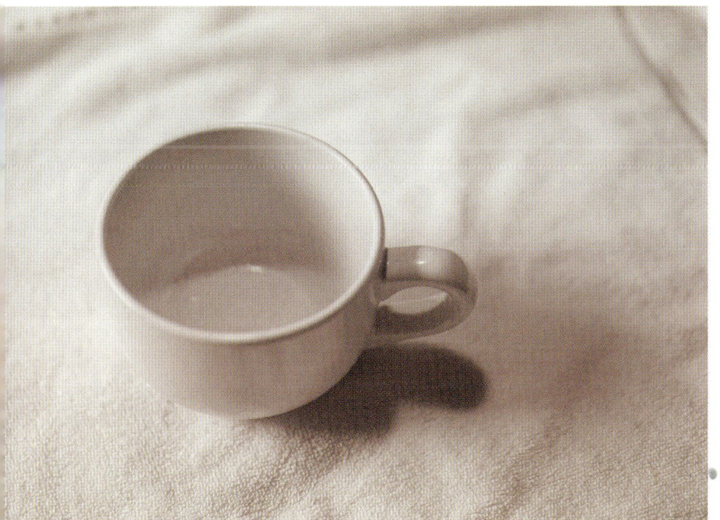

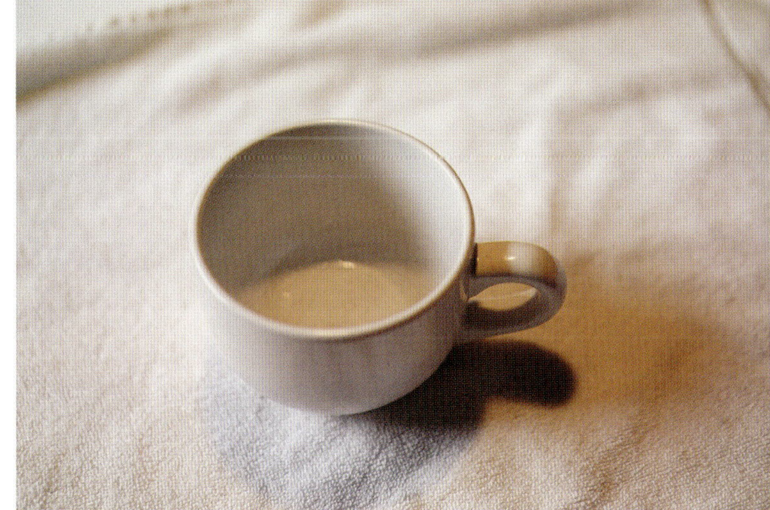

COMPARE AND CONTRAST

The first photograph has been printed strictly as value, so it has no color. The second is a direct photograph showing the true color relationships. Look rapidly from one photograph to the other. Notice the yellowish shadow to the right of the second cup and the blue shadow underneath it. The yellow shadow is a result of the cool light coming in from a window. It looks yellow because of contrast. The blue shadow underneath the cup is caused by a warm halogen light shining from above. The blue shadow is barely discernible in the value image on the left, but you can clearly see it in the color image on the right.

## *Warm and Cool Color Ranges*

When we speak of warm and cool light, think of "warm" as being in the yellow/orange/red range. The "cool" colors are in the blue/purple/green range. Within each color range there are warm and cool differences. Cerulean Blue is warmer than Ultramarine Blue, for example. It's all about comparing. An easy way to understand this concept is to think of a sunny day—you feel warmer in the yellow sunshine and cooler in the blue shade. Or picture yellow or red fire and blue ice.

If colors don't correctly relate to each other, it may prevent the viewer from understanding the purpose of your painting. It may interrupt the experience because something seems off.

# COLOR STUDY COMPOSITIONS

Below are some examples of color study compositions that you can practice with. Start with simple setups like the box and do several until you feel comfortable with that level. Move to a more challenging setup and so on. Don't rush this. This skill is invaluable.

These exercises are a lot of fun. Doing them well means making mistakes, getting messy, experimenting and often working outside your comfort zone. Be self-confident not self-conscious!

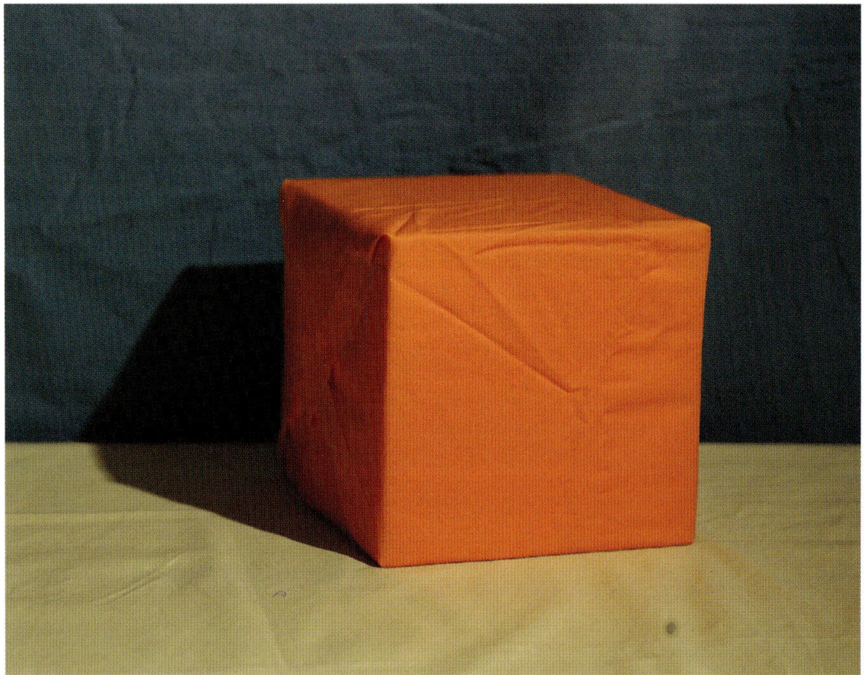

### *Test Time!*

Take the Munsell Hue Test online at colormunki.com/game/huetest_kiosk.

This involves sequencing colors. You can test yourself at the beginning of your color study practice, and then again later on. If you're like most people, you'll score better after studying color through these exercises.

ORANGE BAG
This is a simple setup. There is only one object with clear shadows and easy-to-identify colors.

GREEN BALL
This compositional setup is slightly more complicated because of the drapery folds.

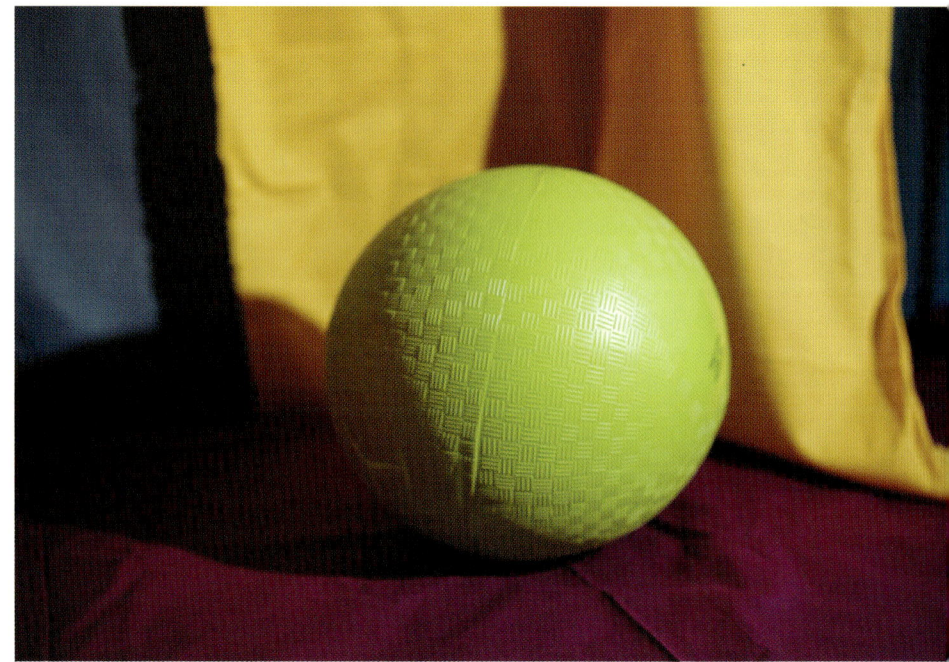

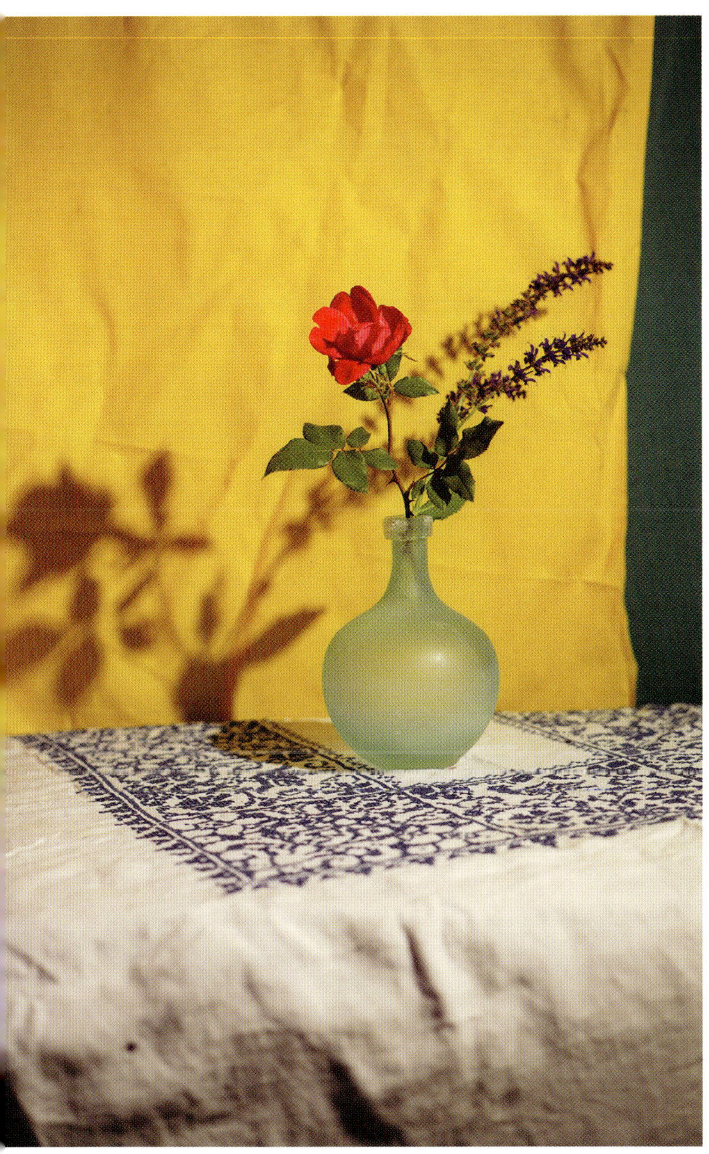

VASE AND ROSE

A color study like this might be done as a study for a final painting. What would be your choice of the first color to put down? There usually are a couple of good starting choices. In this arrangement I would suggest starting with either the yellow or the red. These are two strong clear colors

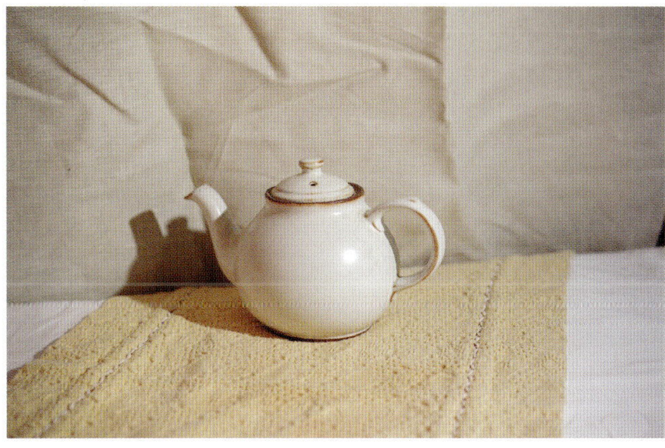

TEAPOT SURROUNDED BY SUBTLE COLORS

This is a challenging composition because the colors are close in both hue and value. It is essential to keep your eyes open and moving rapidly from object to object. It may take several rounds of adjustments.

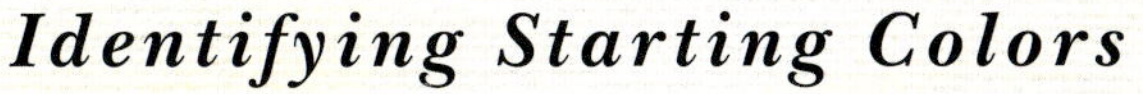

## Identifying Starting Colors

To identify simple starting colors, think about which colors are the most like a tube color. Which colors require initial mixing?

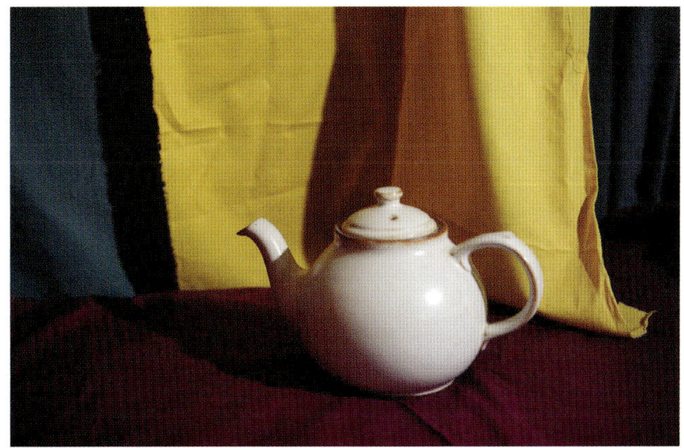

TEAPOT WITH COLORFUL DRAPES

When setting up these color studies, choose things of different value before moving on to more challenging studies. Keep your setups simple. Don't have more than four or five things, including drapery.

*Demonstration*

# SIMPLE COLOR STUDY

Follow the steps to practice a simply color study of a pumpkin.

## *Materials*

SURFACE

stretched canvas

OIL PAINTS

Magenta, Permanent Rose or Quinacridone Red, Cadmium Red Deep, Cadmium Red Medium or Cadmium Scarlet, Cadmium Orange or Cadmium Yellow Deep, Cadmium Yellow Light or Cadmium Lemon, Cadmium Green Light, Viridian or Phthalo Green, Cerulean Blue, Ultramarine Blue, Dioxazine Purple, Cobalt Violet Deep, Yellow Ochre, Indian Yellow, Burnt Sienna or Burnt Umber, Black, Titanium White

BRUSHES

Silver Brush #1003 size 6 extra long bristle filbert; Silver Brush #1034 size 4 long bristle filbert

OTHER

nitrile or vinyl gloves; odorless mineral spirits or Gamsol; stand oil

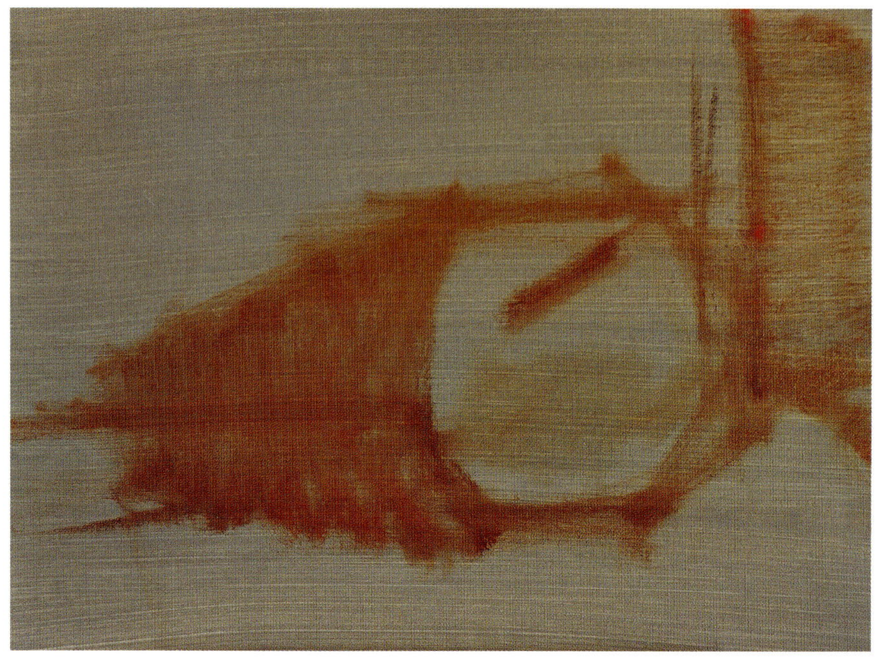

1 BLOCK IN THE COMPOSITION

Block in a simple composition using gesture marks. The paint mixture for this stage will be Burnt Sienna, Ultramarine Blue and a touch of Titanium White. Quickly block in your shadows so you will be aware of their location and leave room for them.

Try not to spend more than a minute or two on this stage. It is important to remember that you will be focusing on color and not drawing in this exercise. If you fall in love with your drawing you will be inclined to be careful and not experimental, which is key to success in this exercise.

## *Stand Oil*

As you work on a color study you will probably build up so much paint that new paint won't be easily applied. Should this happen, use your stand oil. Take a small container and pour a bit of stand oil in and then add a small amount of mineral spirits. The formula will be about three parts stand oil to one part mineral spirits. You may have to adjust depending on your painting. Dip your brush into this mixture and then your oil paint. This should allow you to adjust your colors more easily.

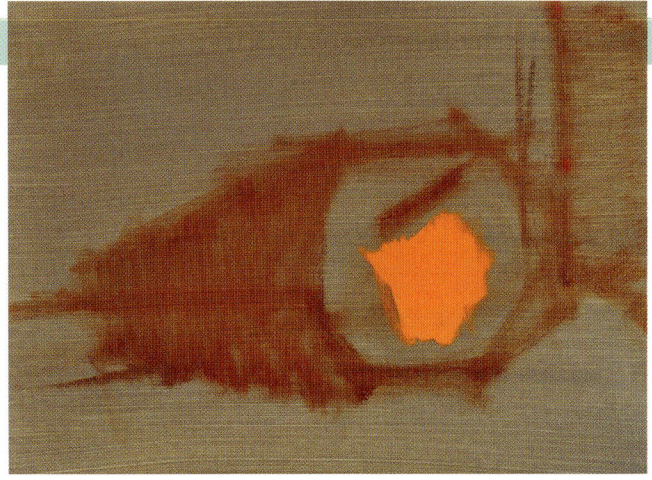

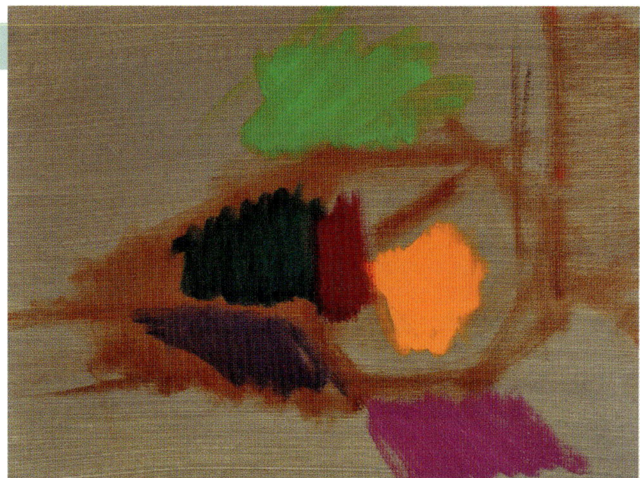

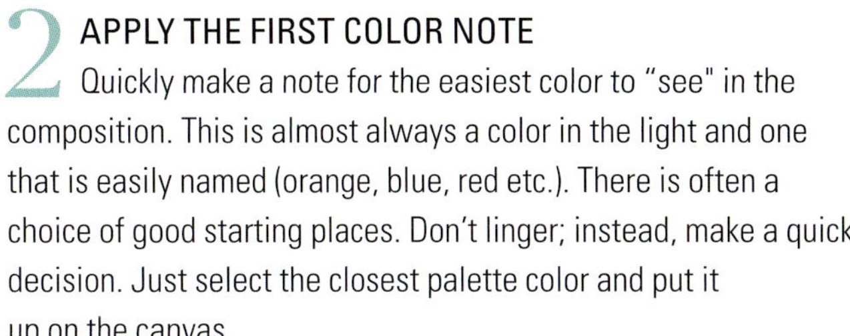

## 2 APPLY THE FIRST COLOR NOTE

Quickly make a note for the easiest color to "see" in the composition. This is almost always a color in the light and one that is easily named (orange, blue, red etc.). There is often a choice of good starting places. Don't linger; instead, make a quick decision. Just select the closest palette color and put it up on the canvas.

Try not to mix more than two palette colors to arrive at your first impression of the color. This rule prevents fussing and second guessing your first reaction to the color. Try not to think about the local or dye-lot color of the object. Everything is influenced by the color of the light that is hitting it. Is it a cool northern light? A warm halogen? The color of the light absolutely influences the local color of the object so don't be fooled by what you think you know as opposed to what you see.

## 3 CONTINUE ADDING COLOR

Move quickly to make a single note for every clear object in the composition. One color for the object in light and one for the object in shadow. Use a single palette color or two mixed for this. Don't dip into the same palette color that you used for another color statement. Move from the simplest, clearest colors to the more difficult. Use as large a color note as necessary for you to judge one color against another. I suggest not filling in the entire area since you're going to be adjusting and spreading the colors as the study progresses and you make adjustments.

Spend no more than five minutes on this stage. Try to move faster than you can fuss or second guess your notes. This is an exercise in adjusting and steering color as well as investigating color relationships. Trust your instincts.

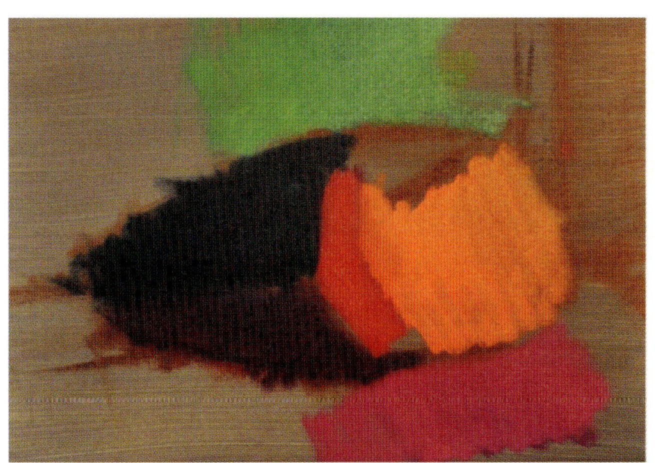

## 4 MAKE COLOR ADJUSTMENTS

Once you have a note for each mass in light and shadow, begin to adjust and correct your initial color choices. Where you begin your adjusting is up to you. I usually begin with the color I'm the happiest with, but see a simple change I can make to bring it closer to the truth. Then I usually head to the color note that has been driving me nuts because it's so off. Remember it is essential that you stand back during the exercise. Move your eyes from one color note to another. Glance at the color you're trying to see. If you stare at the color you won't get the best information about that color as it relates to the other colors around it, and you'll see details. Remember that you're building a color relationship that will depend on all the other color notes in your composition. You are trying to make paint create the illusion of life. Don't spend more than twenty seconds on each color!

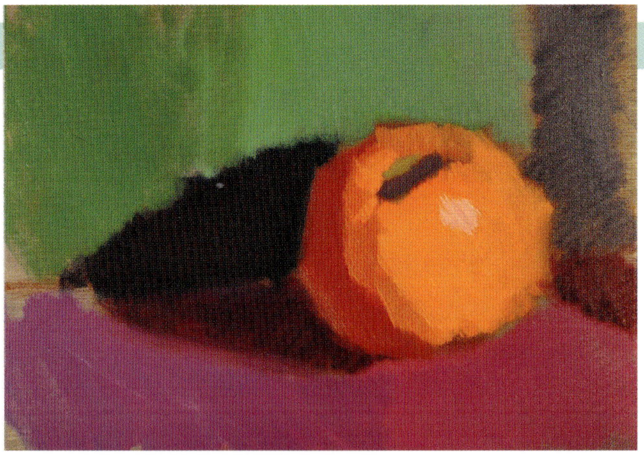

## 5 EVALUATE YOUR PROGRESS

Make several passes around your painting, always standing back and quickly moving your eye from one area to another. Do your color mixing directly on the painting, not on your palette. This ensures that you don't underestimate the impact of the color you're trying to replicate and prevents second guessing. If you have trouble adjusting your paint color because you have so much paint on your canvas, begin to dip into your mixed medium (stand oil and turpentine). Experiment with dancing the paint on top of your canvas and pushing in if you want to mix with the paint underneath. Notice that there is a heavy paint deposit on the canvas, which you can see in the areas that show glare from the camera. Once you can see no further adjustments to your six color areas, you are either done with the color study or you can decide to break your masses into further divisions. In the pumpkin study I decided to move on to finding a highlight color on the pumpkin and also a plane change or dark light area in the light side of the pumpkin.

It is essential that you have a long filbert as the color study progresses so you can regulate how much paint you put on and whether it is deposited correctly on your canvas. If you're working with a short bristle brush, it can push the paint away rather than deposit it on.

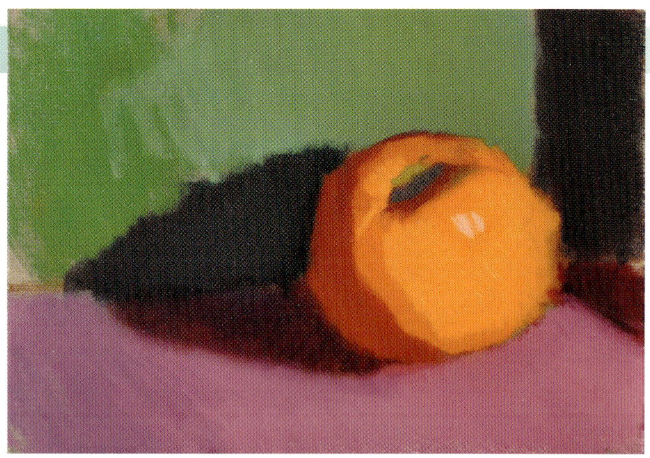

## 6 CONTINUE MAKING ADJUSTMENTS AS NEEDED

Continue to make adjustments to your colors. Stand back and move your eyes from one color mass to another always looking for an adjustment. Be fearless in your color adjustments. This is an experimental study and not a finished painting.

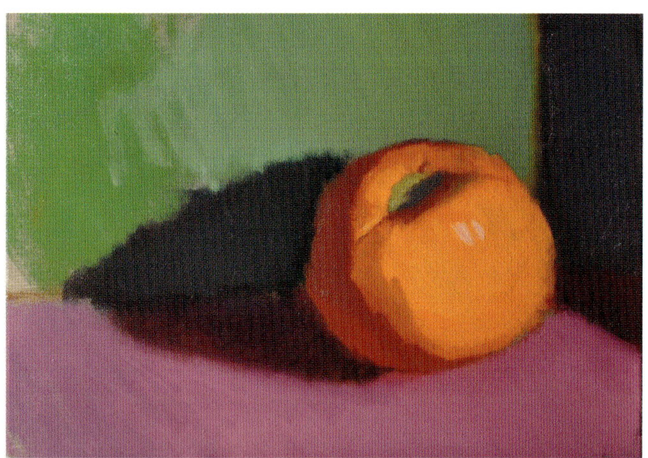

## 7 ADD MORE COLOR

Once you are satisfied with your main color masses, you can add another color to the shadow mass if you'd like. There is a reflected light in the shadow side of the pumpkin and now is the time to try to show that color shift. It's important to squint to determine the value of any reflected light in a shadow mass. There is a tendency to paint reflective light too high in value. Remember that nothing in the shadow will be as light as your darkest note in the light area.

*Demonstration*

# COMPLEX COLOR STUDY

Follow the steps to complete a more complex color study of an orange paper bag.

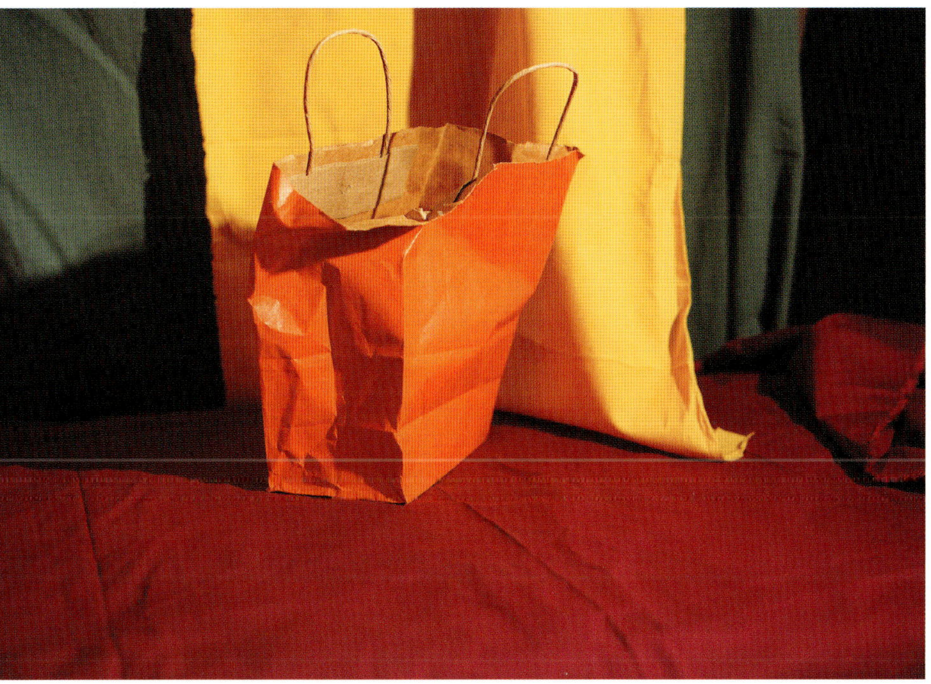

THE SET UP

This vibrant composition includes clear, strong colors. It looks pretty straight forward, but there are still some challenging relationships. The shadow from the bag, for instance, is very close in color and value to the drapery beneath it.

## *Materials*

SURFACE

stretched canvas

OIL PAINTS

Magenta, Permanent Rose or Quinacridone Red, Cadmium Red Deep, Cadmium Red Medium or Cadmium Scarlet, Cadmium Orange or Cadmium Yellow Deep, Cadmium Yellow Light or Cadmium Lemon, Cadmium Green Light, Viridian or Phthalo Green, Cerulean Blue, Ultramarine Blue, Dioxazine Purple, Cobalt Violet Deep, Yellow Ochre, Indian Yellow, Burnt Sienna or Burnt Umber, Black, Titanium White

BRUSHES

Silver Brush #1003 size 6 extra long bristle filbert; Silver Brush #1034 size 4 long bristle filbert

OTHER

nitrile or vinyl gloves; odorless mineral spirits or Gamsol; stand oil

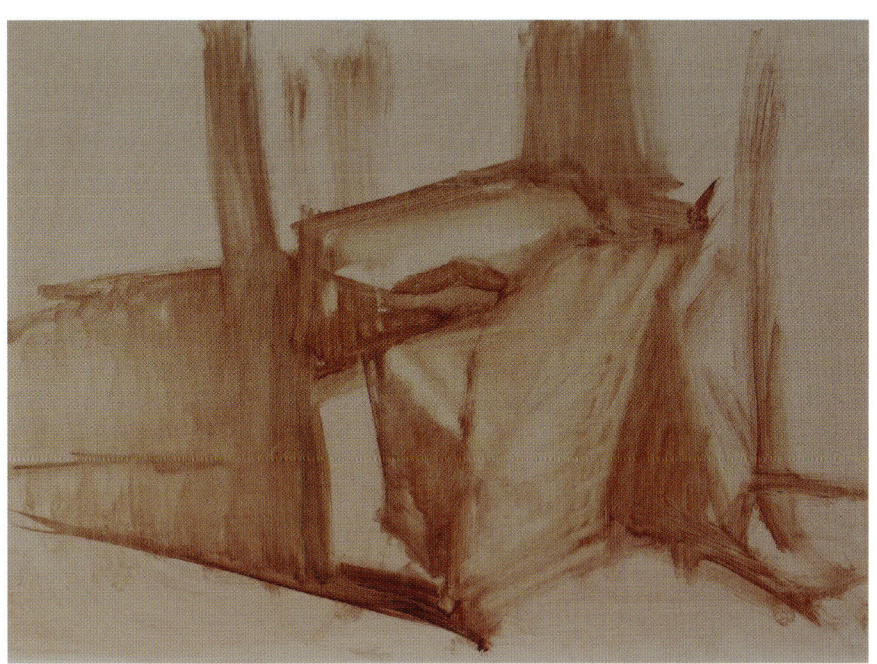

1 START WITH THE GESTURE

Start with a simple gesture and grisaille to indicate the shadows. Make the shapes large enough to allow for adjustment of your colors.

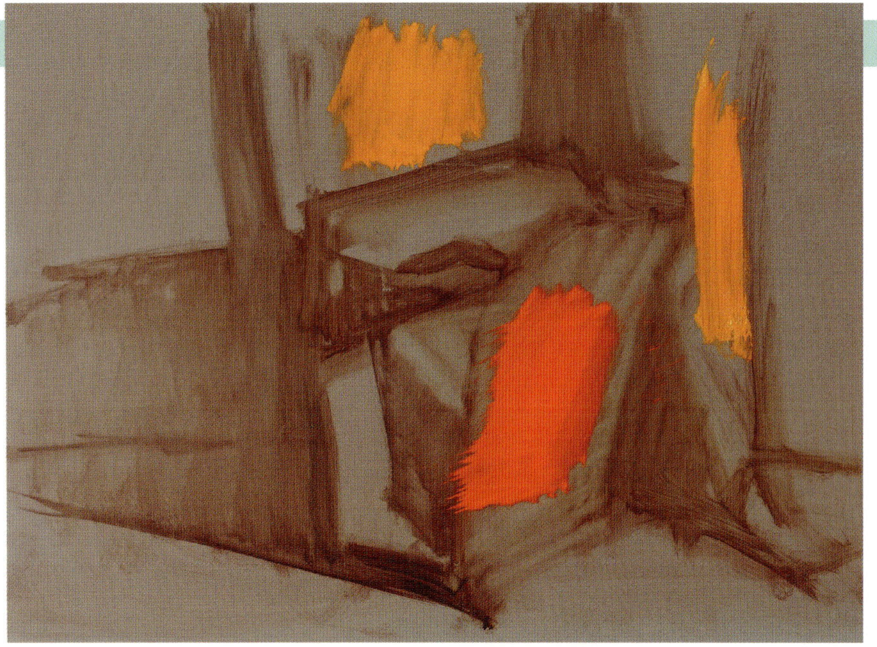

## 2 APPLY THE FIRST COLOR NOTES

Start with the colors that are least complicated and easiest for you to identify. In this case, the colors of the bag and the drapery in the light areas seem to be the simplest and clearest. The notes consist of one palette color each: Cadmium Orange and Cadmium Yellow Medium. Both are warm colors.

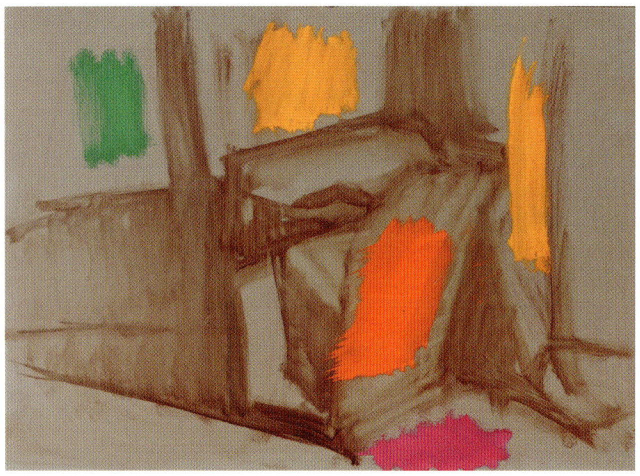

## 3 CONTINUE ADDING COLOR NOTES IN THE LIGHT AREAS

Continue to add simple color notes for all the masses in the light areas.

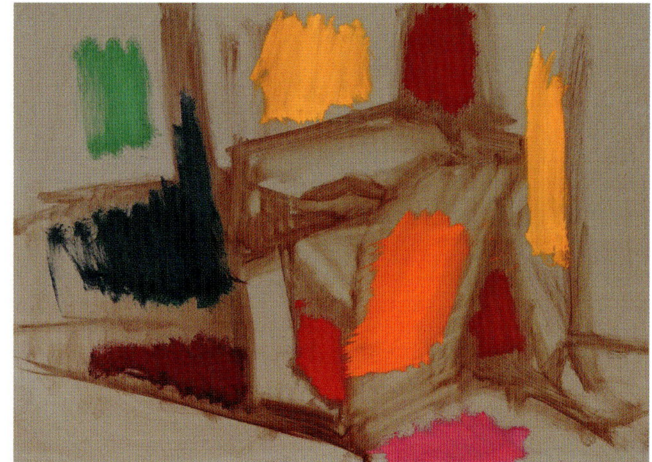

## 4 ADD COLOR NOTES TO THE DARK AREAS

Next apply color notes to the remaining masses in the shadow areas. When finished, you should have colors for each mass in both the light and shadow areas. In this case there are eight.

### *Use Value to Find Color*

If you are at a dead end and having trouble finding a color, locate another color mass in your composition that has the same value, then glance back and forth between the two. Choosing equal values leaves you only with the hue difference to compare. That way you won't be relating both color and value.

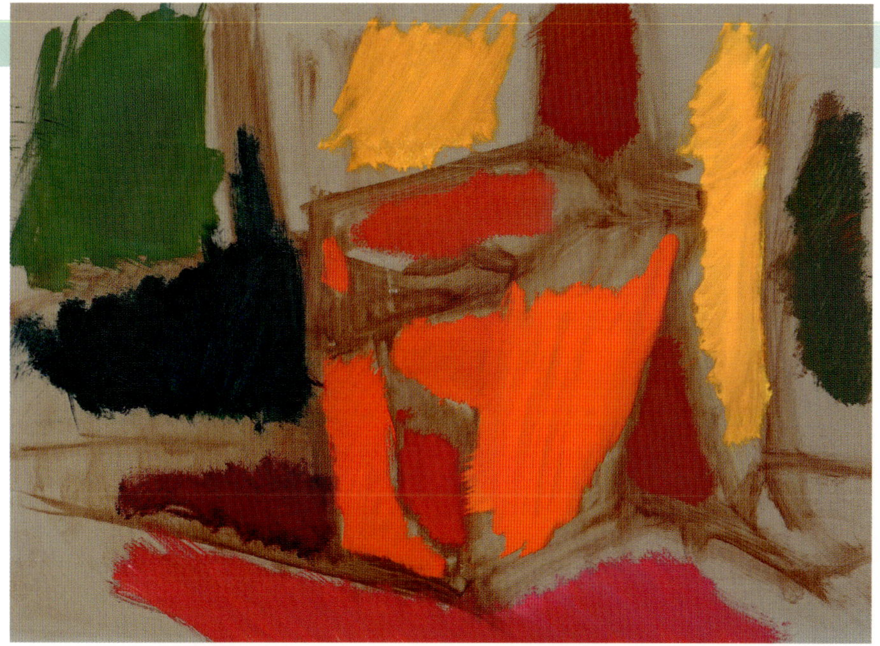

## 5 MAKE ADJUSTMENTS

Adjust your colors. Begin with the color you're happiest with and make any adjustments needed. Once you've got a color note that you're confident with, adjust another color mass to relate to it. As you make each round of adjusting colors, you'll have more and more new colors to compare to.

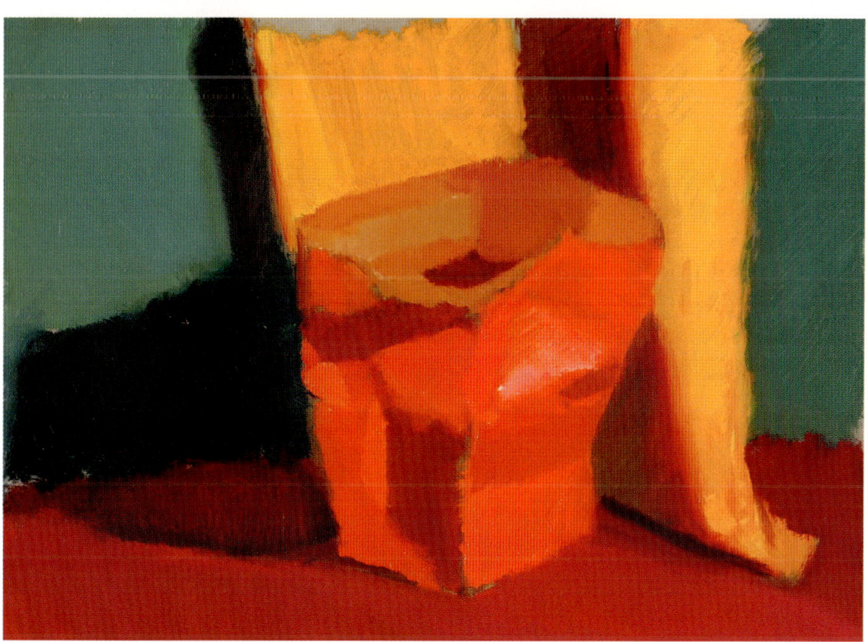

## 6 ADD HIGHLIGHTS

Continue adjusting and spreading the color as you gain more confidence. Try to find variations within the masses. At this point, you can add highlights to break up the masses, if you like. A highlight can be challenging, so I recommend waiting until you have large areas of color you are satisfied with to compare and identify the more complex colors.

### *Don't Paint Too Light or Too Dark*

Be careful that you're not painting darker or lighter than you realize. If you have more light on your canvas, you could paint darker. If you have less light, you could paint lighter. If you notice that the mixture on your palette looks a lot darker or lighter than you expected, put a note down for your darkest dark and lightest light. If a highlight doesn't stand out in your painting the same way it does on your subject, that's an indication you're painting too light overall (i.e., you haven't reached the correct color relationship). If this happens, take your painting into a different light and check the value.

# WARM VS. COOL LIGHT

Take a look at this progression of two color studies of the same subject under two different light temperatures. The first study was done under a natural, cool northern light coming in through the window. The second one was done under a warm halogen light.

## COOL LIGHT COLOR STUDY

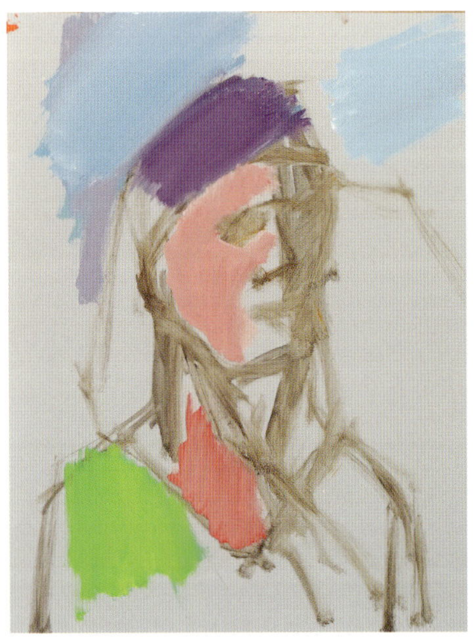

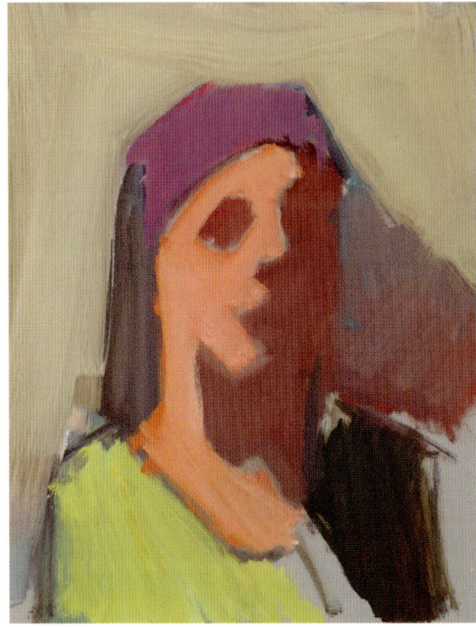

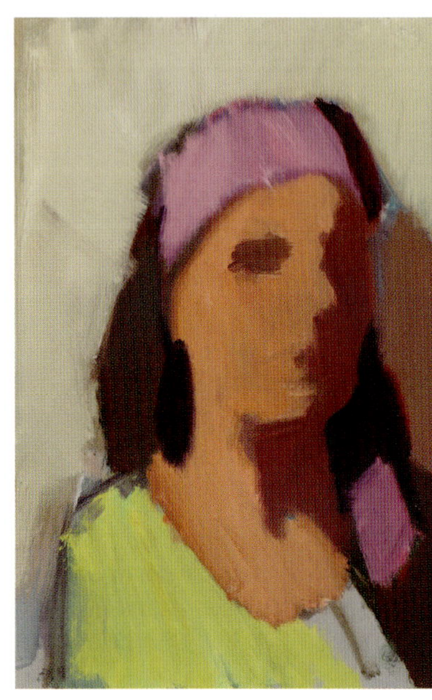

## WARM LIGHT COLOR STUDY

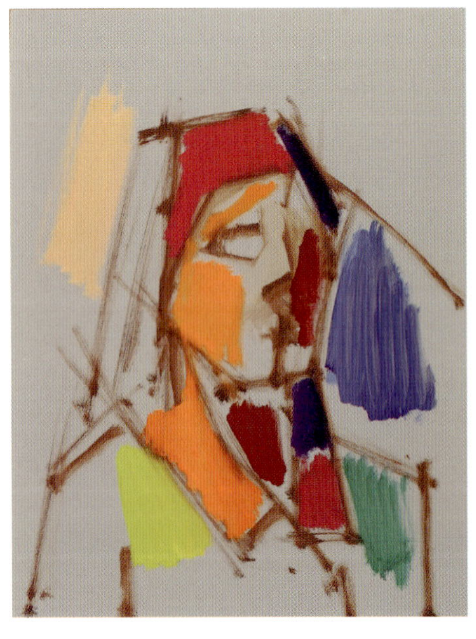

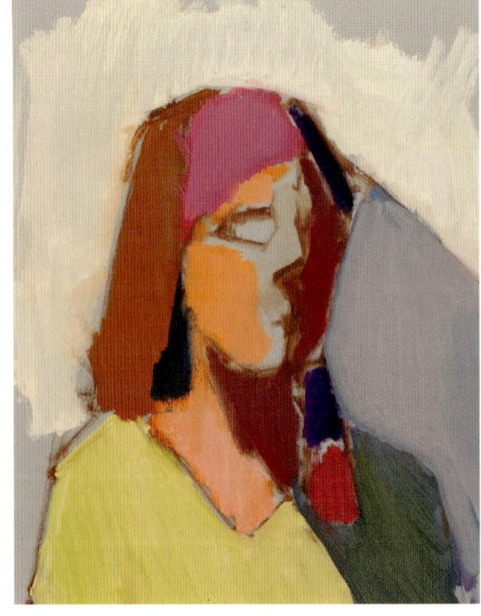

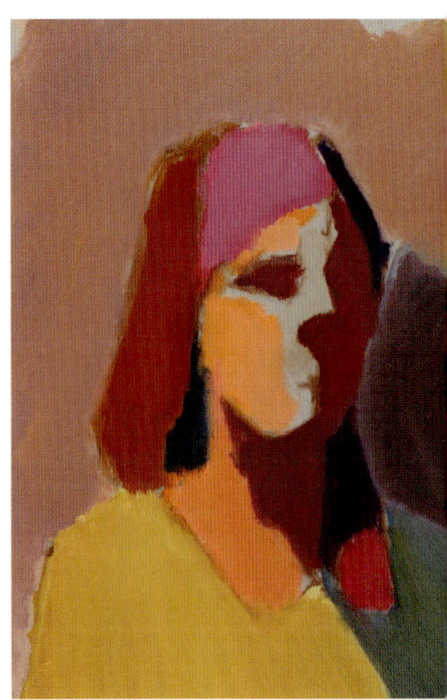

### *Keep It Fun*

These exercises are not meant to be developed into full paintings. Make sure you don't fall in love with your color study. When you can't see any more adjustments move on. Set up another color study arrangement.

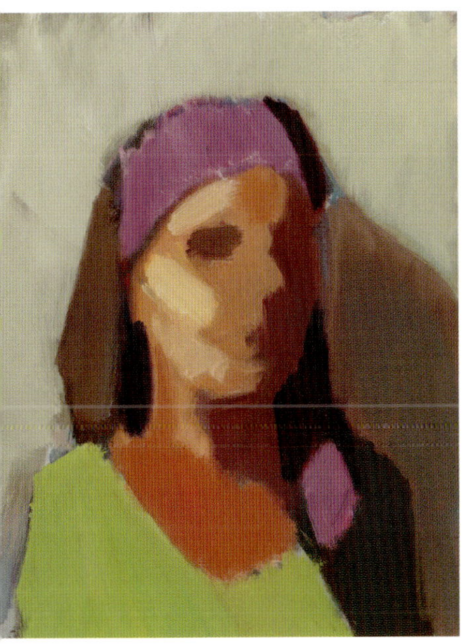

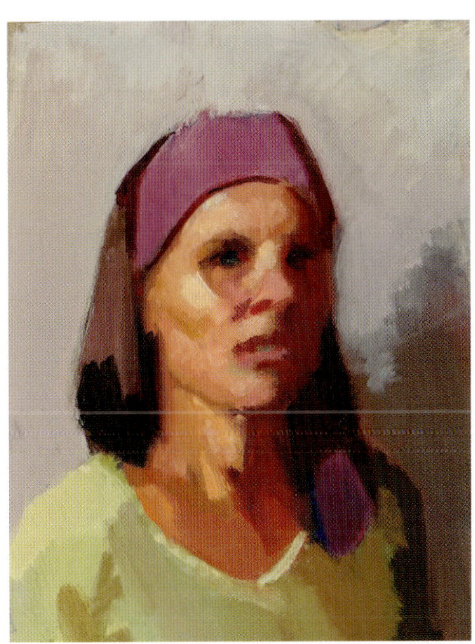

AVOID DETAIL

Remember to avoid detail in a color study. You do not need to be overly concerned with proportions, and you should not spend too much time on the gesture and block-in stage.

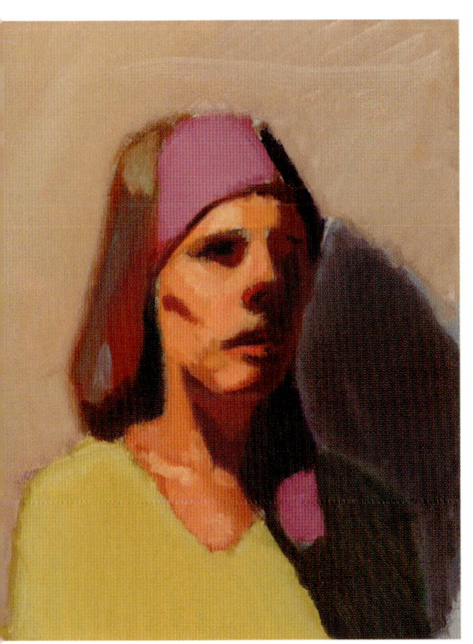

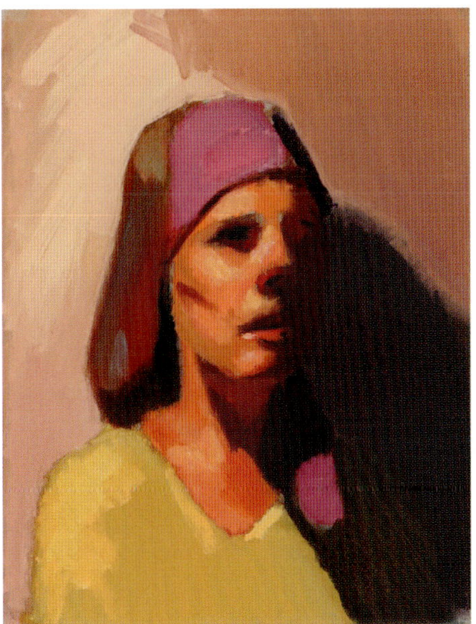

KEEP IT SIMPLE

The goal is to come away from the study with a simple understanding of the color of the light hitting the objects and how it affects them.

Your state of mind should be energetic and explorative. Keep your eyes wide open and moving between the different colors to see the differences.

Here is an excellent comparison of the effect of cool and warm light affecting the same composition. My colleague Kerry Dunn painted these in 2005.

COOL LIGHT

This was painted in natural window light. Notice that the objects in the bluish light are cool and their shadows are warm.

**Color Study 1**
Kerry Dunn, 2005
Oil on stretched canvas
18" × 24" (46cm × 61cm)

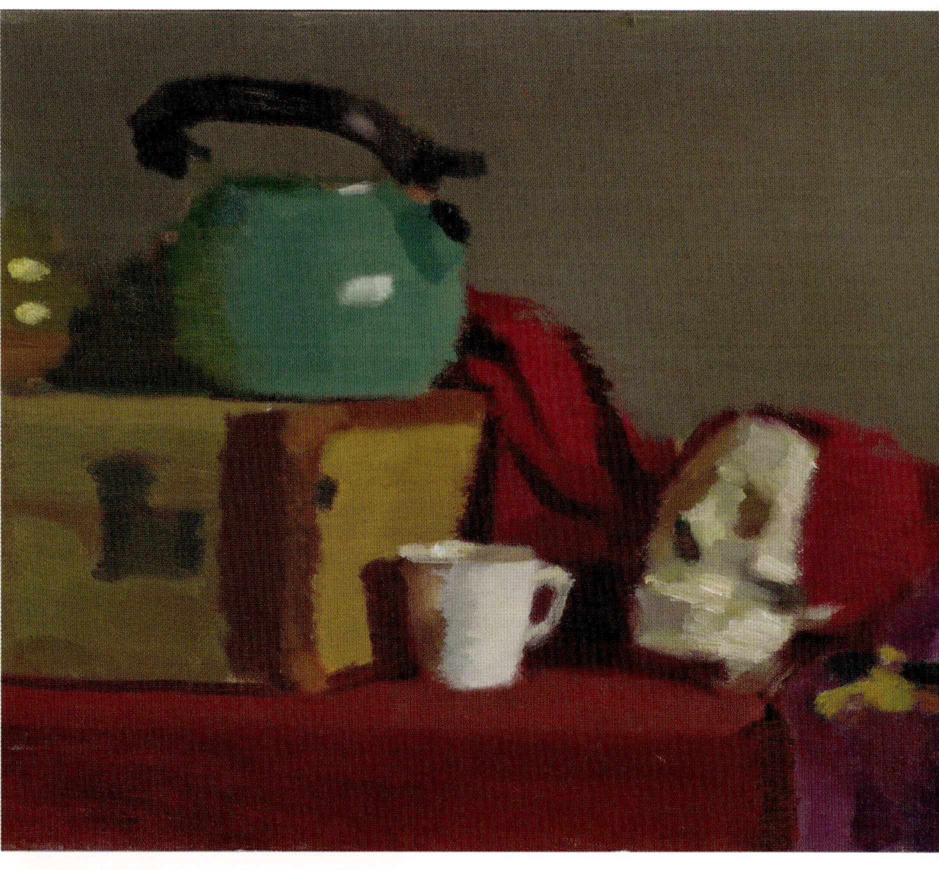

WARM LIGHT

The color differences really stand out when a very warm halogen light is turned on.

**Color Study 2**
Kerry Dunn, 2005
Oil on stretched canvas
18" × 24" (46cm × 61cm)

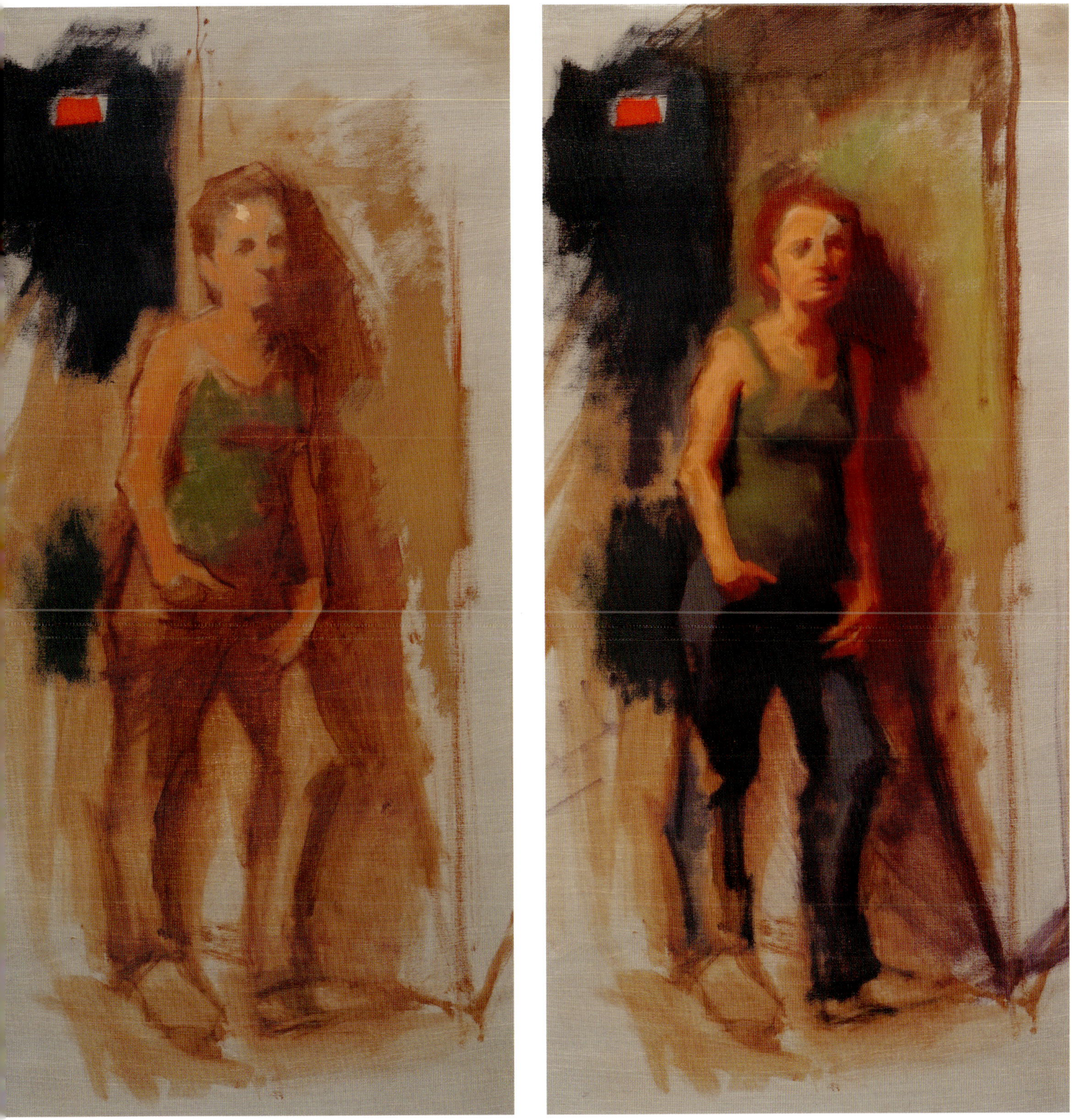

## COLOR RELATIONSHIPS

This is an example of the benefit of studying color relationships. In this painting it was key to have the exit sign look illuminated so I chose that as my first color note. I used the brightest suitable red on my palette and then related the background to it. If I'd waited until later in the painting to paint the sign, chances are good that I couldn't have reached it.

The more color studies you do the more your ability to see subtle differences strengthens. Consequently, you can spend more time on a study, finding more adjustments and undertaking ever more complicated compositions. In the end you'll be able to master any color painting you desire.

**Lauren**
Lea Colie Wight
Oil on linen
28" × 20" (71cm × 51cm)

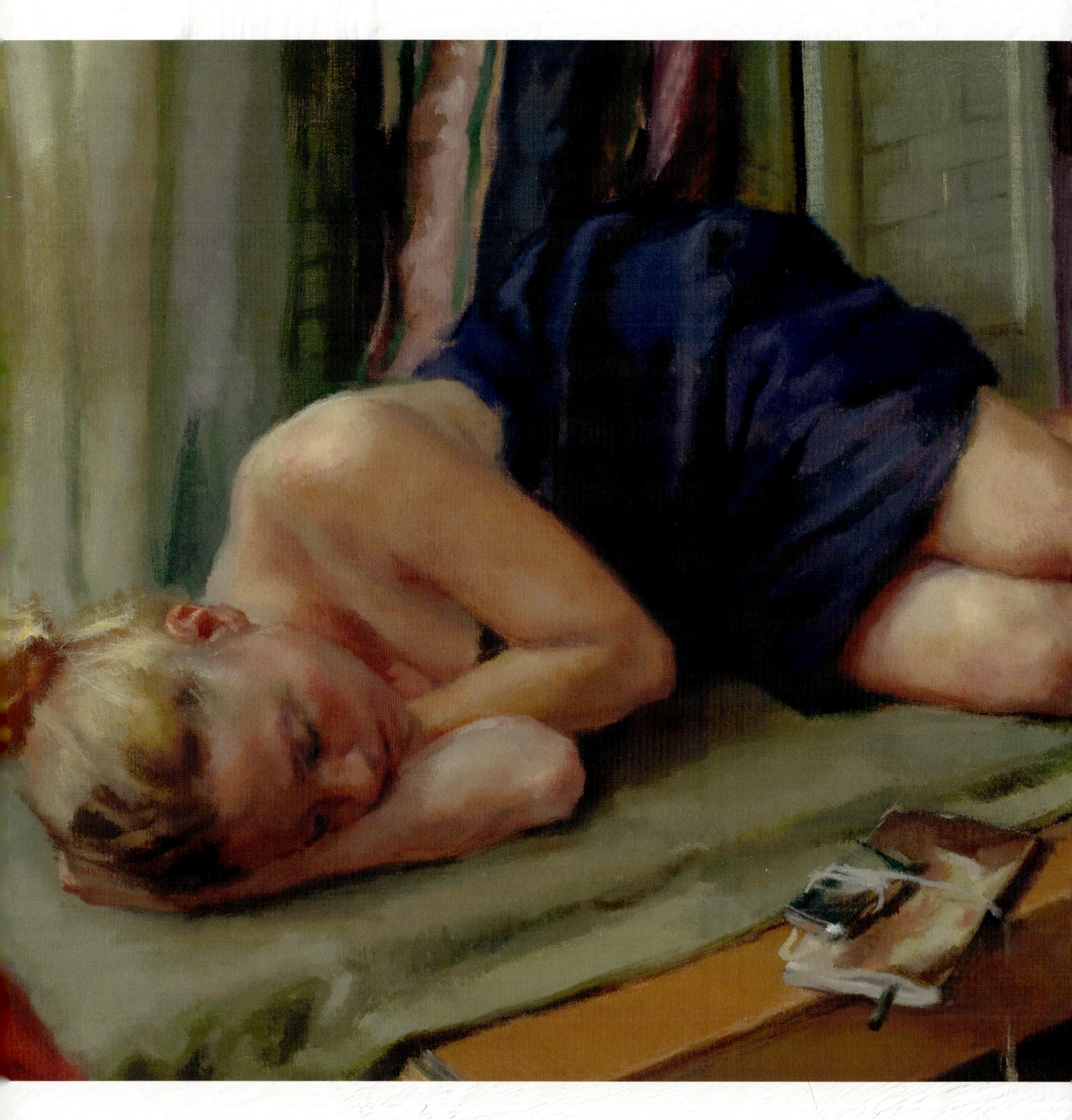

# 5 FIGURES *and* PORTRAITS

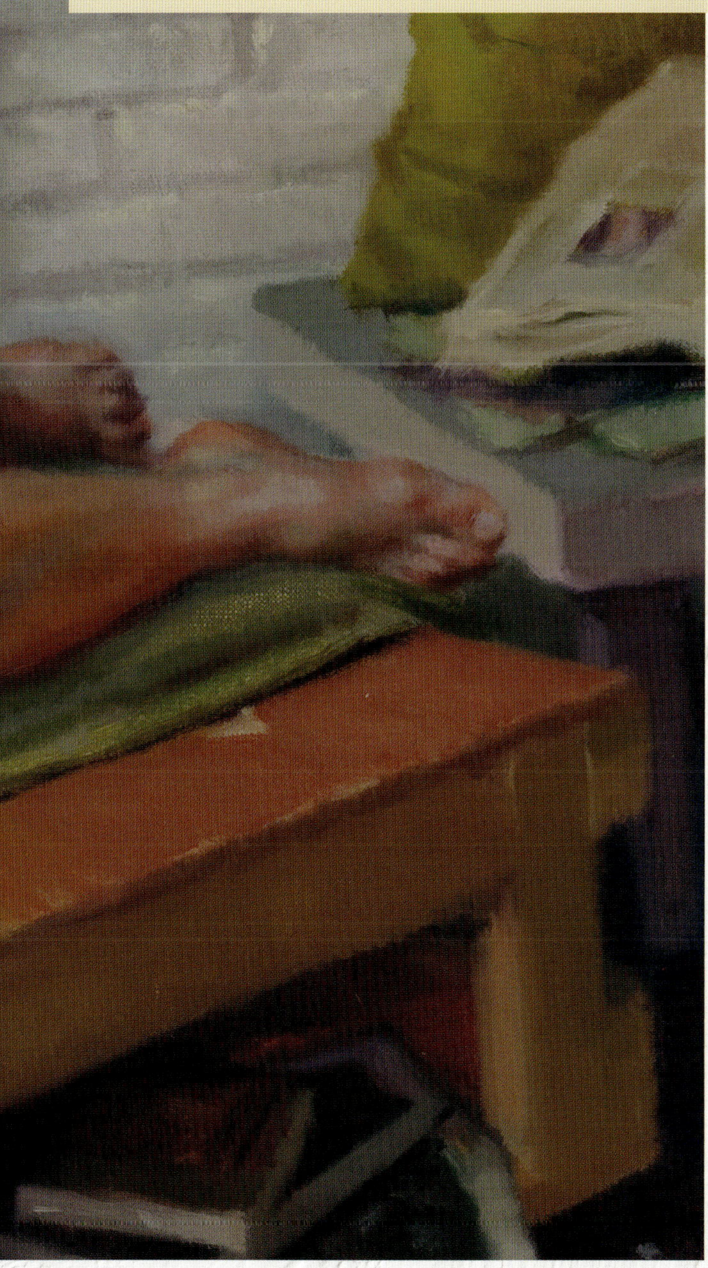

Now you'll begin to put to use all of the methods and techniques that have been studied in the preceding chapters. I liken this to a gymnast in training. The different skills are studied, practiced and mastered individually, then all of that training is brought together in one spectacular routine.

One way to accomplish this is through patience. Take the time to get the goals of each stage correct before moving on to the next stage. Ultimately it's up to you to determine how to weave all the elements of a painting together. How long do you feel you need to stay just in one light value? Should you immediately move to more color? How developed do you want to make your grisaille before laying in color? It's all up to you—you are in control.

**Muse**
Lea Colie Wight
Oil on linen
18" × 30" (46cm × 76cm)

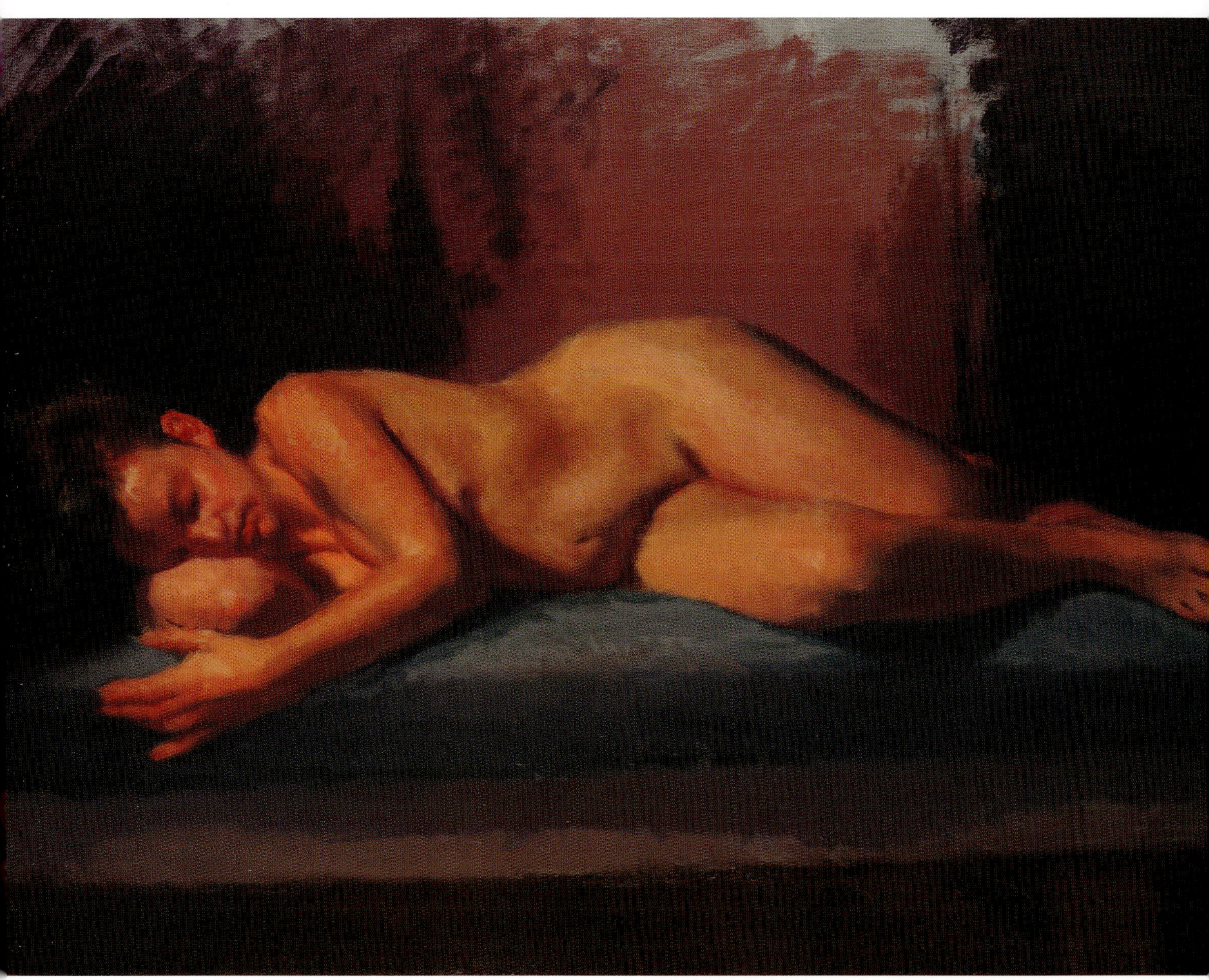

**At Rest**
Lea Colie Wight
Oil on linen
24" × 32" (61cm × 81cm)

*Demonstration*

# FIGURE PAINTING

I believe that rendering the living human form is the best way to learn the art of painting. It is fundamental to learn how to paint nude figures, even if you don't intend for that to be the focus of your personal paintings. A solid understanding of the nude form is essential to painting clothed figures, as well as animals and other forms in nature. It also allows you to paint competently from photographic references without having to rely on a live model.

If you're painting the human figure for the first time, go easy on yourself. It's a challenging job, but it's the pinnacle of painting. You're on the very same road the Masters have journeyed. They worked and learned just like you. The next time you visit an art museum, remember that you share a bond with all the artists whose works hang there.

In this progression, I'll walk you through a full-color figure painting. You'll recognize the methods and techniques covered in earlier chapters. In this case the model is illuminated with a warm, artificial light source, and the easel is in northern light.

## *Materials*

SURFACE
stretched canvas

OIL PIGMENTS
Magenta, Permanent Rose or Quinacridone Red, Cadmium Red Deep, Cadmium Red Medium or Cadmium Scarlet, Cadmium Orange or Cadmium Yellow Deep, Cadmium Yellow Light or Cadmium Lemon, Cadmium Green Light, Viridian or Phthalo Green, Cerulean Blue, Ultramarine Blue, Dioxazine Purple, Cobalt Violet Deep, Yellow Ochre, Indian Yellow, Burnt Sienna or Burnt Umber, Black, Titanium White

BRUSHES
Silver Brush #5001 hake flat or mop brush; Silver Brush #7110 sable cat's tongue sizes 4, 6 and 8; Silver Brush #1034 long bristle filbert sizes 2, 3, 4 and 6; Rosemary brush #278 sizes 2, 4 and 6

OTHER
nitrile or vinyl gloves, odorless mineral spirits or Gamsol, paper towels, spray Retouch varnish

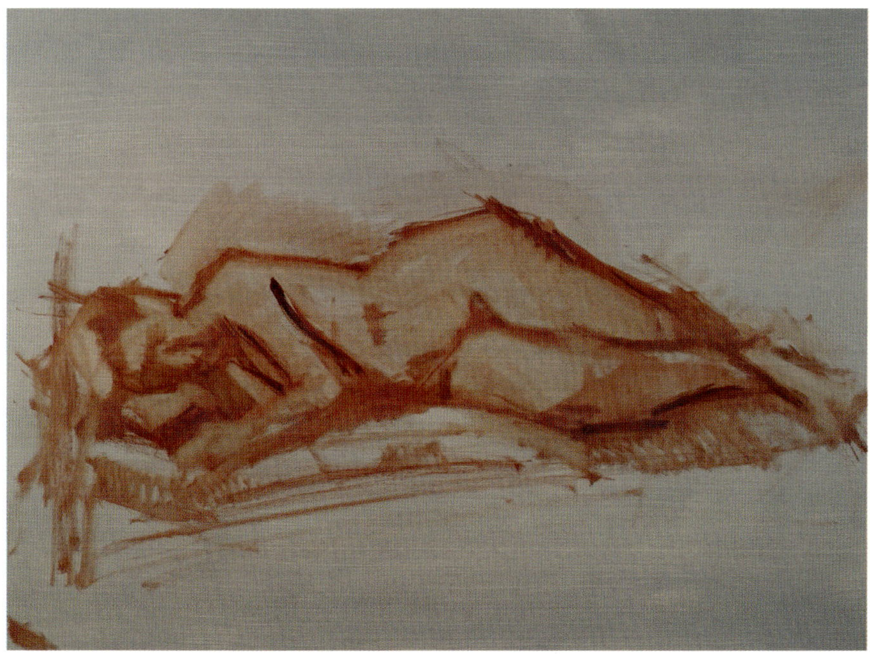

1 BEGIN WITH THE OPENING GESTURE
Make your opening gesture and first drawing adjustment. There are a few different approaches you can choose. The most important thing is that your marks indicate the major action of the pose. Toggle back and forth between gesture, abstraction and form. Try to think of the body in three dimensions. The proportions are quite open to change.

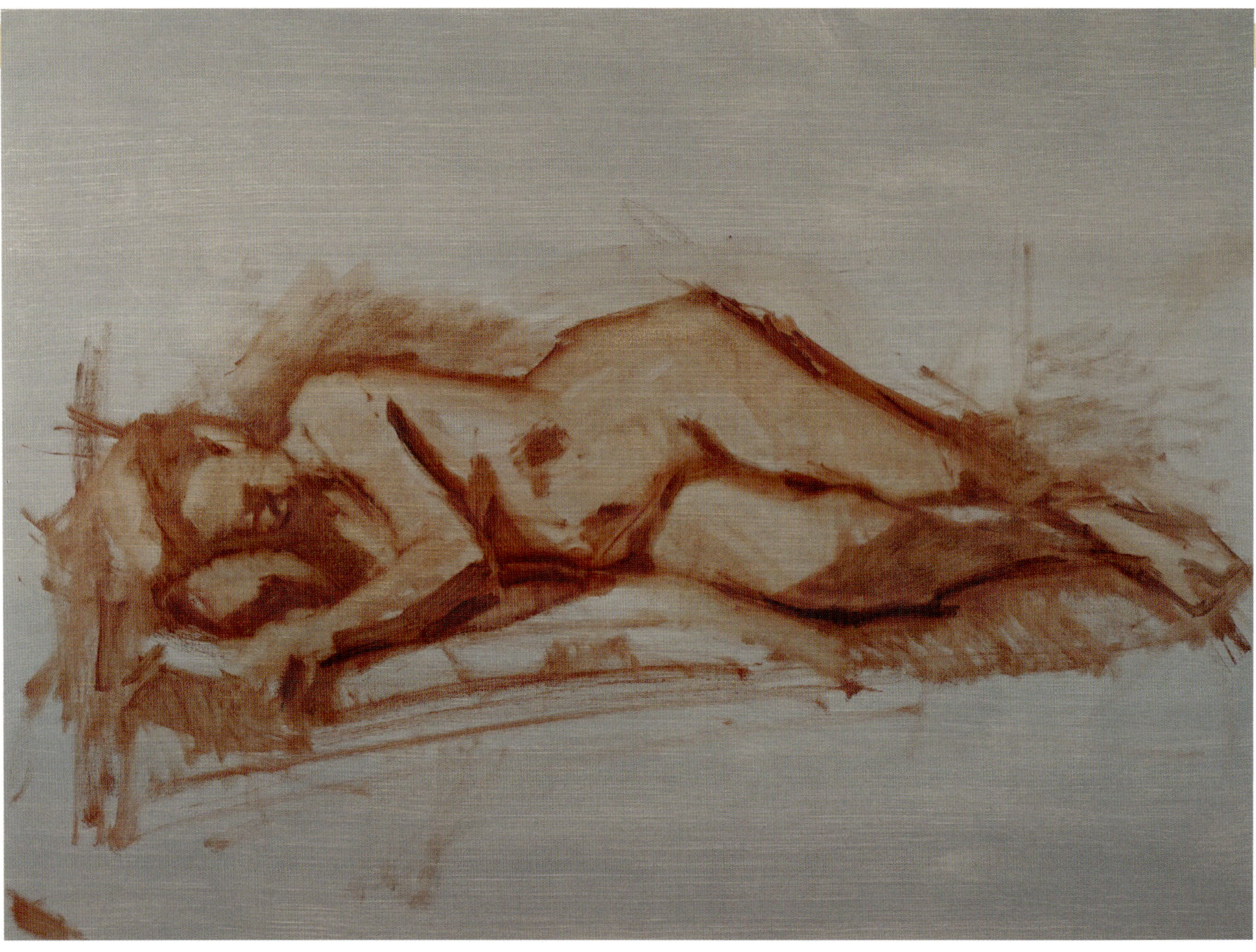

## Cause and Effect

Both sides of the body act as a single unit so what happens on one side has an effect on another. When one side of a form is compressed, you will find extension on the other. For example, when an elbow is bent, one side is compressed and the other is pulled taut over the bones.

In this pose, the figure's left side is compressed and her right side is extended.

### 2 DEVELOP AND ADJUST THE GESTURE

Develop your drawing using abstract shapes to judge proportions. Find the adjustments by standing back and observing both the model and the painting from a distance of about ten feet (three meters). In addition to proportions, focus on reinforcing the gestural movement of the pose.

Work all over the figure in a general way. Judge the entire figure to ensure that your proportions stay correct. In this stage it can be easy to get lost focusing on one area and wind up with a feature the wrong size. This could lead to the figure becoming too large or too small.

Wipe out any extra lines in order to see your decisions more clearly and to pull your drawing together.

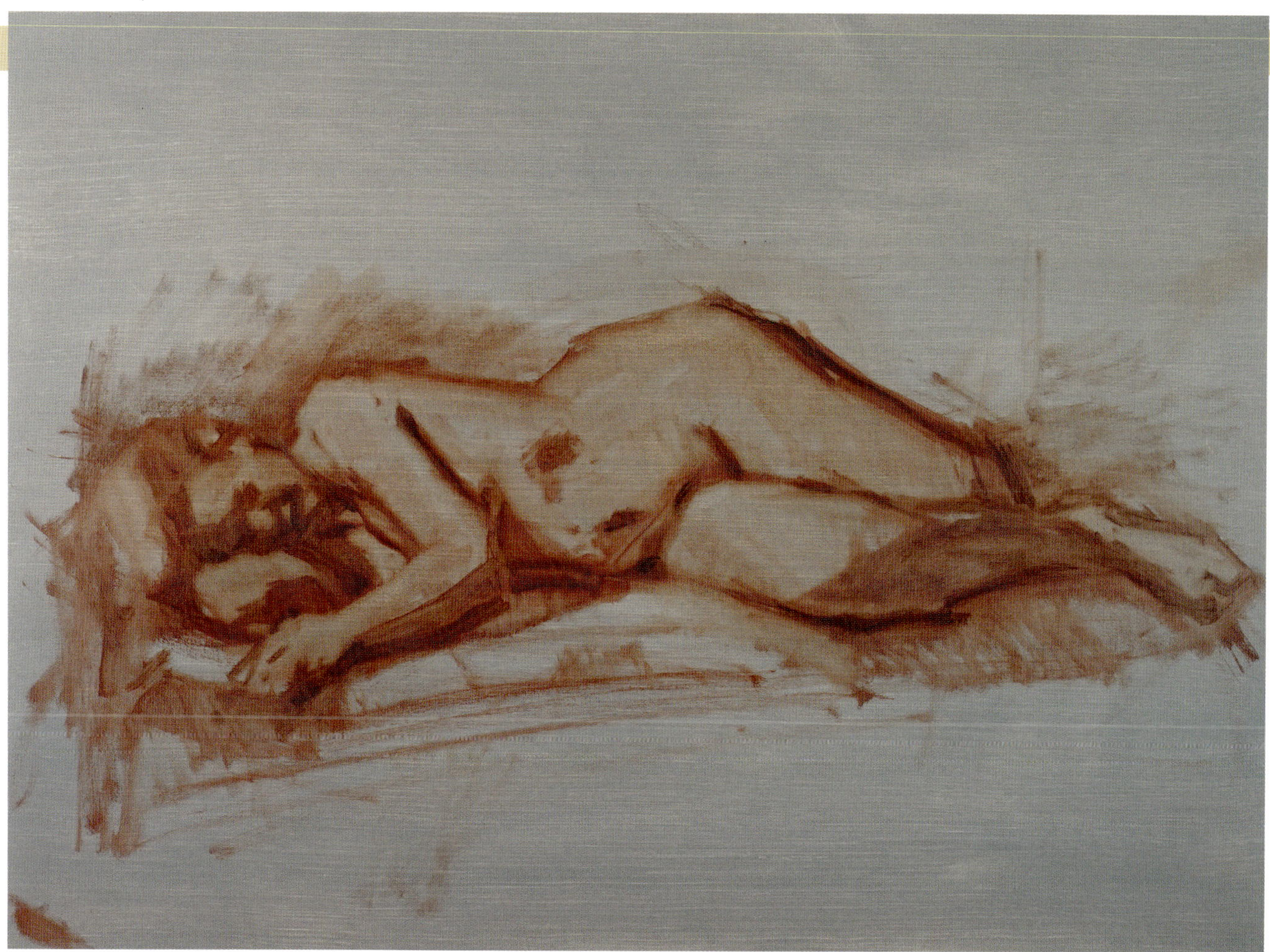

## 3 LOOK FOR CONNECTING LINES AND MASS IN SHADOW PATTERNS

Step back and look for long connecting lines through your composition. This particular pose is full of these opportunities. Notice the way the line running from her left shoulder to her waist carries through to the top of her right thigh. Identifying these relationships makes your drawing process much easier. Look for the angle between the hands. Find the anatomical landmarks such as the bottom of the ribcage, the neck insertion, the pelvic landmarks, the hands and feet, the basic head shape, the centerline and so on.

Block in a simple shadow pattern. Squint to see the shadows and terminator (the area between the darkest dark and the darkest light). If you can't easily see the separation of light and shadow in a given area, walk around the model until you get to a position where it is more obvious. Carry that information back to your easel position. Usually you will be able to see a clue once you view it clearly from another position. This is one of the real advantages of working with a live model.

Feel your own body for skeletal and form clues.

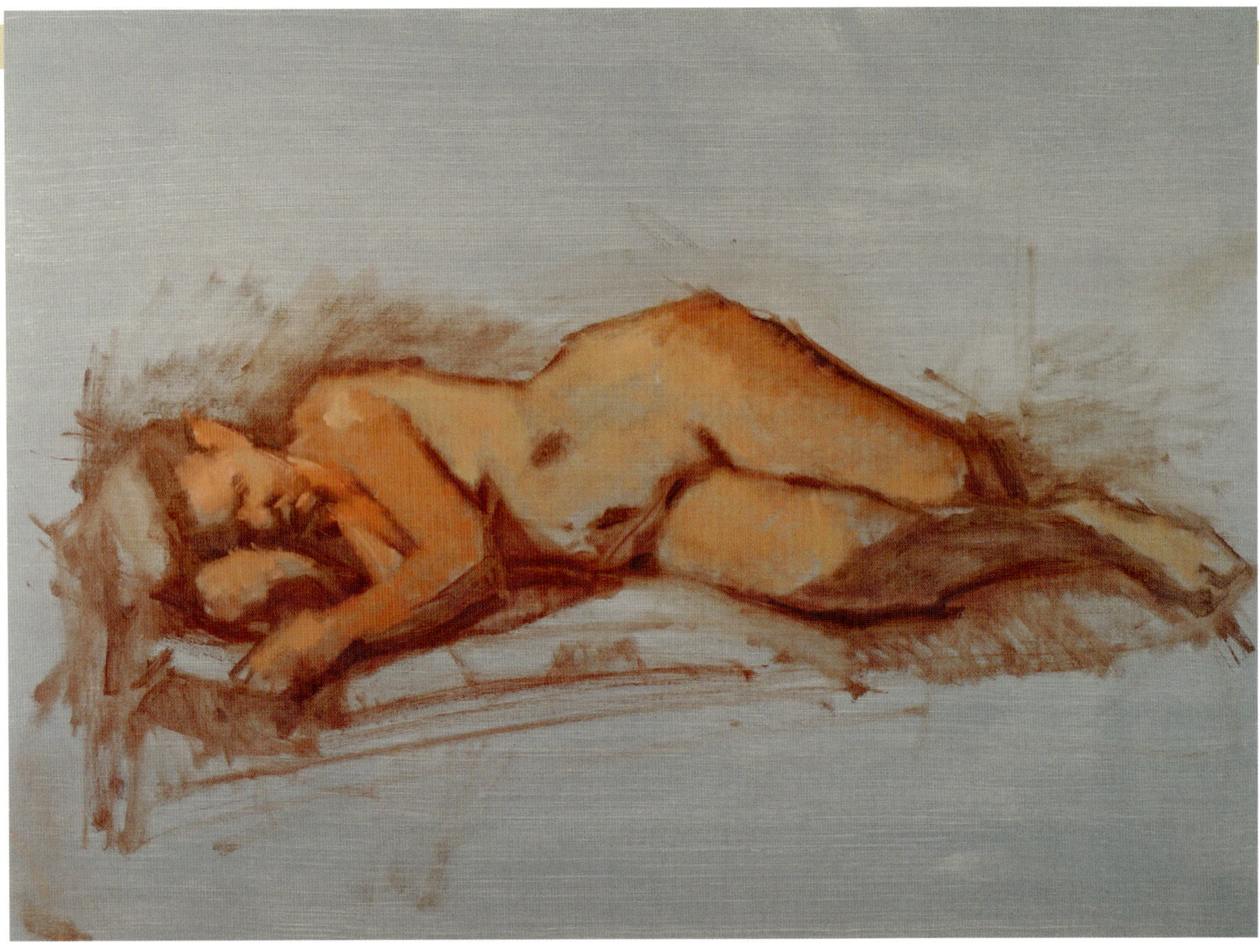

### Use Your Own Body As Reference

Remember that your body is the perfect reference. Bend to one side and feel both sides of your ribcage to hip relationship—compression and extension at work. Use yourself as a textbook to find the landmarks and bony structures in your own body.

## 4 CONTINUE BLOCKING IN THE DRAWING AND REFINE THE GRISAILLE

Continue to block in your drawing until you feel you've gotten an accurate drawing with the major elements placed. At this point you want to have a solid map of landmarks and large plane shifts. Address some of the features you think you'll want to pay attention to when you begin blocking in color.

Spend some time refining the grisaille. Focus again on the long connections through the body. The shadow on the model's neck moves down and connects with her spine beautifully. Keep looking for that as the painting develops.

Now you are in the closed grisaille stage. Begin adding color for the skin in light to shape and build form. Try to keep a thin layer of paint, not filling in entire areas. If you choose to block in more than one color, as I did here, limit your color masses to three or four. Always look for the biggest differences that describe the big color or planes. Try to get in the ballpark color-wise, but don't get sidetracked trying to find the exact color of her skin. You'll be adjusting the color as you develop the form.

Step back and judge the simplest breakdown. In this case there are three main areas: the shoulders, arms and head, the torso and the legs. There is a plane change between the upper torso and the abdomen. From the legs to the abdomen there is a big plane change that shows up in both value and color because of the angle to the light.

You be the judge of how quickly you develop this beginning stage and keep it organized. If you overdo your development, just simplify your form and stay with a few colors. Keep the big planes clear.

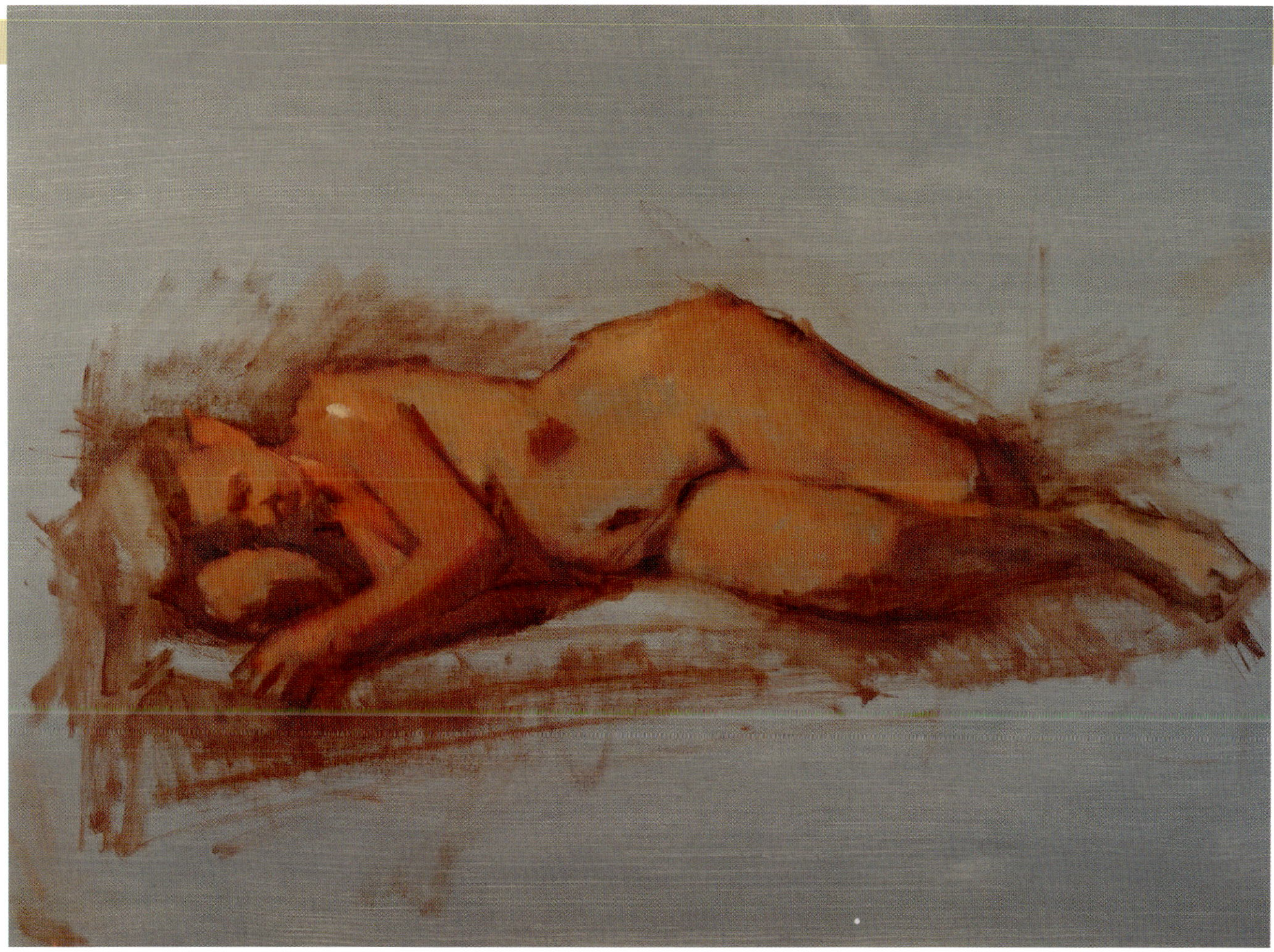

## 5 CONTINUE TO WORK THE COLORS, MAKE ADJUSTMENTS AND BLOCK IN MAJOR PLANES AND LANDMARKS

Work the simple colors. Include the highlight to help find the value. Develop your drawing and adjust the proportions. Find things to change. Each time you stand back and compare your painting with your model, look for something you can improve upon—just don't switch to detail work. Look for the largest things you can improve. When you don't find anything that stands out as incorrect, move to the next stage.

Here, there are several elements to consider about the way her head lays on her elbow and the centerline of her head without being about to locate her hidden ear. When a head is nodded or tilted down, the relative position of the ear to the nose changes, among other things. The distance between the chin and the arm won't be helpful, since the arm can and does move slightly back and forward and the shoulder can be relaxed or drawn up. Think about what parts can move independently of the main structure. The more you're used to working from a live model the less difficult these shifts will be.

Once a decision has been made, block in the major planes and landmarks. An awareness of skull structure will allow you to make educated decisions as to the tip, tilt and turn of the head.

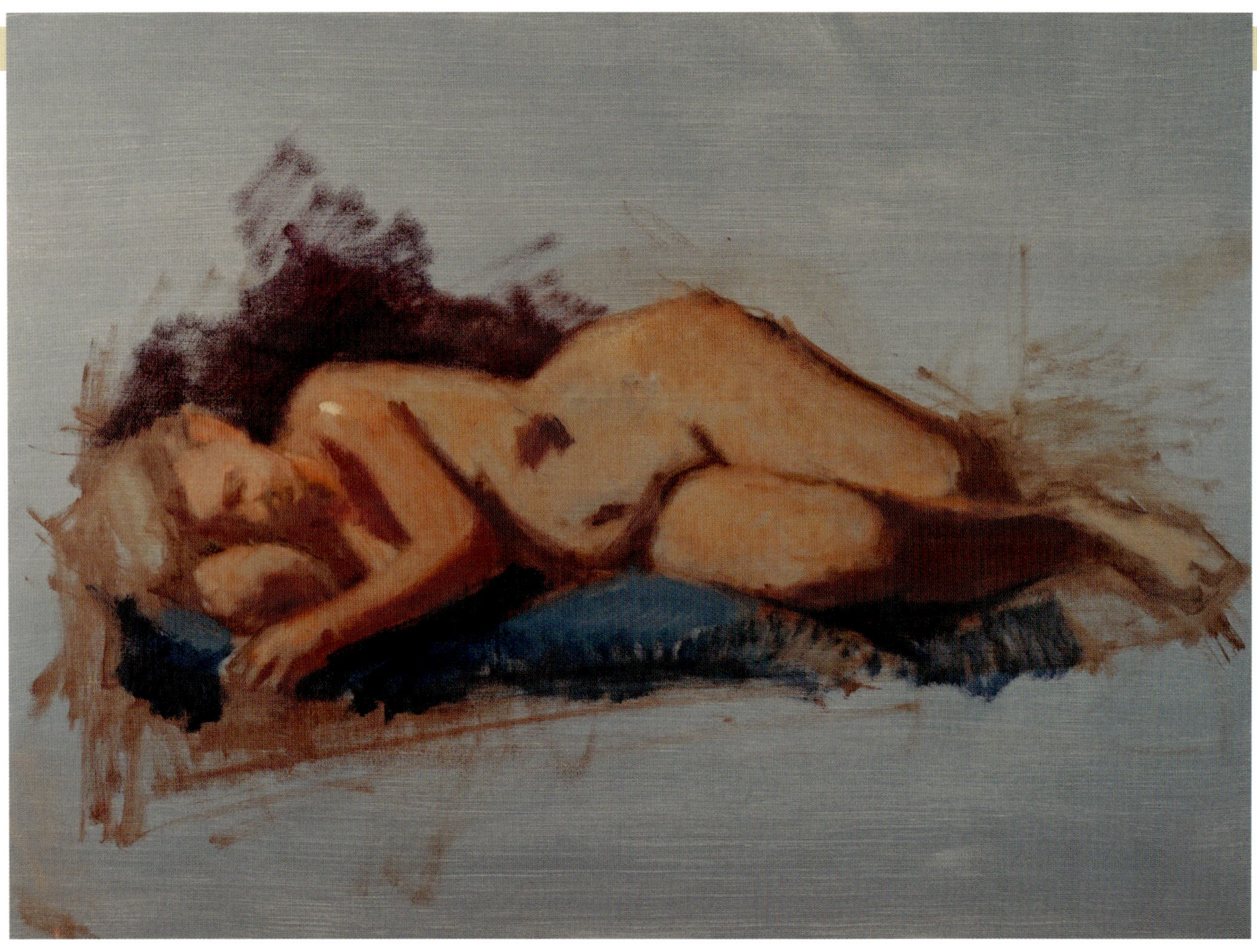

### Don't Get Hung Up on Details

Once detail is added to an area it is very difficult to see the entire painting in a general, overall way. We keep believing in the detail, which makes it hard to see big problems.

6 DEVELOP VALUE AND COLOR, ADD SURROUNDING COLOR NOTES
Add more colors when you're confident in the large shapes and can't see anything major to change. Within the figure, limit yourself in the number of new colors and values. Keep it simple and avoid details.

As you start to make better decisions about the color and value to be developed, you'll need some surrounding color notes. This model has bright green areas in her hair. Just paint your first impression of the color and don't deal with anymore than that, since hair shape changes. Make these additional colors clear and strong. As you keep painting and adjusting, these colors will become less vibrant. However, if you approach this through strong colors, you can be assured that they won't become monotone. All shadow colors should be placed now.

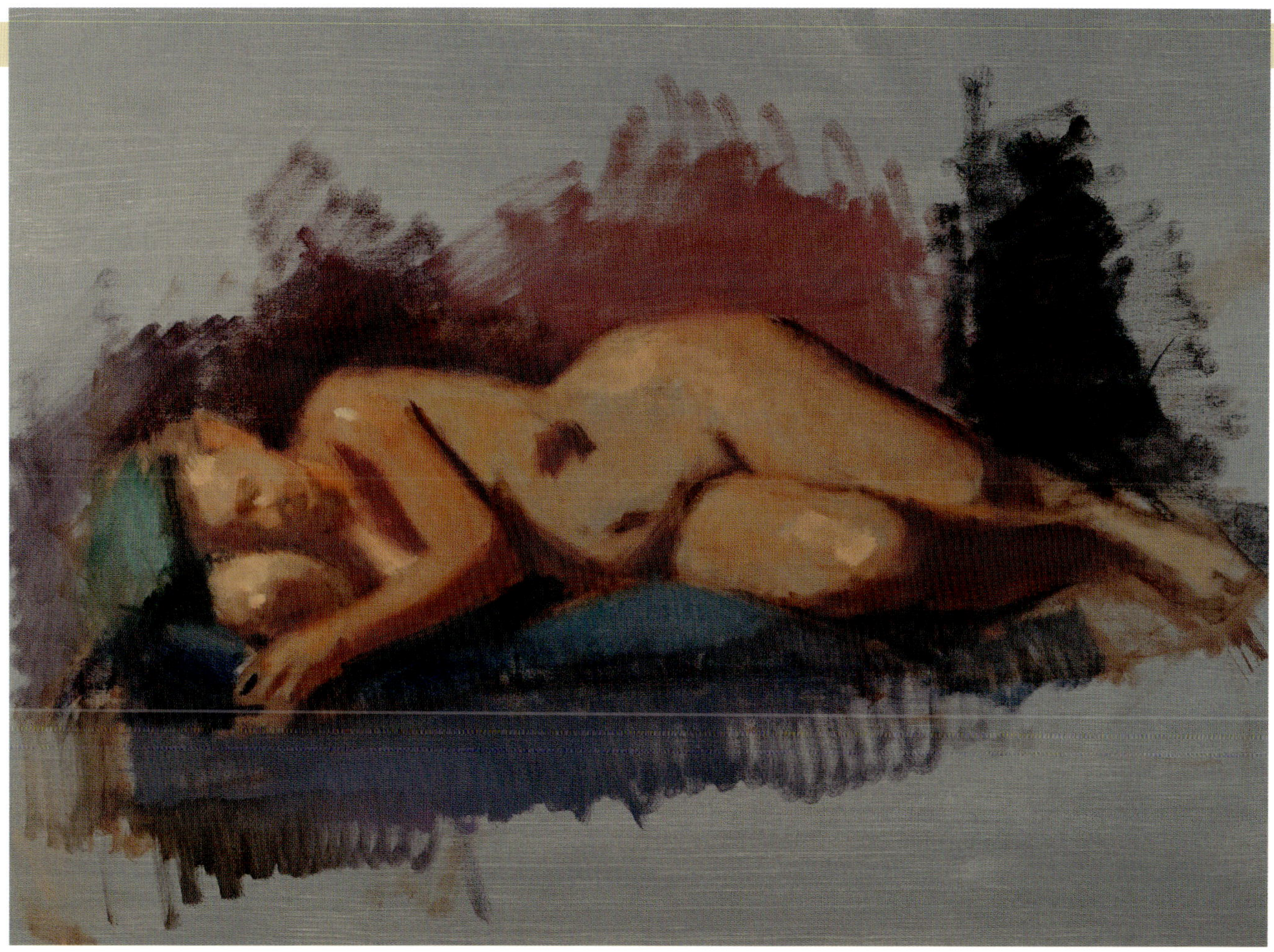

## 7 CONTINUE ADDING COLOR NOTES

Now add some color notes for the colors surrounding the figure. Focus on laying in a few significant colors. Up until now you've been working to shape your figure using your first guess as to the figure colors. These clear colors will help you make good decisions about the color and value of her body. Make your colors clear and strong. Remember that these will be adjusted and changed as the painting progresses. Keep your edges soft.

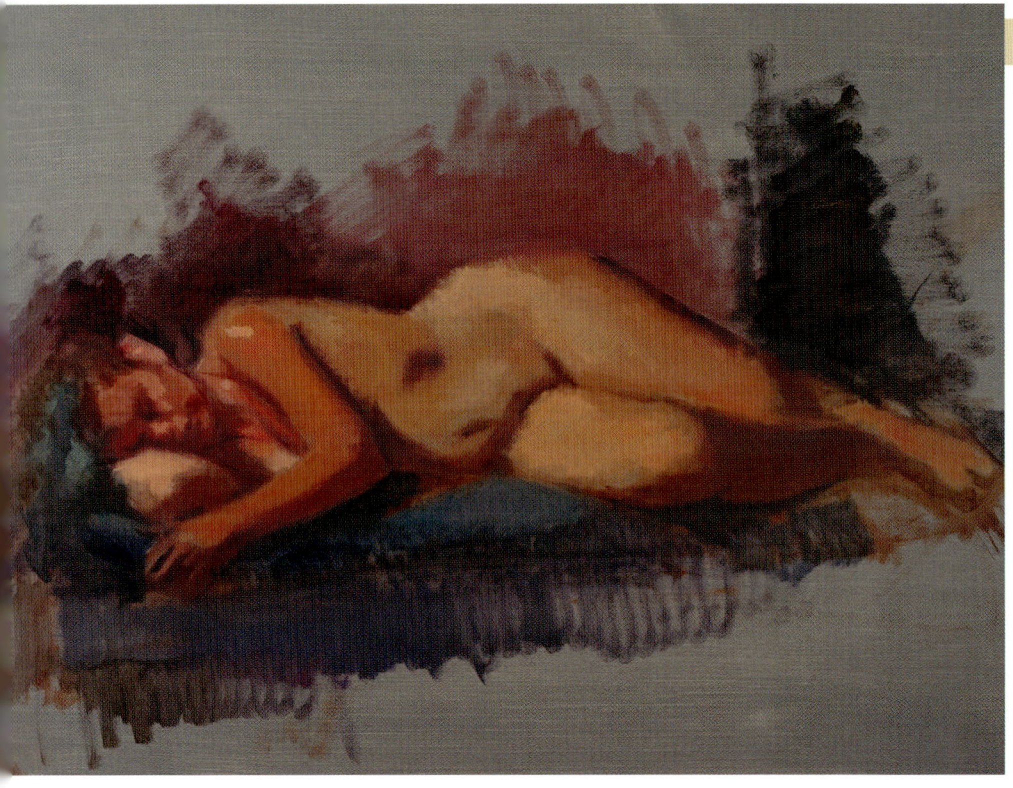

## 8 CONTINUE WORKING THE BODY AND MAKING ADJUSTMENTS

Continue working all over the body. In this case, additional higher planes of color were developed on the abdomen. The shape of her legs was adjusted, and more color notes were added.

Make another pass over the body, adding small unique color notes as you see them to make sure they don't get compromised as the painting develops. Check the gesture, the drawing, the color and the value relationships. Once you don't find anything to change in the existing stage, add the next large missing piece.

Paint wet into wet in the areas surrounding the main area you're working on to make the transition between the planes more natural. This let's you merge the two areas using moveable paint without getting a scratchy look. The form can be pushed and pulled to adjust and refine the shapes.

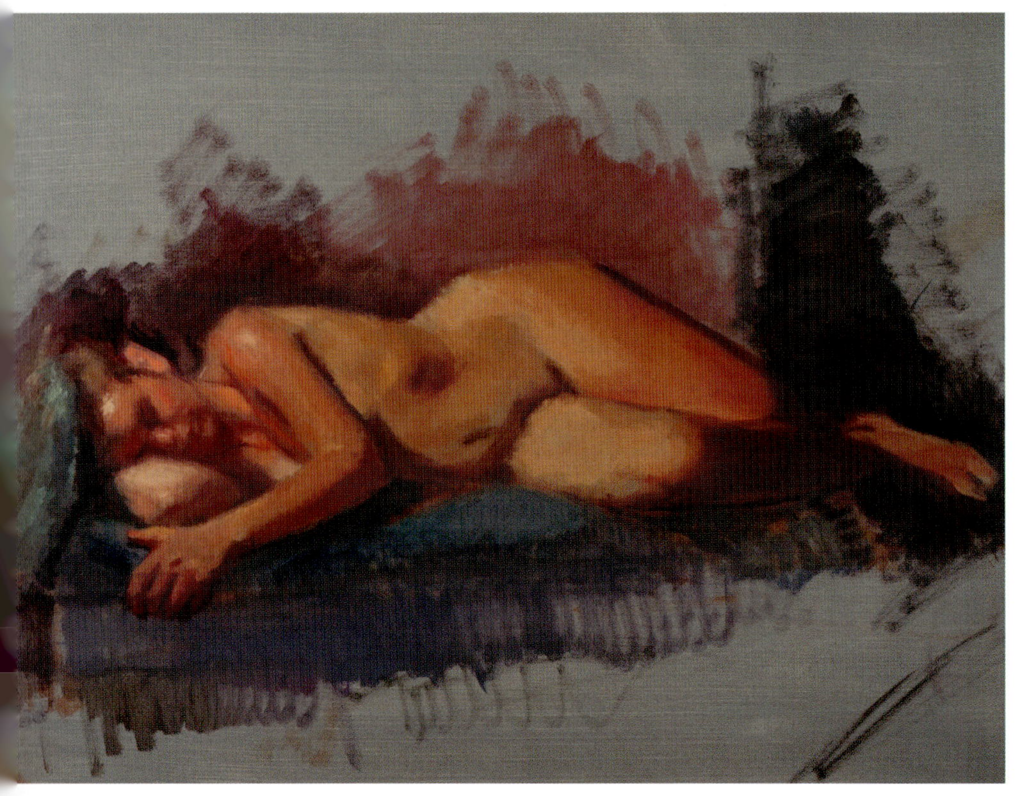

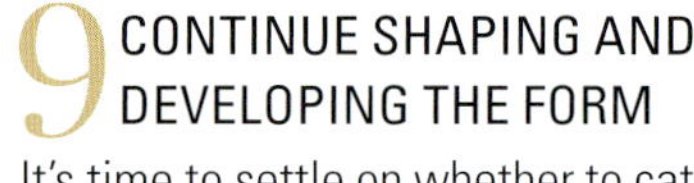

## 9 CONTINUE SHAPING AND DEVELOPING THE FORM

It's time to settle on whether to catch her sleeping or contemplative, as shown by her eye position. Base decisions like this on the different esthetics you've noticed as the painting progresses.

Continue developing the form, further refining her head and face. Here, a highlight was added to the forehead, and another layer of paint was added on her face. This shows the smaller planes and additional colors as seen on her cheekbone. The same holds true for her torso—there are additional colors and smaller planes. Her foot is beginning to come into focus, and there is a gentler turn of form all over.

Explore color and shape for the hair. Be bold and general, but don't settle on the final shape. Decide on the final hand shape and position you want before asking your model to hold it.

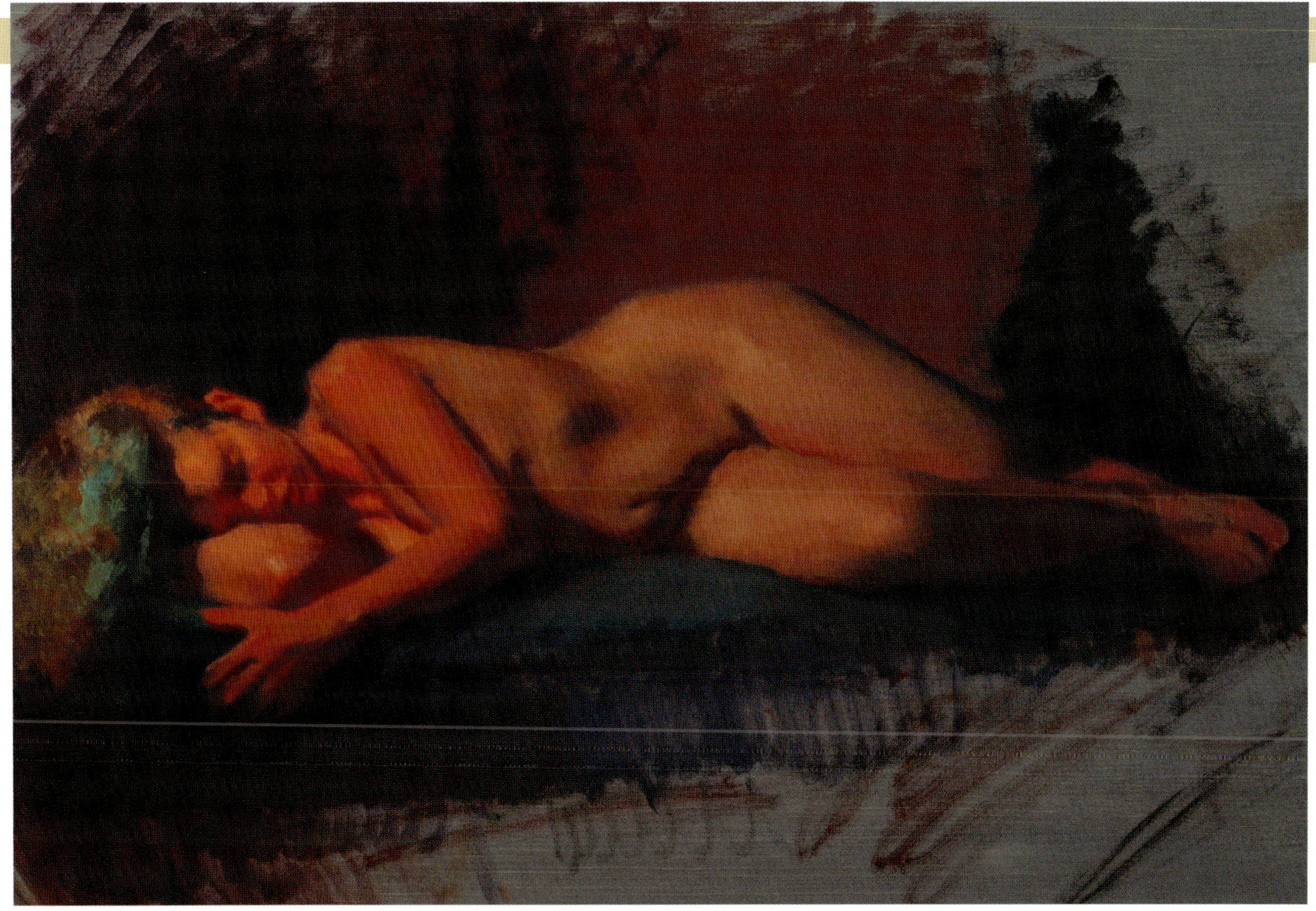

## 10 EVALUATE YOUR PROGRESS AND MAKE FURTHER ADJUSTMENTS

At this stage you should be working the entire painting as a whole and making changes and adjustments as you see the need.

When you add information to an area, make sure you still see the large plane changes. As with all the stages of a painting it's important to stand back and look at the whole figure to check a few essentials. Can you still tell what direction the light is coming from by the shape of the shadows? In this composition the light comes from the left and above. Keeping the direction of your light source in mind will help you to see shadow positions and plane changes. Remember that shadow and light shows three-dimensional form.

Consider how you want the viewer's eye to move around the painting. What are your focal points? What areas do you want to accentuate?

### *Shifting Positions*

With any prolonged pose, it is unavoidable that the model will shift from time to time. These subtle shifts can be very hard to detect, but it is important to get good at spotting them in order to adjust your model.

It is even more important to become aware of the way the model shifts throughout each pose. Does she relax and sink in as time passes? Does she stiffen because of discomfort? Should you draw with your brush in the beginning of each pose and then focus on color and working within established form toward the end? Think of a strategy and try not to adjust your model for each tiny change.

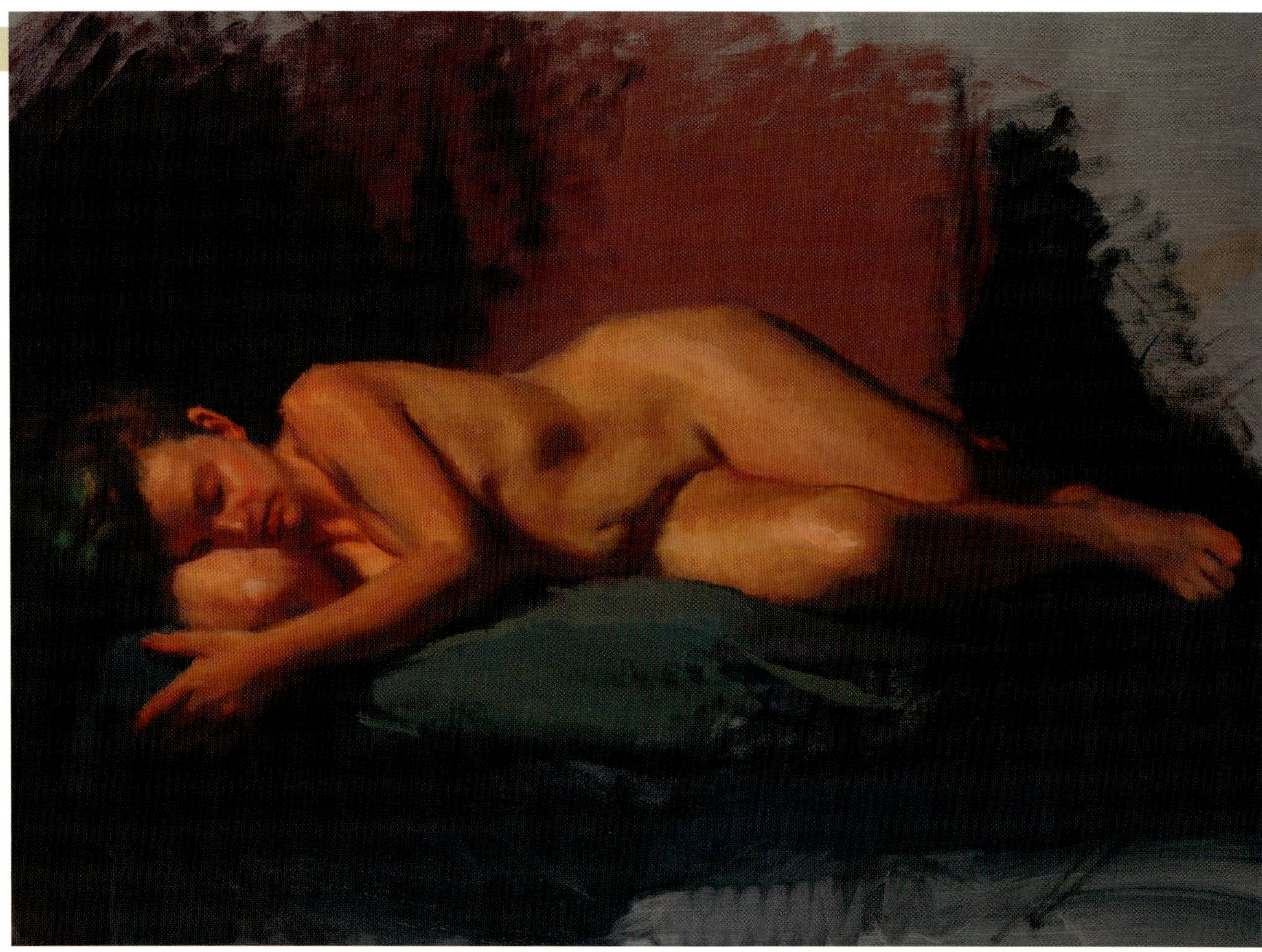

### Painting Hands

When a model resumes a pose after taking a break, there is often a change in the position of the hands. It's OK to play around and experiment with some different hand positions before making a final decision. As long as you keep the color and value generally working, it won't be distracting.

## 11 SHARPEN THE FOCAL AREAS

Begin to focus closer on one or two areas. Sharpen the focal points. In this case, I focused on her legs and her shoulder region.

It's necessary to paint into the surrounding area so that the edges remain soft. When you're painting the human form, try to think dimensionally. Her knee is closer to you than her hips. Her elbow is pointed toward you and is bent. Think of where her right shoulder is and where her neck enters her shoulder area. Try to see her from above. If you visualize the body this way, it results in lifelike form.

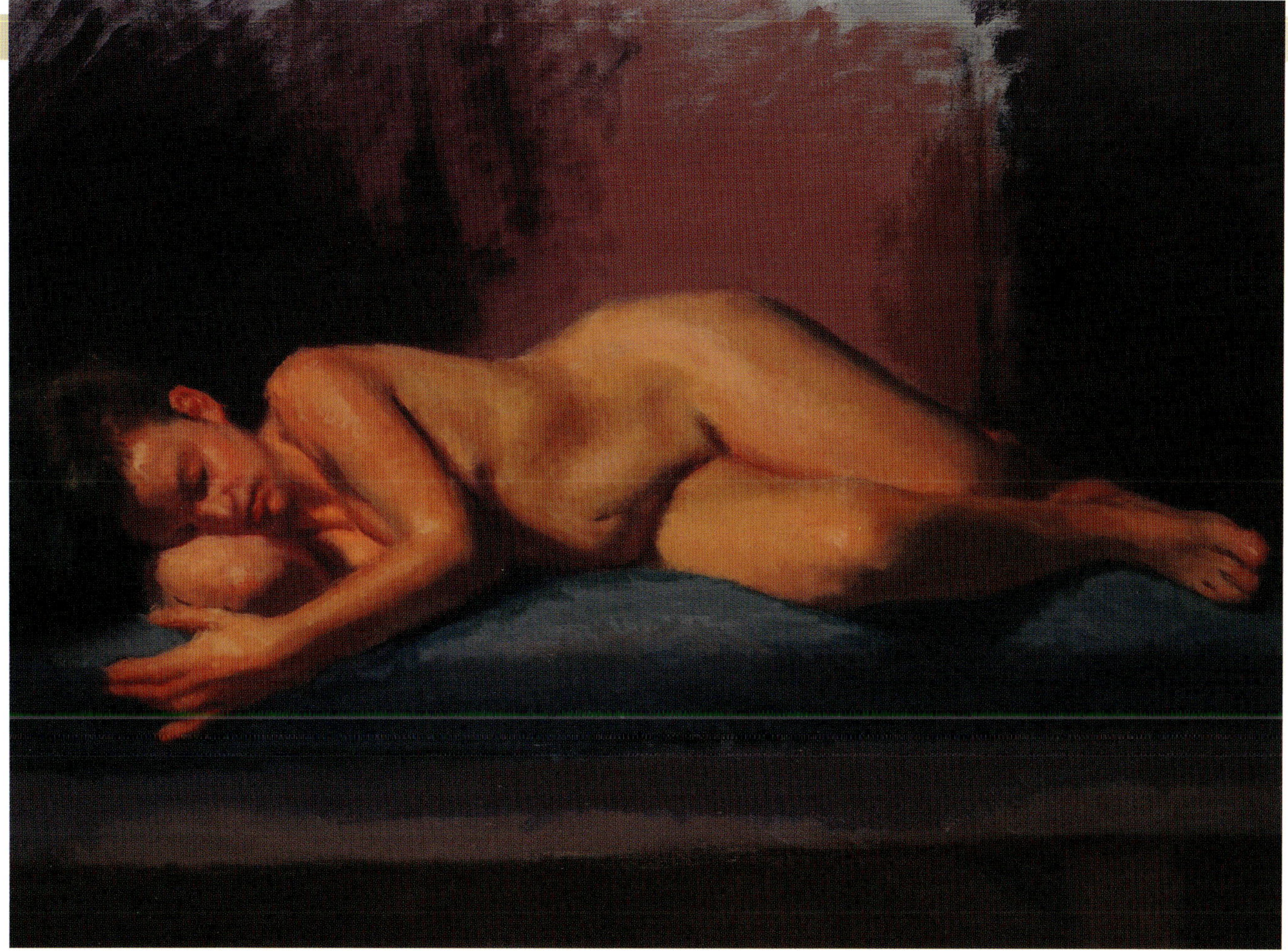

## 12 WORK THE DETAILS AND MAKE FINAL ADJUSTMENTS

Work on smaller areas and other areas in the painting that have been neglected. Here, that is primarily the platform she is lying on. I noticed that the shadow under her ribcage was too dark, which created too deep an indentation. If she'd been inhaling sharply that dark value might make sense. This is a great example of how value changes create dimension.

Walk away from the painting for a week or two, then evaluate one last time to make your final judgements and adjustments. When you are actively working on a painting, it's hard to be objective.

### *Allow for Drying Time Between Sessions*

When scheduling your model, leave a day or two in between sessions to allow time for the paint to stabilize on your canvas. This time can vary depending on the environment, how absorbent your canvas is, what the drying time of your paint is and the amount of paint you've used.

# LIGHTING CONSIDERATIONS

When setting up a simple pose using artificial light on your model, block out any other light source. Try to keep ambient light to a minimum. Keep your shadows clearly separated from your lights.

When you're painting under natural light, be aware of outdoor light changes. The weather and time of day influence how much light illuminates your canvas.

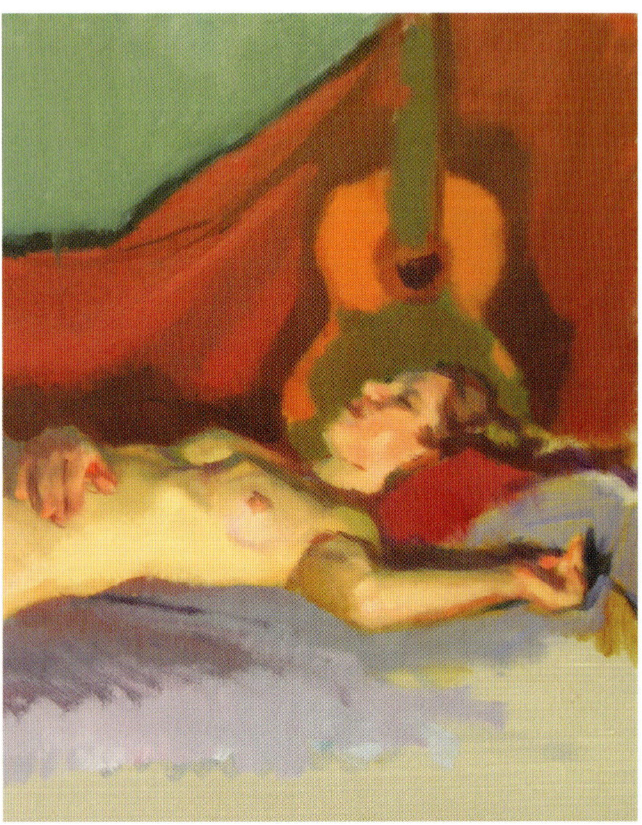

**Music**
Lea Colie Wight
Oil on linen
20" × 16" (51cm × 41cm)

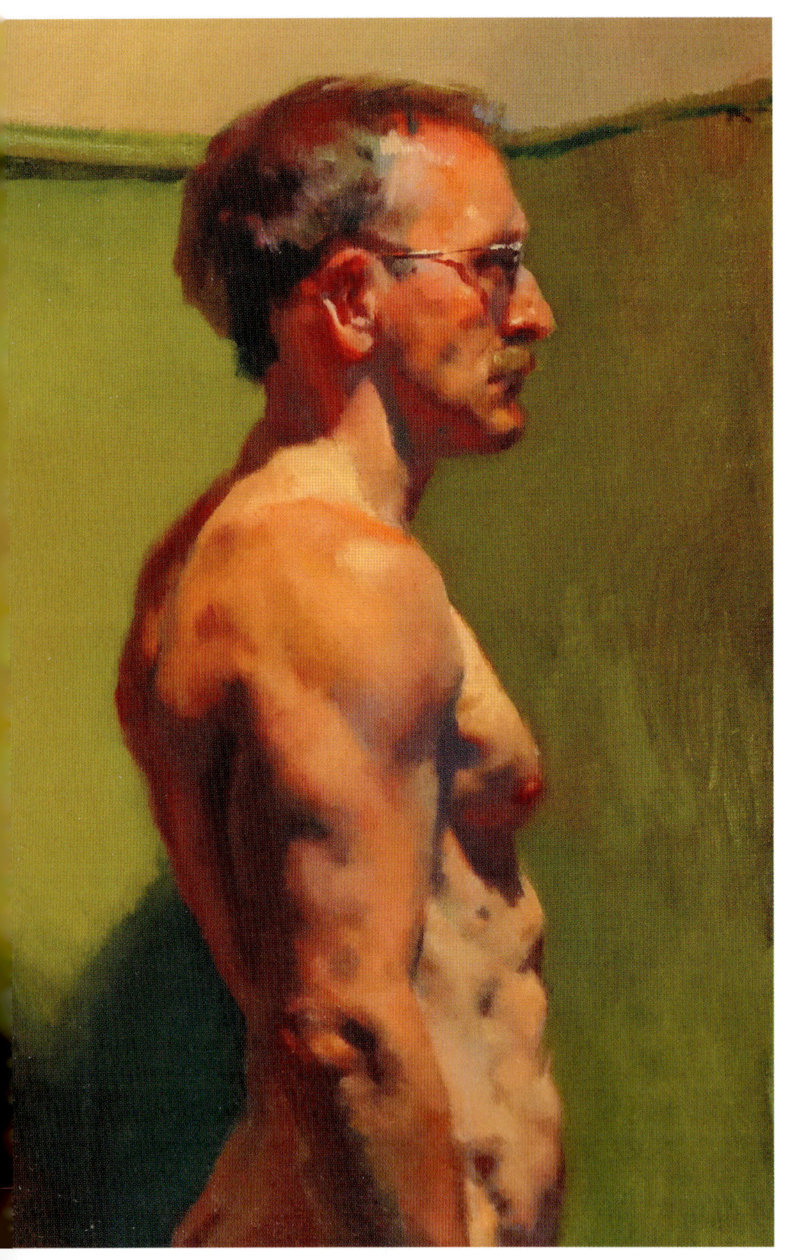

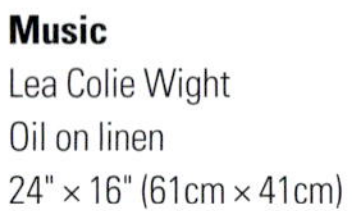

**Music**
Lea Colie Wight
Oil on linen
24" × 16" (61cm × 41cm)

### *Make a Plan*

Make notes at the end of each painting day. This should include any observations about how the day went, what you were happy with, any breakthroughs, any challenges.

Plan the day ahead so you have a game plan. Without a plan and a clear direction, the next painting day can be unproductive. If you can remind yourself in the morning of what you wanted to accomplish that day, you're off to a good start. It often happens that what was clear at the end of the last day is forgotten in the morning.

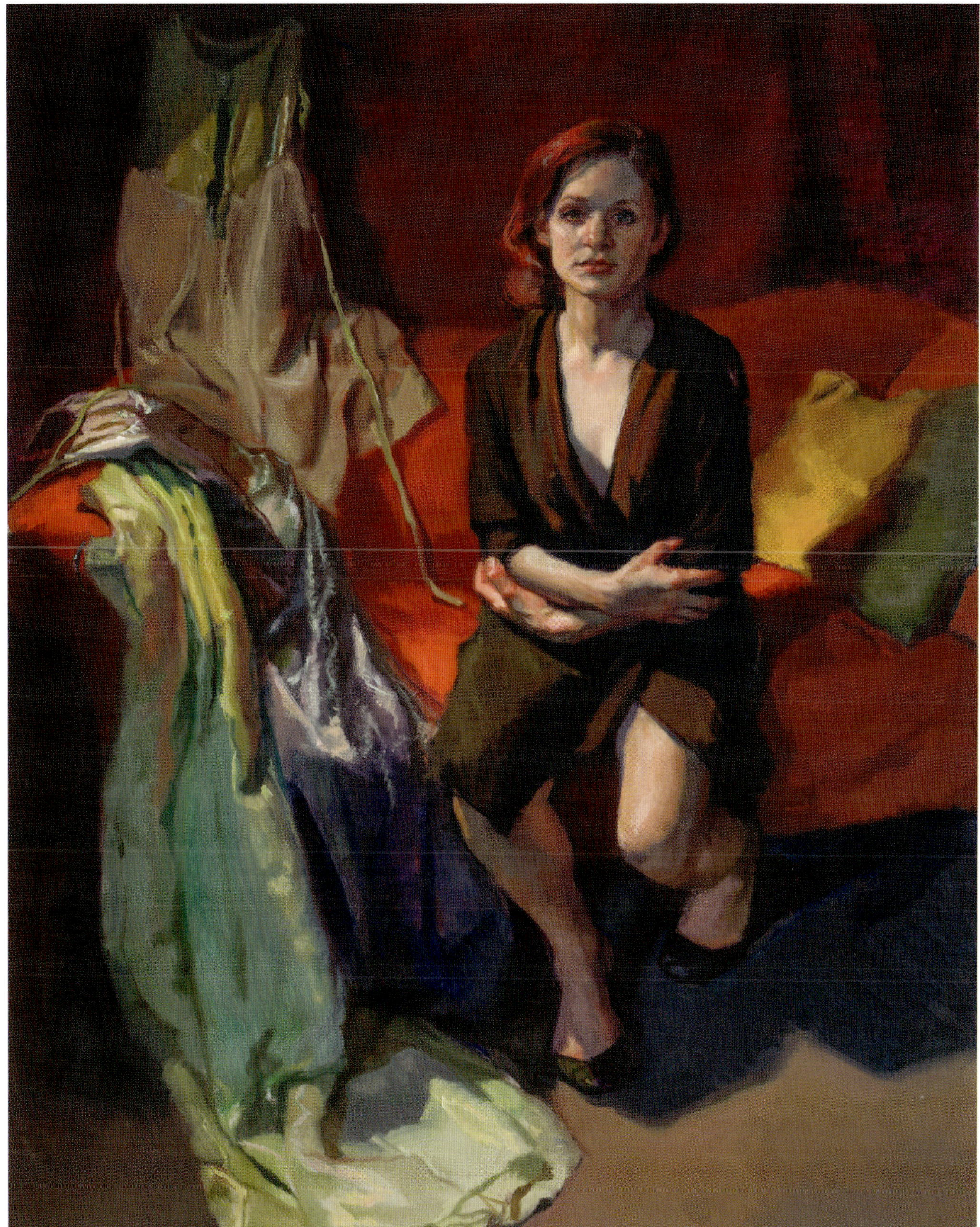

## PAINTING WITH FORM KNOWLEDGE

This piece illustrates the importance of being able to paint the figure even when clothed. As you paint, visualize the form beneath the clothing and let your knowledge guide you. Painting with form knowledge allows the viewer to focus on the personal expression and beauty of the subject.

**The Embrace**
Lea Colie Wight
Oil on linen
40" × 30" (102cm × 76cm)

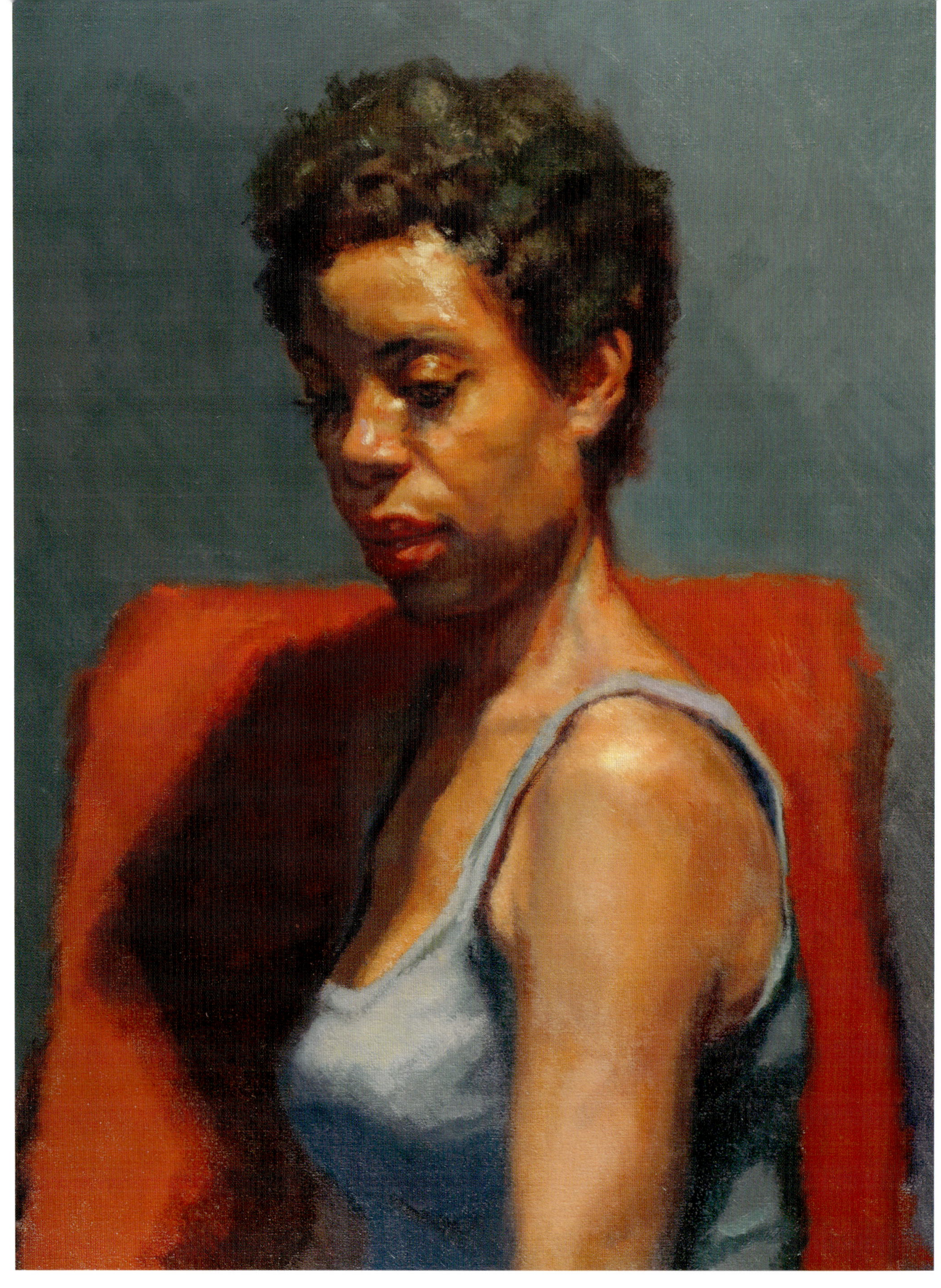

**Carol**
Lea Colie Wight
Oil on canvas
24" × 18" (61cm × 46cm)

*Demonstration*

# PORTRAIT PAINTING

Artists have been creating portraits since ancient times. This is a profound legacy that painters and sculptors of today carry on. It is arresting to come face to face with a portrait painted centuries ago and feel that connection. The intensity of a subject's gaze can make you feel as if you're right there in the studio watching them, brush in hand.

This demonstration will show you the step-by-step development of a portrait, where you'll see the lessons you learned earlier in the book put to use. When you set up for your painting, you will have some choices to make. What setting do you want your subject to be in? What will your light source be? What colors would best set off your subject? Do you want your painting to include the subject's hands, or just the head and shoulders? Some portraits include only the head and neck, cropped according to a shirt opening.

If you decide on a head and shoulder composition, make sure to pay close attention to the shoulders, neck and surrounding landmarks, even if they are handled with minimal lines. If you aren't sure of these, make a quick sketch so you know where they are. Use your own body as a guide or refer to an anatomy book or website. If you try to fake it, it will almost always show in your final painting.

## *Materials*

SURFACE

streched canvas

OIL PIGMENTS

Magenta, Permanent Rose or Quinacridone Red, Cadmium Red Deep, Cadmium Red Medium or Cadmium Scarlet, Cadmium Orange or Cadmium Yellow Deep, Cadmium Yellow Light or Cadmium Lemon, Cadmium Green Light, Viridian or Phthalo Green, Cerulean Blue, Ultramarine Blue, Dioxazine Purple, Cobalt Violet Deep, Yellow Ochre, Indian Yellow, Burnt Sienna or Burnt Umber, Black, Titanium White

BRUSHES

Silver Brush #5001 hake flat or mop brush; Silver Brush #7110 sable cat's tongue sizes 4, 6 and 8; Silver Brush #1034 long bristle filbert sizes 2, 3, 4 and 6; Rosemary brush #278 sizes 2, 4 and 6

OTHER

nitrile or vinyl gloves, odorless mineral spirits or Gamsol, paper towels, spray Retouch varnish

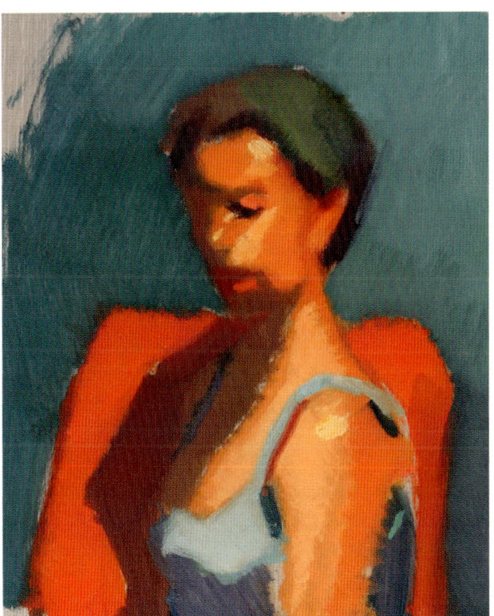

1 BEGIN WITH VALUE, COLOR AND COMPOSITION STUDIES

I strongly recommend executing value, color and composition studies before you dive into your portrait. Doing these studies will take some of the experimentation out of your painting and will let you start strong and confident.

### Choosing Canvas Size

I recommend painting the subject's head close to life size or a bit smaller. This will give you ample room to develop your painting and paint smaller passages.

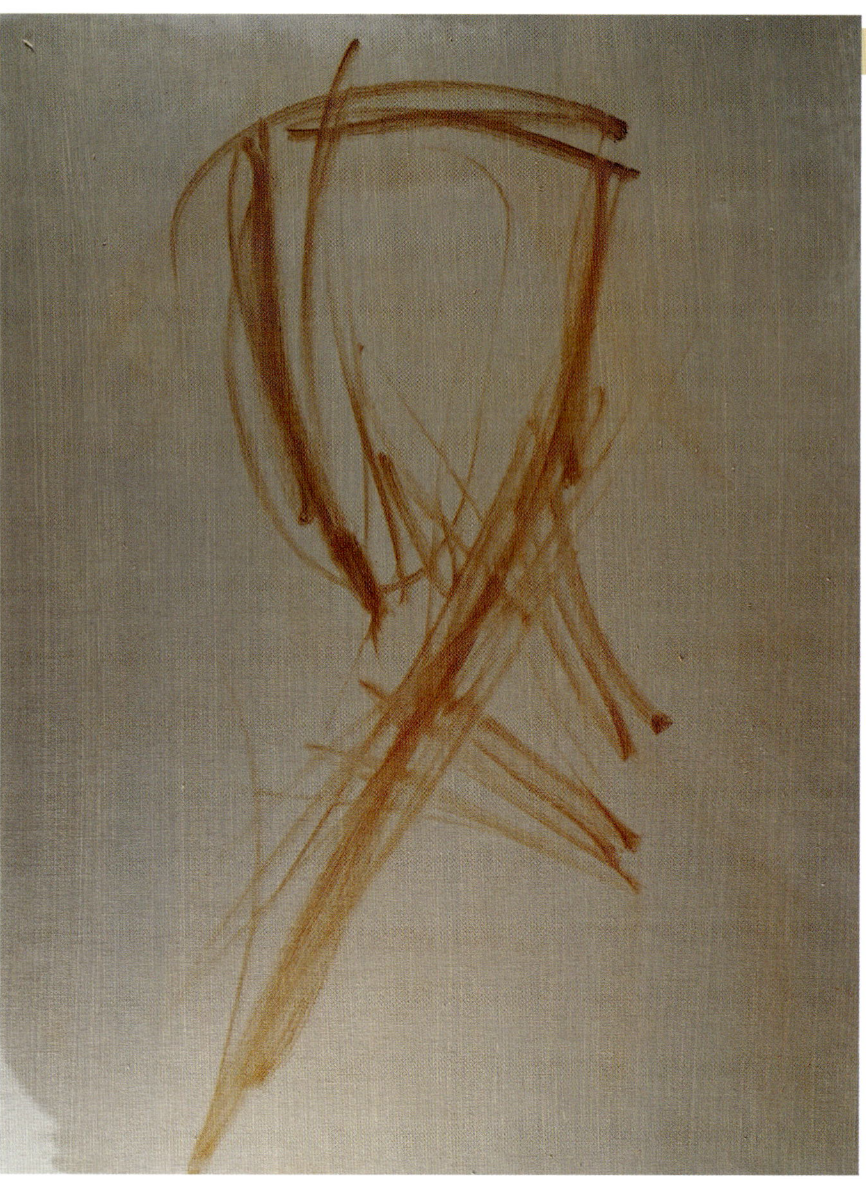

## 2 BEGIN WITH THE OPENING GESTURE

Look back and forth between your subject and your canvas. Visualize your composition. Try to envision where you are going to crop and what the final painting will look like. This simple step results in better proportions in your final painting.

Hold your brush at the end of the handle with a grasp much like you would hold a pencil. Stand at arm's length from the canvas and make a few energetic strokes to show the main information about the pose. For these opening stages, use a neutral brown color such as Burnt Umber or Burnt Sienna mixed with Ultramarine Blue.

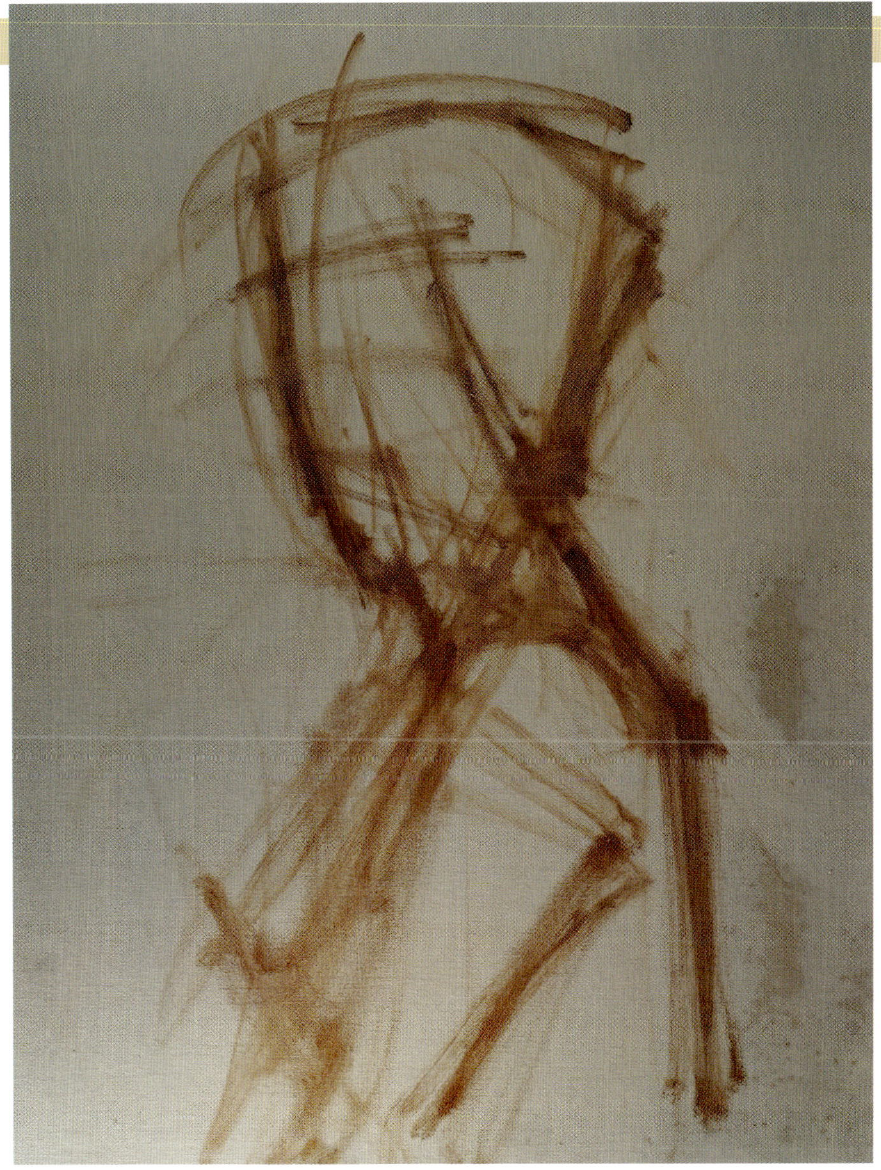

### 3 DEVELOP AND ADJUST THE GESTURE

Step back and squint at your subject to simplify what you're seeing. If you could add two or three more lines, which would be the most important? Add those lines, then step back and squint between your painting and the subject again. Try to identify large lines that might need to be adjusted.

This is a helpful stage, because it's much easier to identify things that may need to be moved before you have a lot of detail distracting you. This way of seeing sets you up with correct information to follow, and you can confidently develop your painting knowing your big information is right.

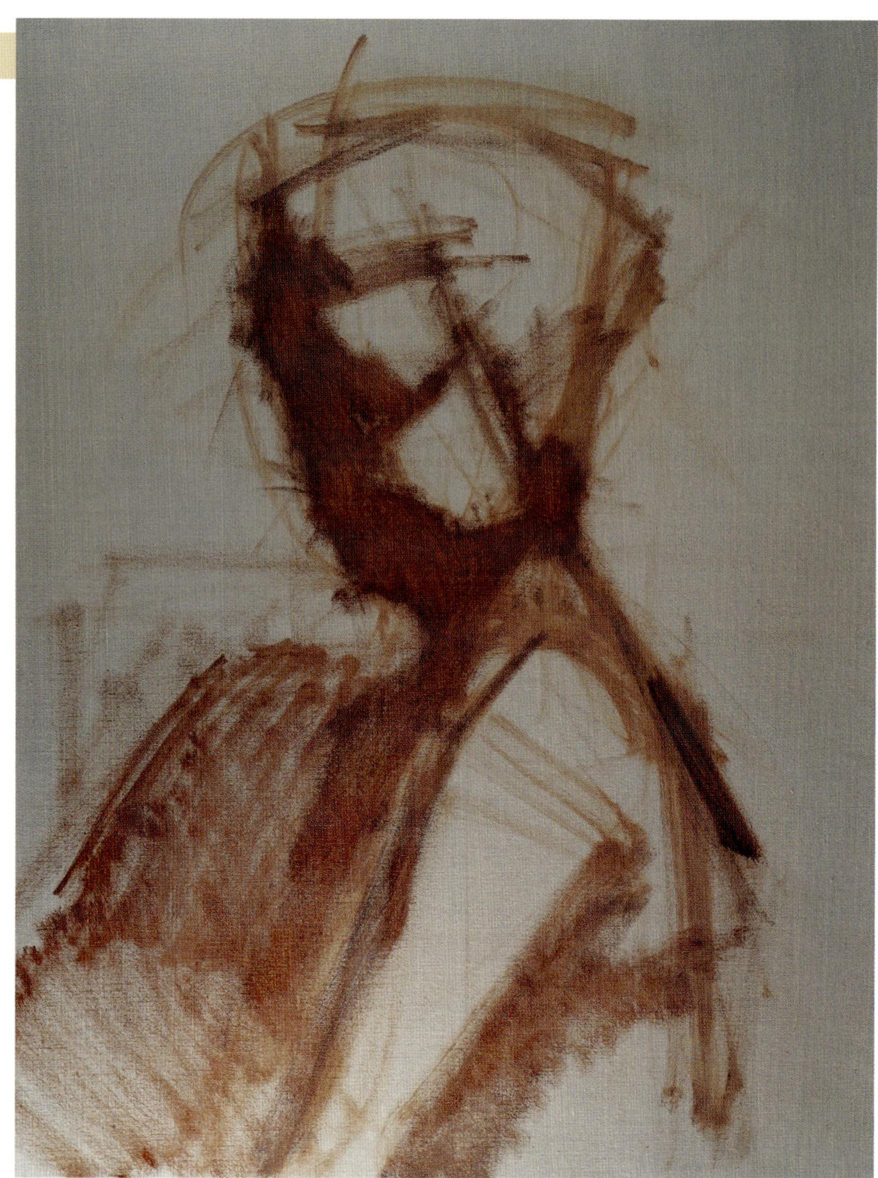

## Sum of All Parts

Always consider the neck as an integral part of the head and show where it inserts into the torso. Make sure you indicate where the shoulders end in order to tell the viewer what the size of the subject is. Is he a linebacker? Do her shoulders continue forever? Even when your focus is on your subject's head, these things are important to consider.

### 4 BLOCK IN THE SHADOW MASSES

Use the side of your brush to spread and shape the shadow masses. Then use a paper towel to wipe off and shape your shadows. Squint to find smaller variations in your shadow masses.

Continue to step back and look from your painting to your subject and back again. Think of your painting as representing three dimensions. Think about sculpting the very basic planes of the head. Toggle your awareness back and forth between simple abstract shape and three-dimensional awareness.

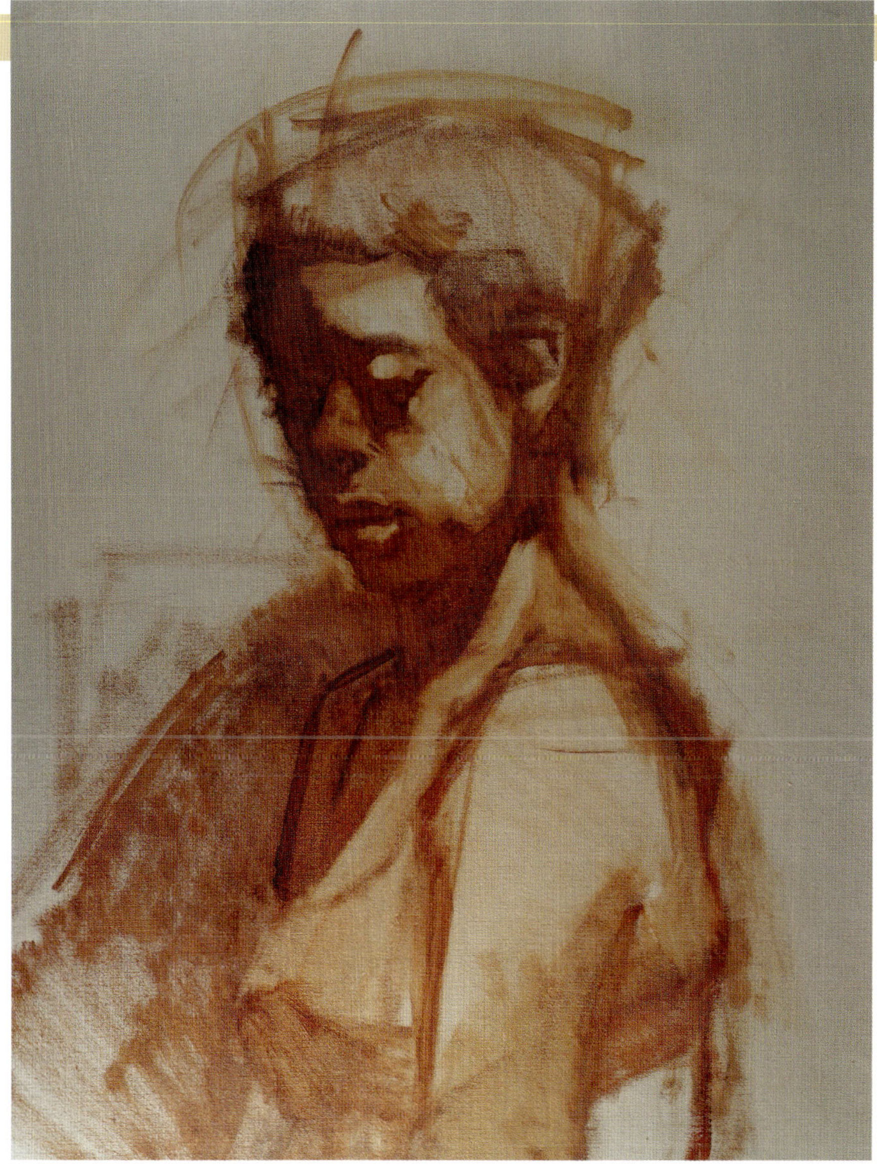

## 5 CONTINUE SHAPING THE SHADOWS AND DEVELOPING THE LANDMARKS

Continue shaping and correcting your block in. Begin to develop the darker accents in shadow in order to separate the very darkest areas within the shadow masses.

Develop the major landmarks—the nose, shoulders and so forth. Remember to keep squinting and looking back and forth between subject and painting, only now begin to open your eyes up enough for the smaller shapes to begin revealing themselves. You are creeping up on the information and always looking for the next largest statement.

In this case, there was a shifting of the pose. My model's arm moved. I could have asked her to adjust, but I didn't mind the change since it was still in the early days of the pose. (I have found that the more comfortable a model is, the more their personality will emerge.) This new position, while not as dynamic, is quieter and creates a more introspective portrait.

Continually checking the entire painting lets you catch pose shifts as they occur. If I'd been working on one detail after another, I probably wouldn't have noticed this change. At this point I've taken my grisaille block-in as far as I need to.

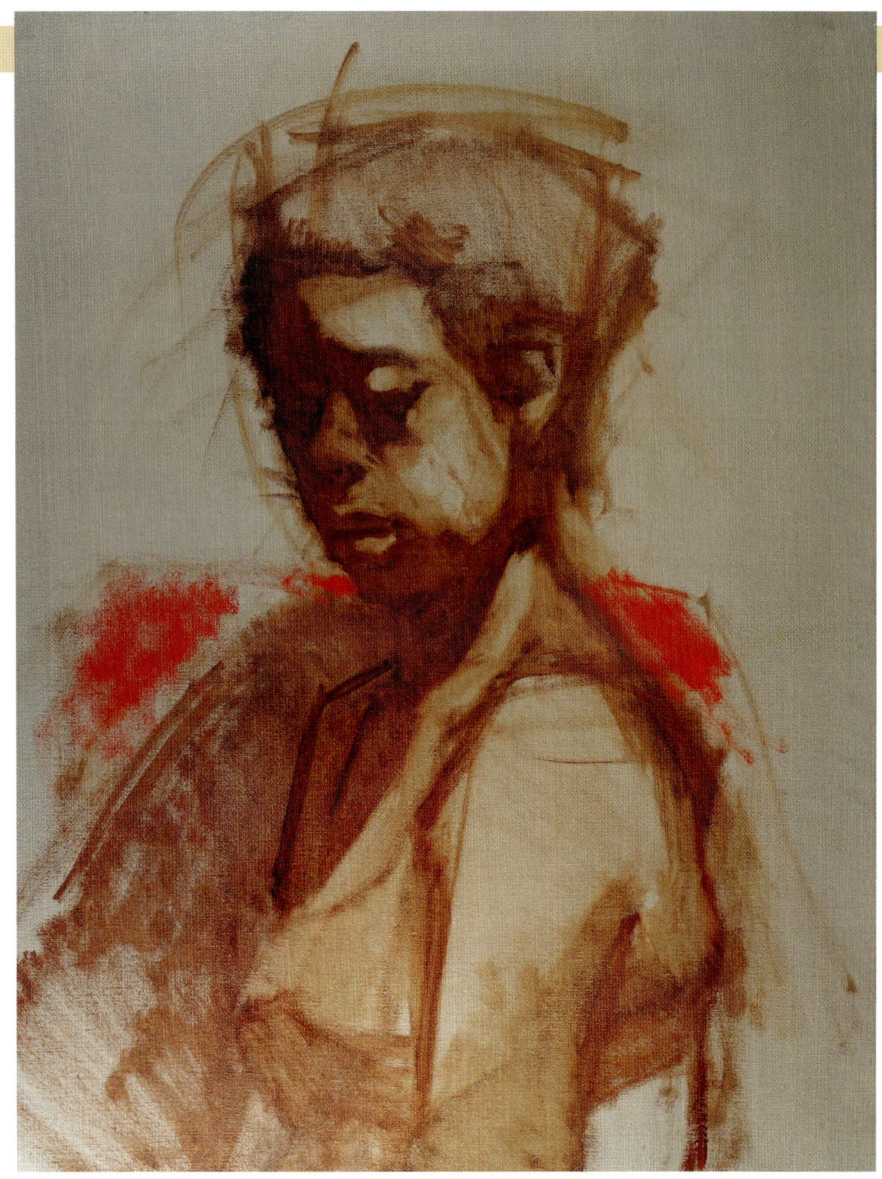

## 6 ADD THE FIRST COLOR NOTES

It's time for some color. Keep the paint thin and start with the easiest to see and purest, strongest color. In this case, it was the red of the chair that the model was sitting on. Now you have a good clear color to relate the more complex colors to.

### *Overstate, Don't Understate*

Don't automatically downplay your initial color notes. Before you begin adjusting, wait and look at the overall value and color difference after the addition of other colors. As you adjust your colors again and again, you'll be able to show the subtle colors that are actually still there.

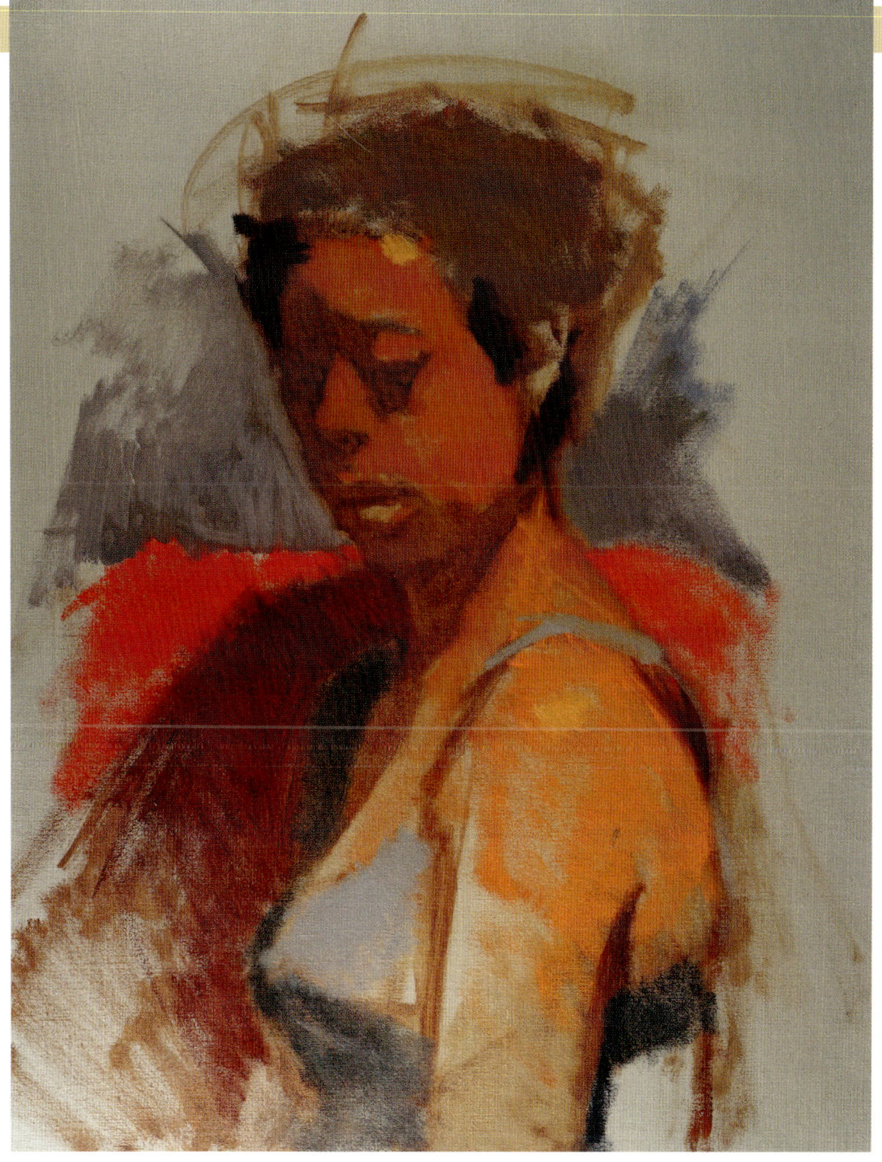

## Finding True Value Ranges

It can help to add a piece of white paper somewhere in the vicinity of your model and your painting. Having a pure white reference to compare to your lightest areas will help you make sure that you're painting in the correct value range.

When painting with a lot of light on your canvas, you may tend to paint darker because the paint appears brighter than it really is. The opposite is true when painting in a very low light situation.

Adding a highlight should be one of your first notes.

### 7 CONTINUE ADDING COLOR, HIGHLIGHTS AND DARK ACCENTS

Add two more colors. Add color notes for the remaining masses including the shadows. Avoid using browns. Instead, try to mix from pure chromatic palette colors.

Find a lower value color on the model's skin so that you can layer the lighter planes on top as the painting is developed. Here, the color was darker than I intended, but I decided to wait and see if it would work as a base color.

Now is a good time to add a highlight and dark accent so you can see your general value range. I added the color of Carol's shirt, hair and the shadow she cast on the chair. Adding the highlight on my model's forehead gave me the information that my initial color choice wasn't too far off and would probably serve as one of the darker areas of light as her head planes turn away from the light. I added lighter notes for my model's arm and neck.

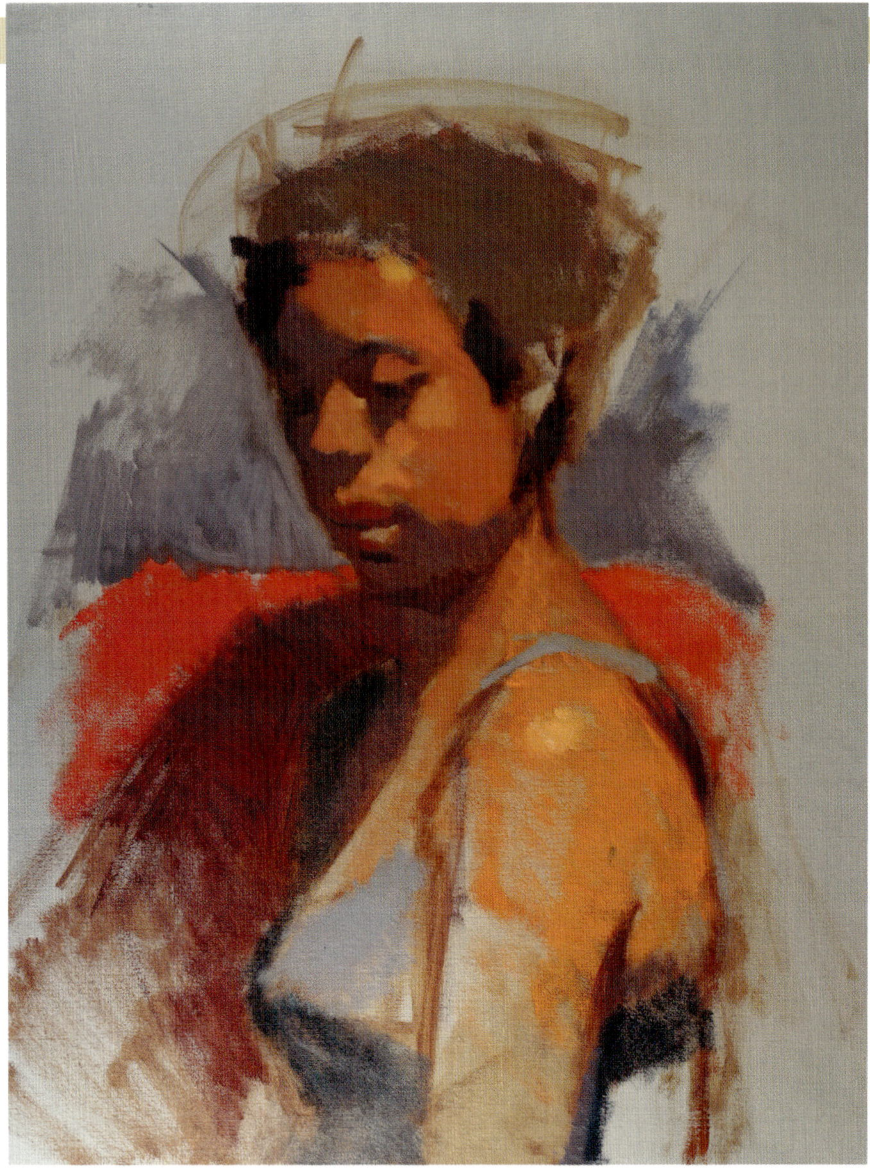

### *Evaluating Your Progress*

When you step back and evaluate your painting, ask yourself whether any area looks left behind.

## 8 ADD HIGHER VALUES

Once you are satisfied with the basic colors of the masses, it is time to add higher values. I chose the area where the model's face planes are turned upward toward the light. Think of the basic planes of the head and notice which main planes are receiving more light than others. Remember once again to look for the simplest statement you can make.

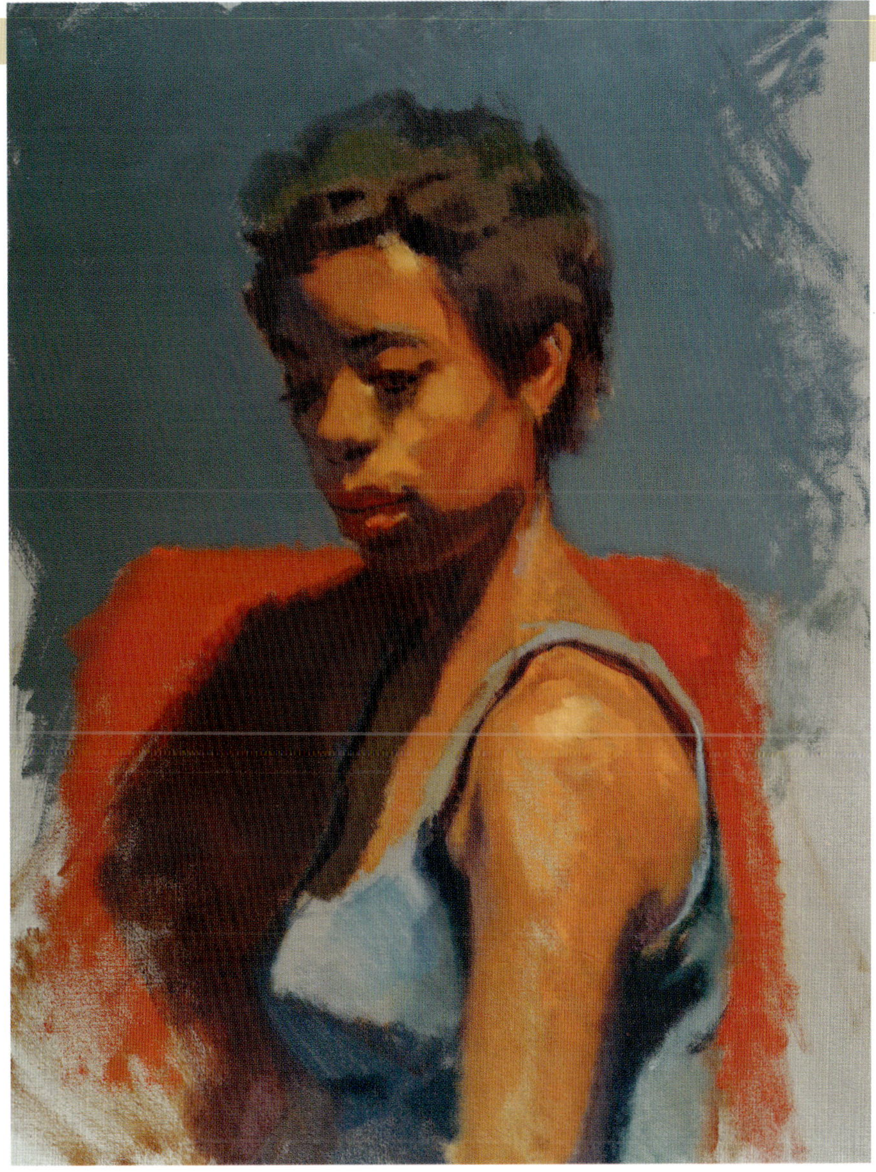

## 9 CONTINUE DEVELOPING SHAPE, COLOR AND FORM

Continue developing and adjusting colors and values. Work on many different areas while always looking for the next thing that seems to be behind in development. Some of the areas I worked on were deepening the shadow on the chair, layering and shaping more paint on the model's neck and chest, finding additional structural form in the cheek, adding a note for the light on her lip and strengthening the darks all around the painting. In these later stages, it is really important to calmly stand back and compare.

Never let go of the awareness you maintained in the opening stages of your painting. Is your gesture still there? Look for those extended lines of movement. Is the long line of her back in place? Does it extend through the hair line as it does in this composition? Always look for some adjustment you can make that will make your painting flow

## *Painting Hair*

It is a common problem to lose the shape of the skull when painting hair. Hair follows the planes of the head. Look for the general pattern of the hair and avoid painting individual strands. You may find it helpful to make your color application horizontal rather than vertical.

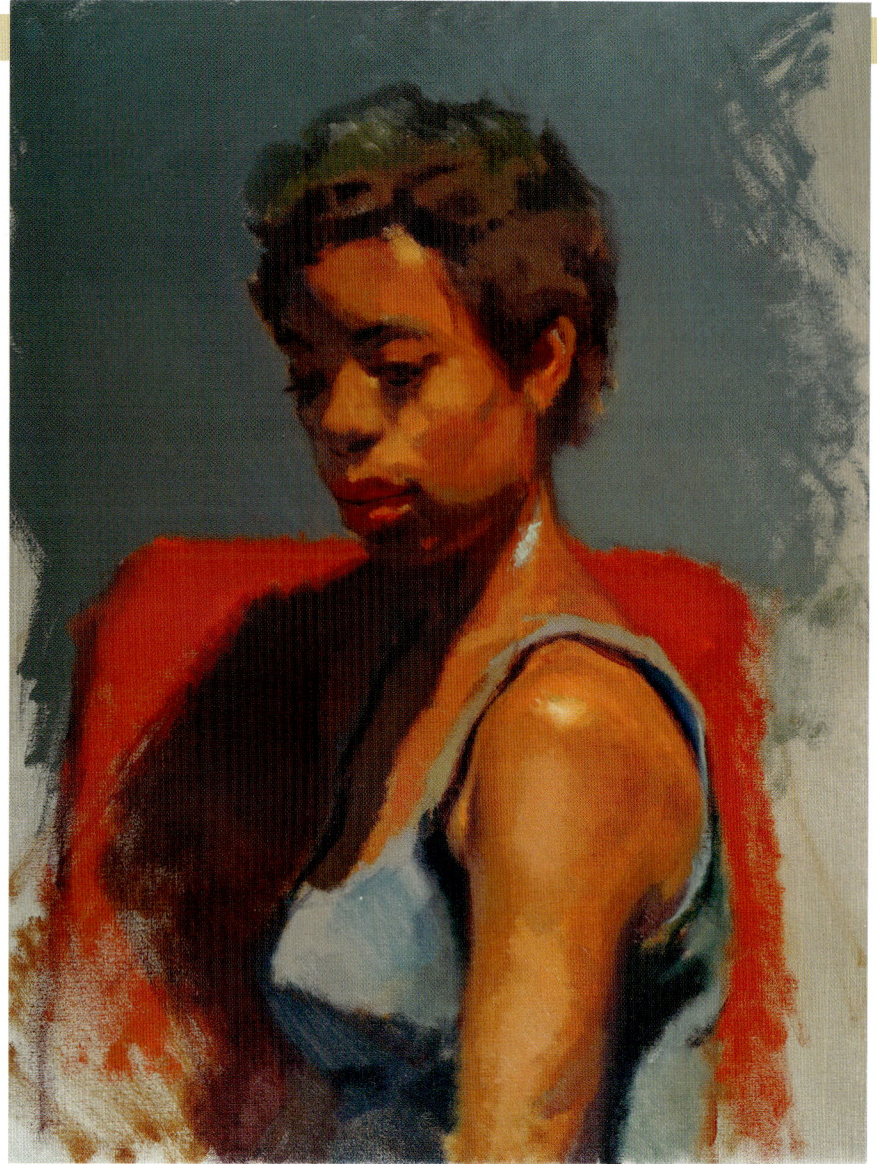

10 EVALUATE THE COMPOSITION AND MAKE ADJUSTMENTS
Stepping back and looking objectively, I noticed that I'd changed the shape of my model's hair, so I adjusted that. The background color as well as her shirt were expanded and adjusted. Continue to add development once you're satisfied with the current stage. Start thinking about your focal point(s) and begin to add more information there. This will be a gradual process through the next stages up until the finish.

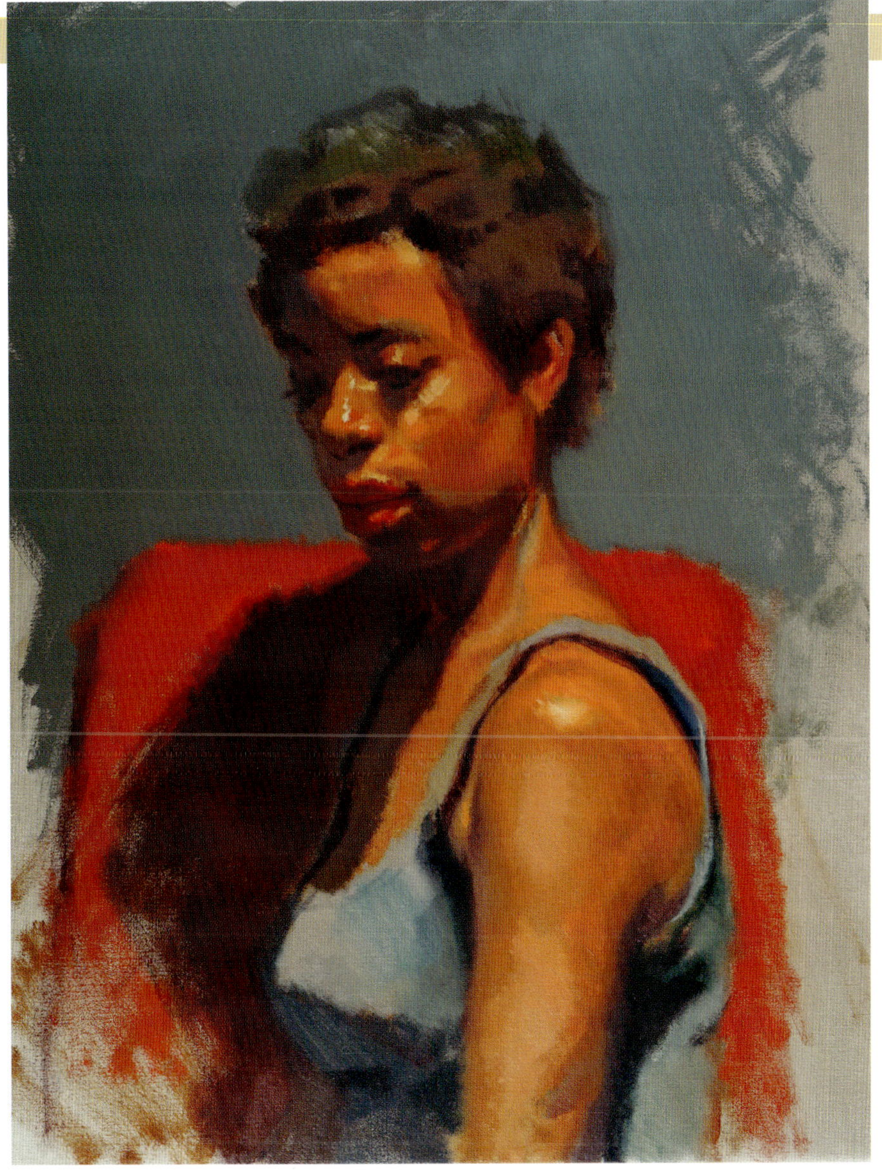

### *Eyes As a Focal Point*

The eyes convey the personality of the subject, so it's natural for viewers to linger there. Because of this, the eye is usually the focal point in a portrait. (Although this is not always the case.)

In this portrait, the focal point is the model's right eye. If this were a pose with both eyes in the light, I would have selected one eye to focus on.

## 11 DEVELOP THE HIGHLIGHTS

Highlights can be challenging, and many artists may be tempted to be conservative when addressing them. A highlight, though, is one of the more beautiful aspects in a painting because it really shows the color of the light bathing your sitter. It appears cooler in a warm light and warmer in a cool light. It is usually the complementary color of the surface it appears on. The color of a highlight can be intimidating because it is very clear, but also very hard to get just right. My advice is: Don't put it off. After all, it's only paint. Don't wait until you have a beautifully developed painting that you don't want to experiment on. Just go for it.

When I glanced quickly, my impression was turquoise. This initial strong color will be adjusted until it sits correctly in its place, but hopefully will retain its color identity. Think of pushing the color over the edge and then reeling it back to its place. If you paint a color study before you start, make sure this is one of the colors you investigate.

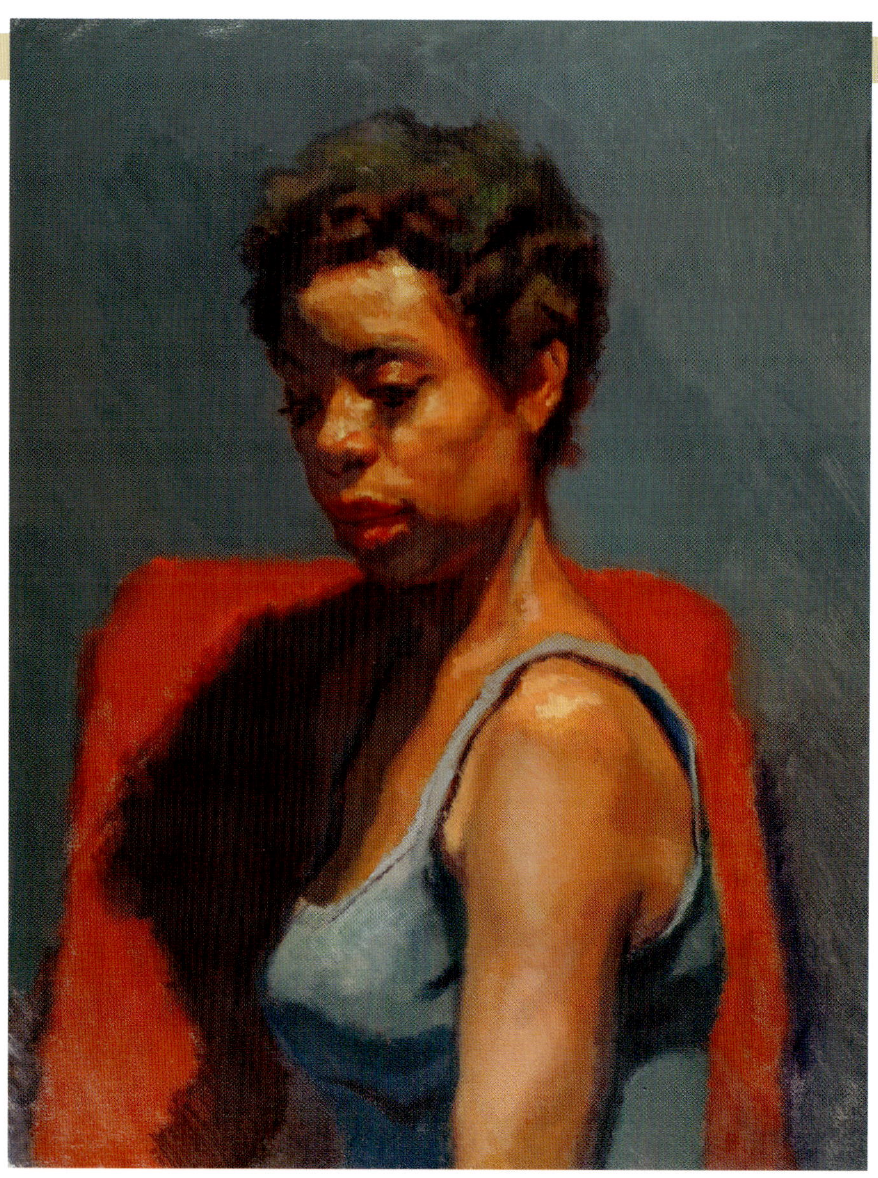

## 12 SHARPEN THE FOCAL AREAS

Up until now, notes and adjustments have been made all over the painting at each session. In this stage you'll spend more time on a smaller area, such as the model's arm, neck or head. Continue to adjust the colors to create the illusion of three-dimensional form and to make the value and color change accomplish that.

When you want to create a natural turn of form in a smaller area, it's good to work wet-into-wet. In other words, work with wet paint on the entire area. For example, if you are working from the shadow into the light on the model's forehead, it is necessary to cover the terminator area with a new coat of paint. To avoid a hard edge it can be effective to scumble your paint and lighten your brush pressure so that there is a gradual passage into the dry paint area. It's advisable to let this happen in a quiet area where there is a lot of the same color.

In this case, I re-covered the shadow on her forehead along the edge next to the light. The next color I mixed was the dark light just next to the shadow, then I dragged it over on the light side farther than I saw it.

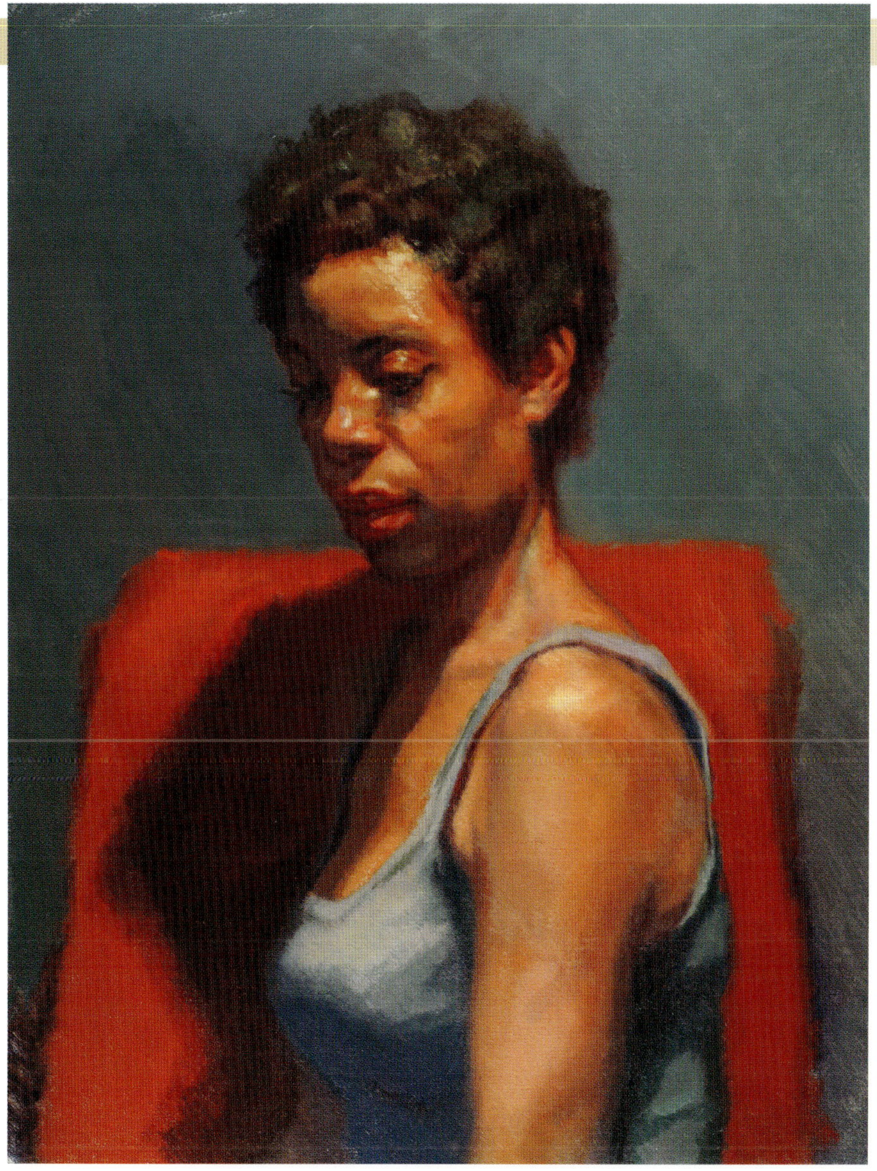

## 13 WORK THE DETAILS AND MAKE ANY FINAL ADJUSTMENTS

The final stage of a painting is when I feel the subject really comes into focus. Watch for plane changes that look too abrupt or sharp. One such area in this painting occurred where the light met the shadow on the model's face. To make this passage more natural, I added a deeper turning color. When you work on a passage where light meets shadow in this way, often you have to relinquish your exact shadow shape while finding the correct color that runs just on the light side of the shadow. Once you find that color, go back to your shadow color and redraw the shadow shape.

The beauty of working wet-into-wet is that it allows you to push one color against another to reshape the border between them. I also made notes of higher value along the model's cheek bone, as well as some strong notes of color on her nose. Step back and glance back and forth between subject and painting to find these additional notes. Calm focus wins the race.

**Family**
Lea Colie Wight
Oil on linen
38" × 26" (97cm × 66cm)

This is one in a series of paintings I did about mothers and children. I love the closeness and protectiveness of the family. It was a joy to paint. Although the mother sat for the entire painting, I was unable to convince the girls to sit the whole time. I blocked them in and painted them for a while at each sitting. I worked from reference photos for the finishing stage.

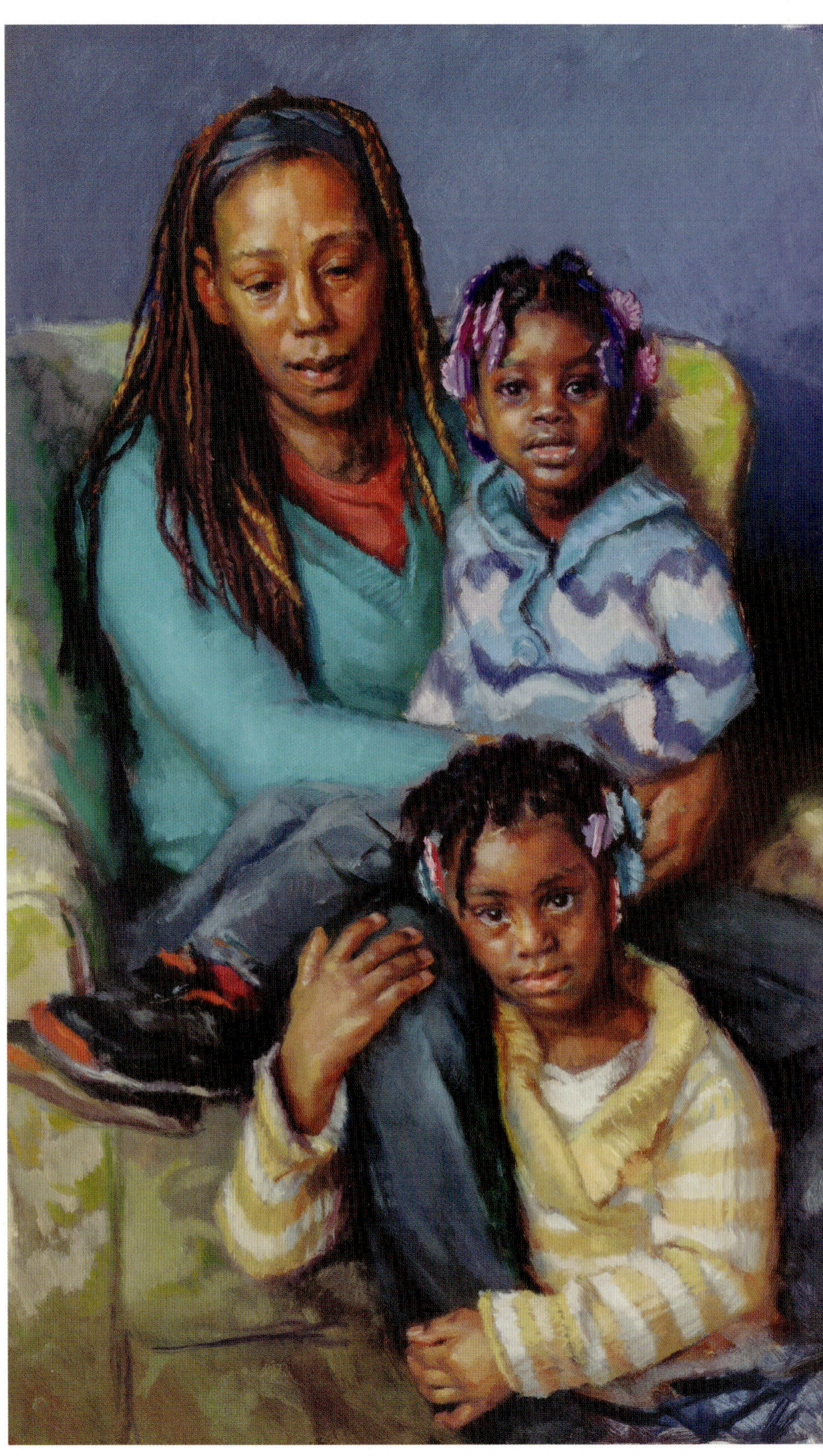

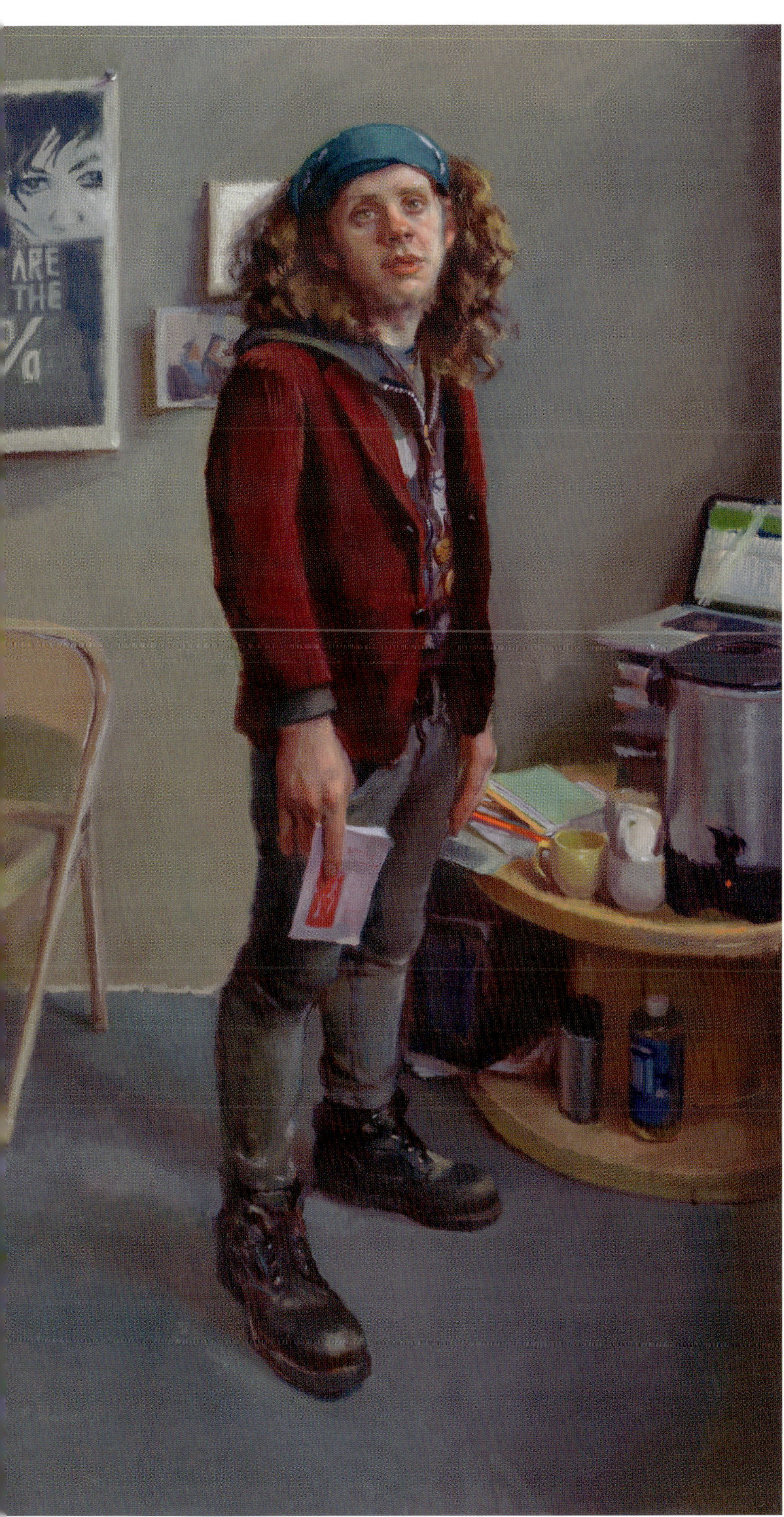


**Disciple**
Lea Colie Wight
Oil on linen
44" × 24" (112cm × 61cm)

I began this painting with a different idea in mind, but as I worked with this young man he revealed more of himself to me, and the painting changed. He wore his regular clothes and brought in objects that had personal meaning to him. He told me his history, his goals for the future and what moved him. The title *Disciple* is descriptive of his inner being. This morphosis can happen with a long painting. If you allow it, I think it results in a better painting.

These paintings were done by master artists whose dedication, knowledge and skill allow them to create powerful works in their own voices. They have built these paintings based on the methods and techniques shown in this book.

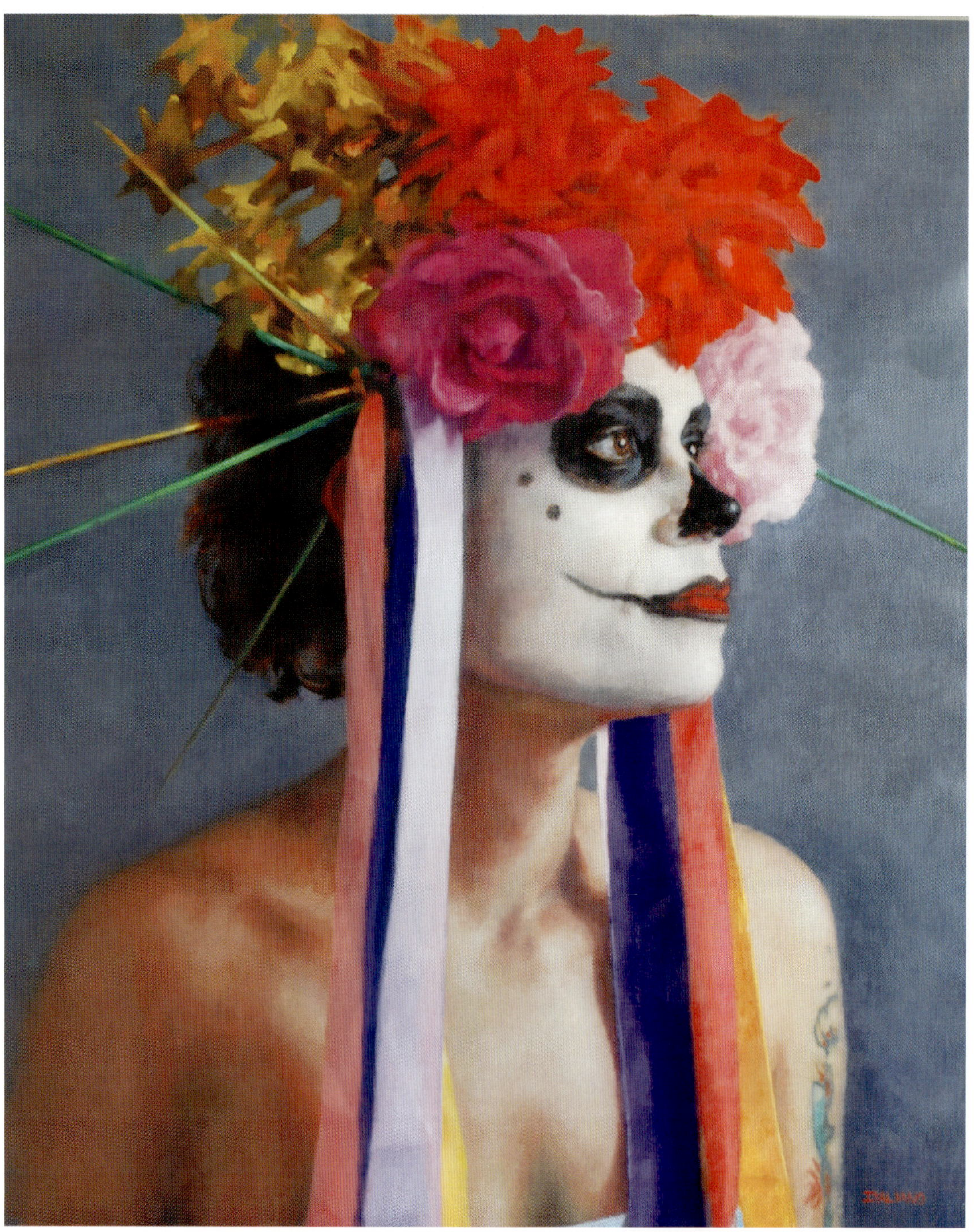

**Remembrance, Day of the Dead series**
Natalie Italiano
Oil on canvas
30" × 24" (76cm × 61cm)

Natalie's extensive experience working from life enabled her to create this beautifully evocative portrait.

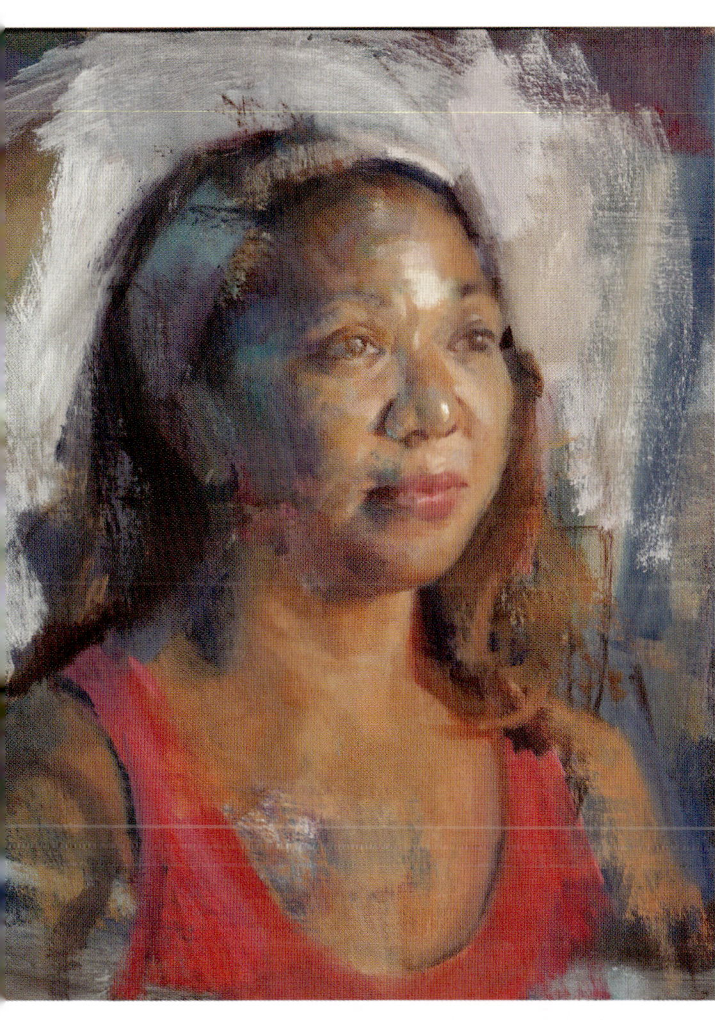

**Marlisa, My Neighbor**
JaFang Lu
20" × 16" (51cm × 41cm)

The beauty and personal expression shown in this painting is based on knowledge and confidence.

**Self Portrait**
Darren Kingsley
Oil on canvas
20" × 20" (51cm × 51cm)

This painting illustrates the power of color in expert hands.

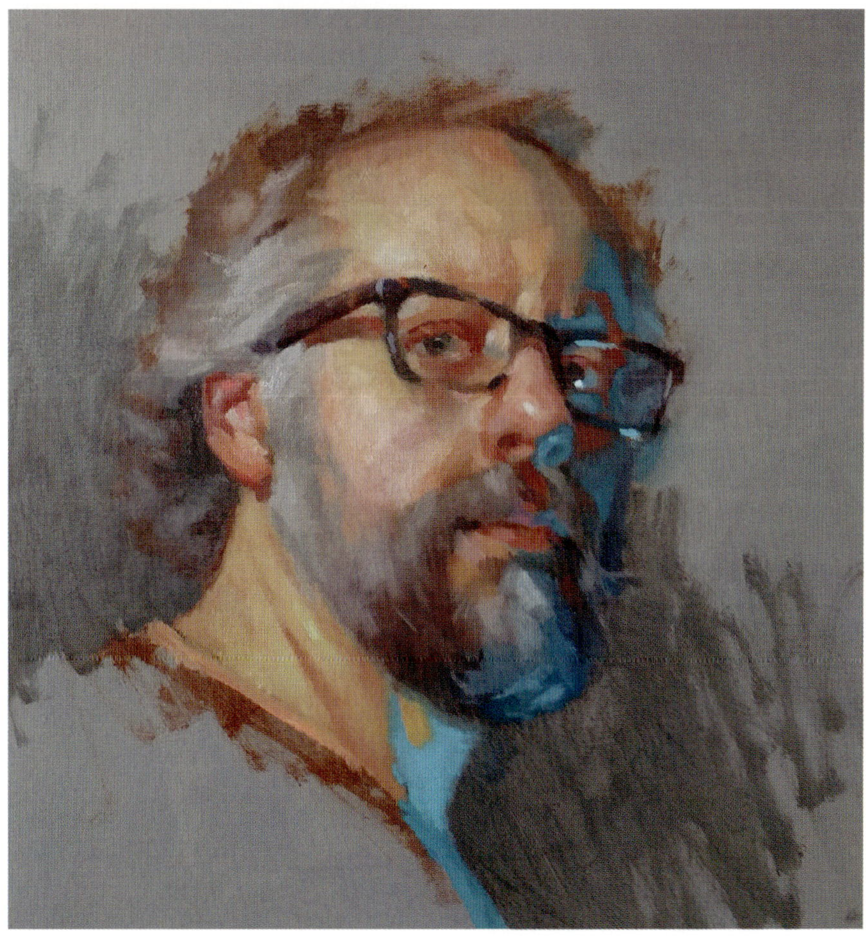

# 6 STILL LIFE *and* LANDSCAPES

A painting is rarely an effortless process of building one stage upon another until it's finished. Should your paintings progress smoothly all the way from the first brushstroke through to the signature, that's wonderful. If it's a bumpy ride, well, enjoy that.

If you're like me, and your usual painting practice is experiment, change, correct and repaint frequently, then you might find the upcoming painting demonstrations a bit challenging at times. If you do run into problems, take strength in knowing that you already have all the tools you need to get your painting back on track. So if an element needs to be moved or resized, just do it. Remember that all of your hard work, practice and training have given you real skill. It's not a fluke when you paint something well!

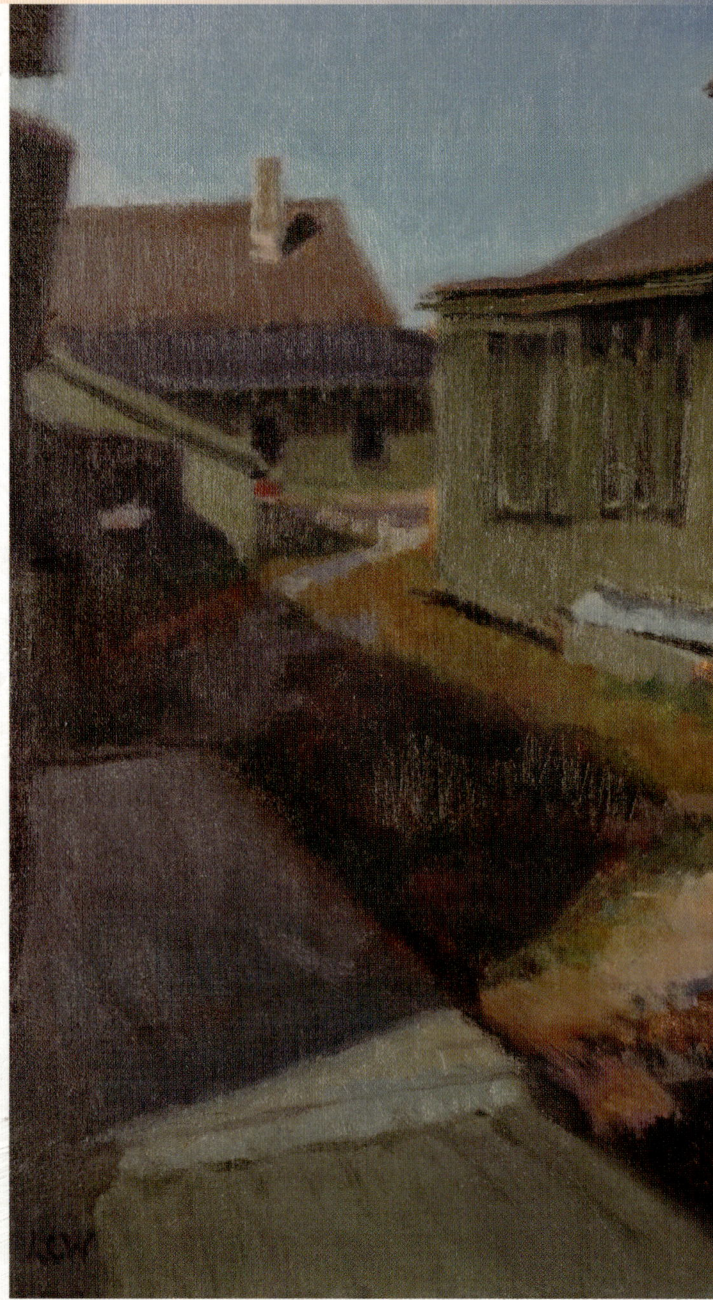

**Boatyard 2**
Lea Colie Wight
Oil on canvas
18" × 24" (46cm × 61cm)

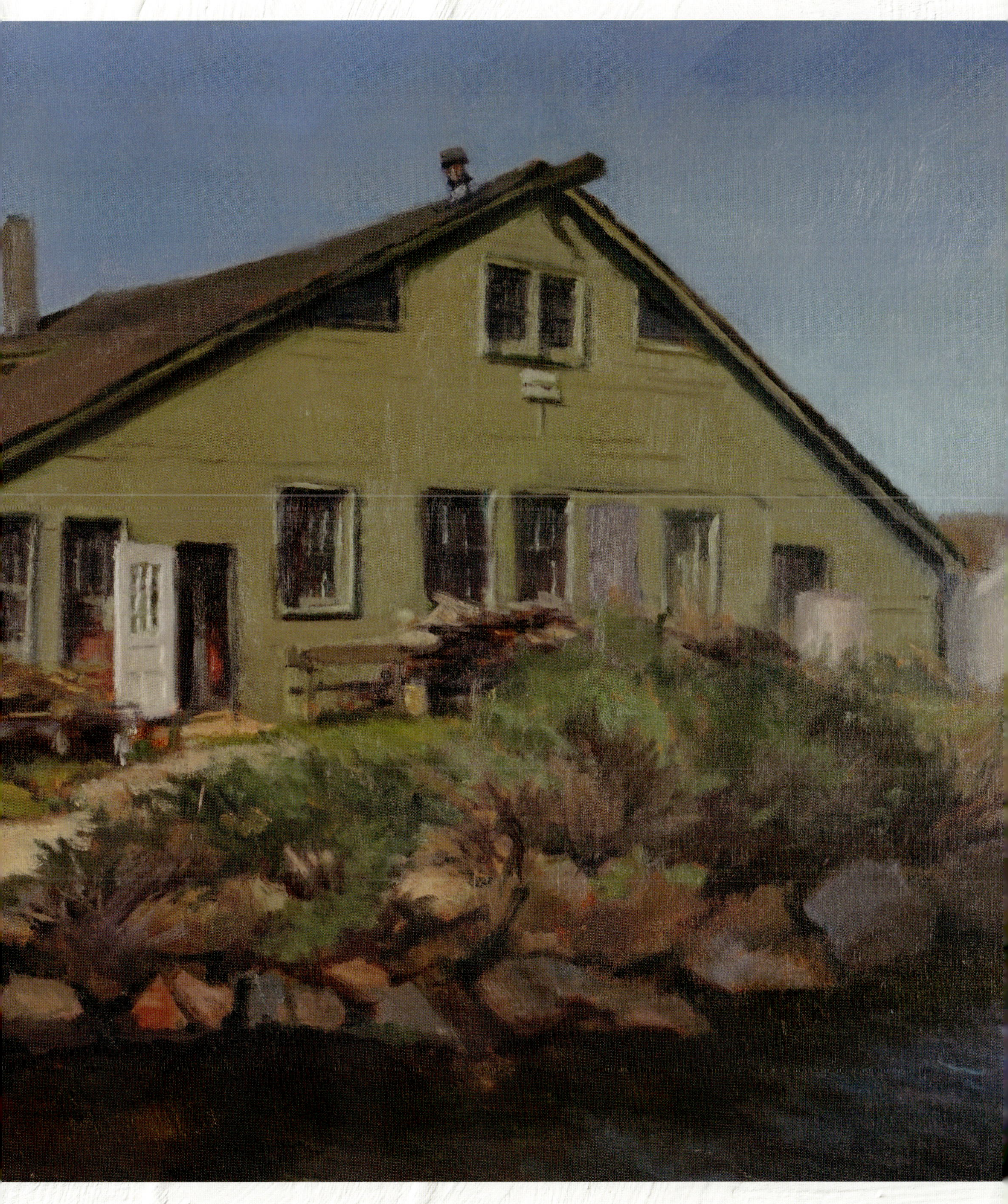

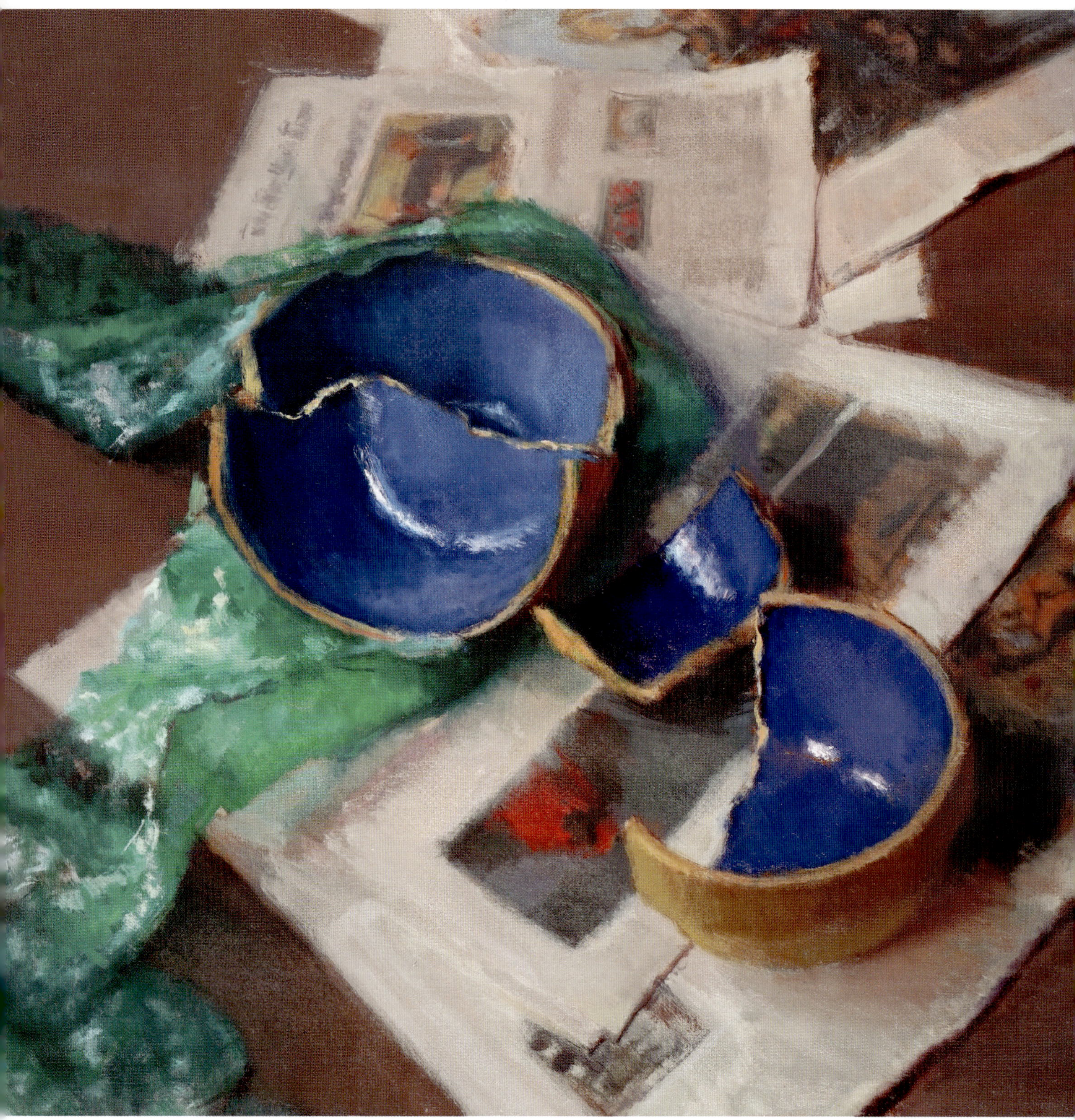

**Broken**
Lea Colie Wight
Oil on canvas
24" × 18" (61cm × 46cm)

*Demonstration*

# STILL LIFE PAINTING

If you're new to painting still lifes, it's best to set up a simple composition. When you're comfortable with simple setups, then you can go further and choose compositions that have challenges like glass, patterned fabrics or metal objects.

When you feel you're ready to paint a formal still life, it's natural and desirable to have a personal affinity with your subject. This subject could be objects that you have a personal connection with and spark memories, or it could be objects that make a statement. This is what will keep you engaged all through the painting.

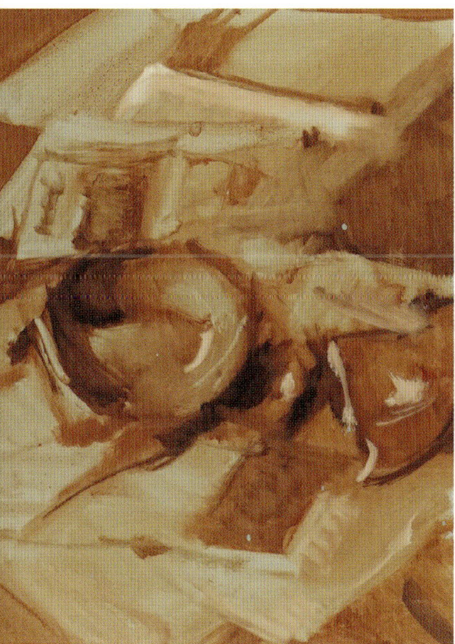

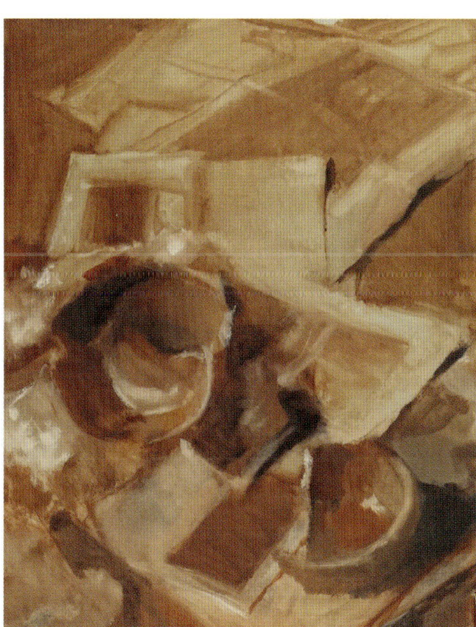

### 1 BEGIN WITH COMPOSITION STUDIES

Settle on your composition by doing small studies. By default, you'll be working out your main value relationships. The studies above began with a gesture painting and moved into a simple value study.

In the first study, the bowls are placed closer together, but the placement is unbalanced. I wanted the composition to flow from the top right corner to the bottom left corner, but the bowls blocked rather than supported the pathway through the painting.

In the second study, the placement of the bowls is staggered, resulting in a much more successful composition.

## *Materials*

SURFACE

stretched canvas

OIL PIGMENTS

Magenta, Permanent Rose or Quinacridone Red, Cadmium Red Deep, Cadmium Red Medium or Cadmium Scarlet, Cadmium Orange or Cadmium Yellow Deep, Cadmium Yellow Light or Cadmium Lemon, Cadmium Green Light, Viridian or Phthalo Green, Cerulean Blue, Ultramarine Blue, Dioxazine Purple, Cobalt Violet Deep, Yellow Ochre, Indian Yellow, Burnt Sienna or Burnt Umber, Black, Titanium White

BRUSHES

Silver Brush #5001 hake flat or mop brush; Silver Brush #7110 sable cat's tongue sizes 4, 6 and 8; Silver Brush #1034 long bristle filbert sizes 2, 3, 4 and 6; Rosemary brush #278 sizes 2, 4 and 6

OTHER

nitrile or vinyl gloves, odorless mineral spirits or Gamsol, paper towels, spray Retouch varnish

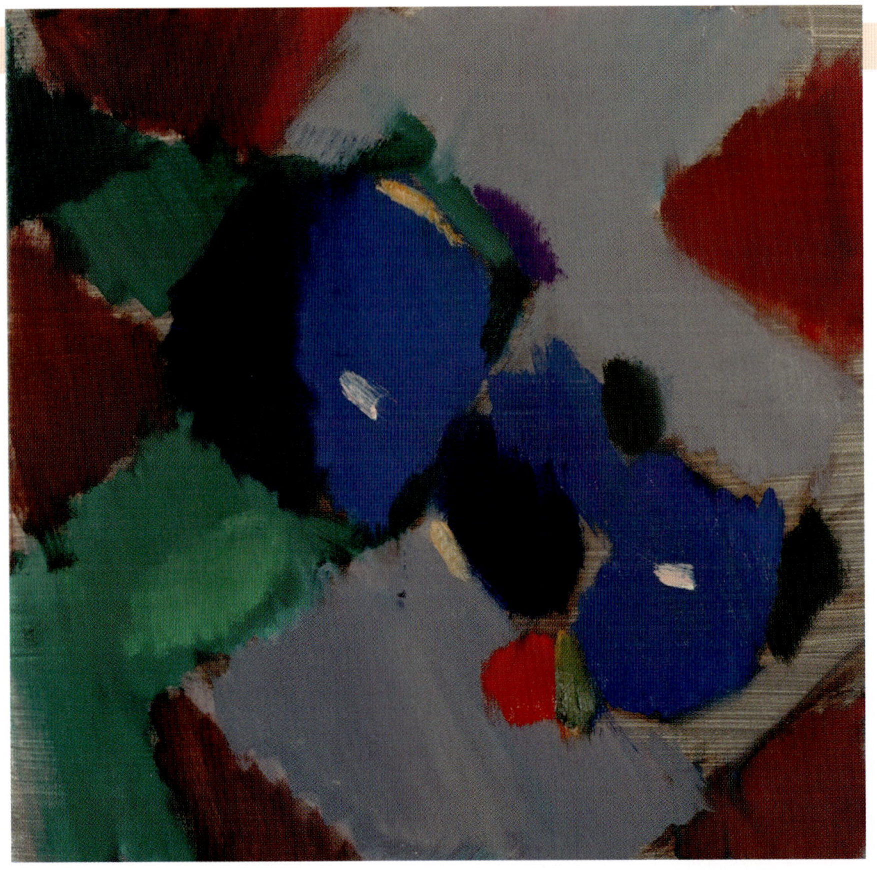

## 2 DO A COLOR STUDY

Next complete a simple color study of your composition. This will allow you to block your beginning colors in on your final painting with confidence. Don't forget to start with the easiest color to see and work your way through to the more subtle colors. Work around the colors without lingering on one. Once you've got a handle on your main colors, you've finished your study.

### *Take Time to Decide on a Composition*

It is often a good practice to wait for a day before making a final decision on your composition. This helps you judge your composition more clearly and impartially.

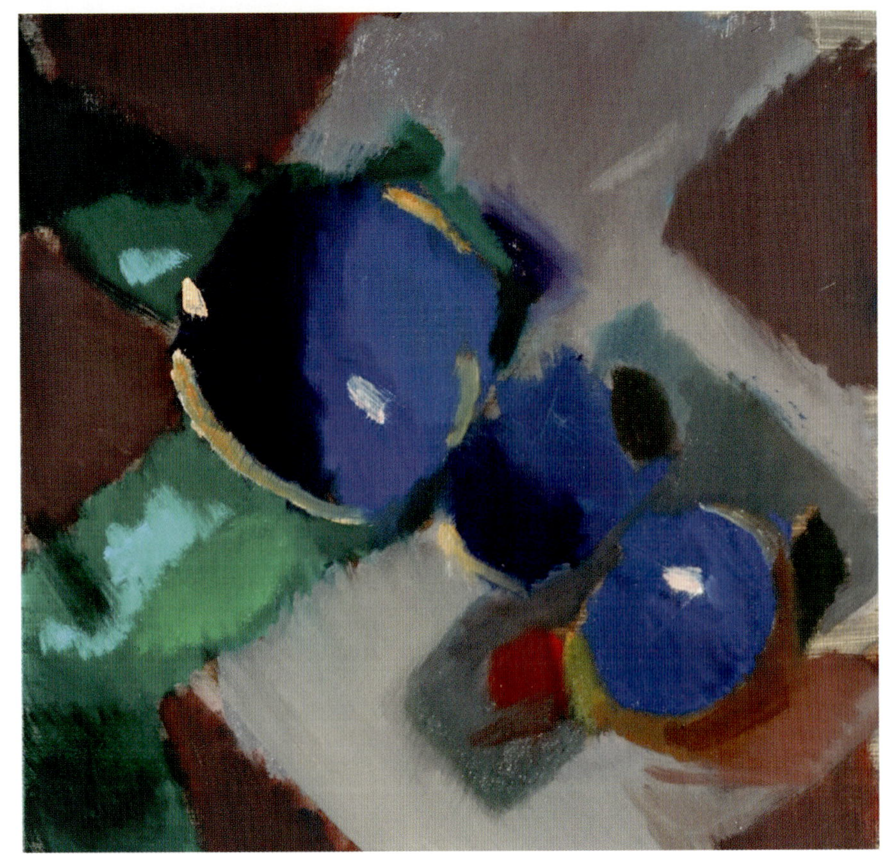

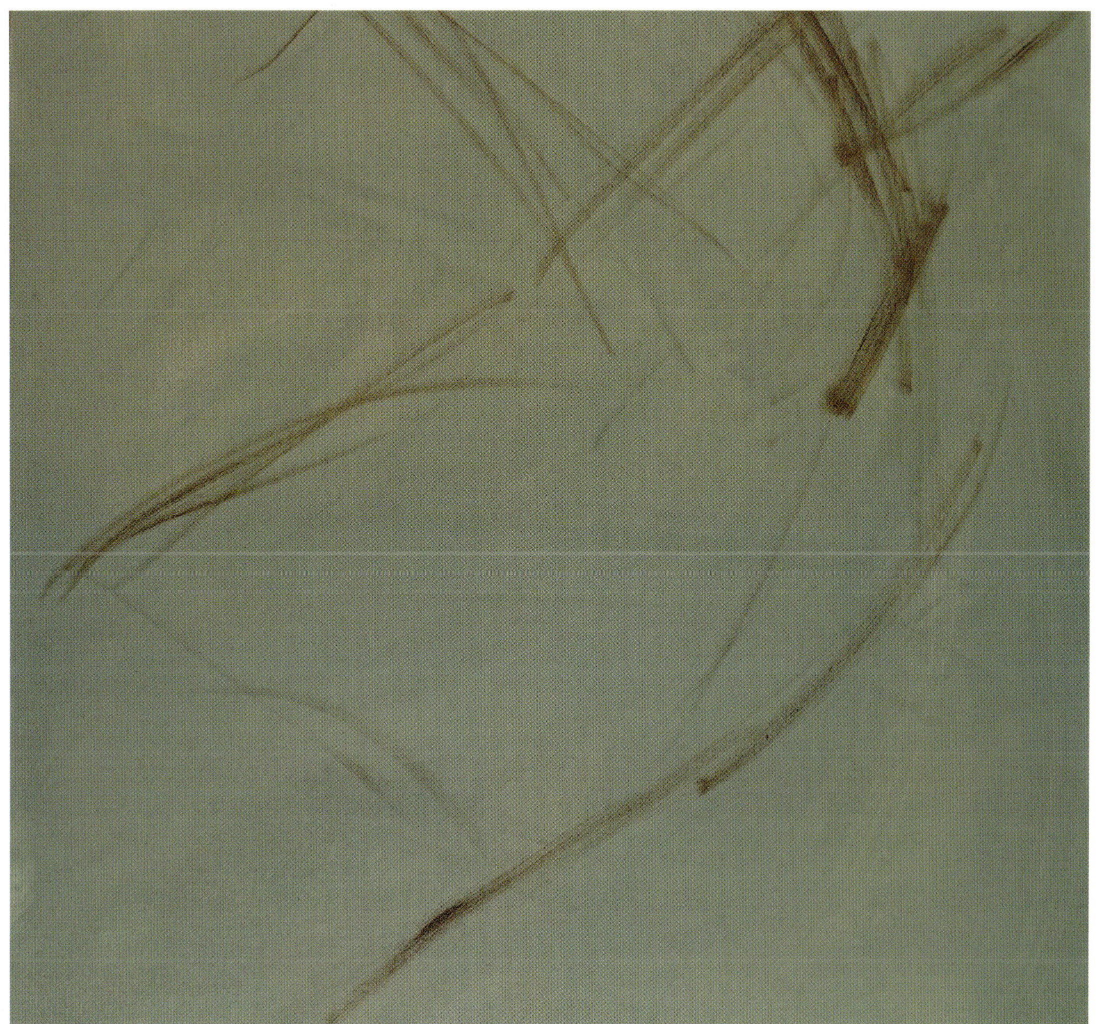

## 3 BEGIN THE GESTURE

Take some time and try to see your composition on your canvas. Keep your initial gesture simple, free and loose. In chapter 3, you learned about capturing the energy and movement of your subject. Still life, figures, portraits, landscapes—whatever your subject, the gesture is your largest impression of what is before you. It will develop into your finished painting.

This is an exciting moment. Don't hesitate or worry that your lines will be wrong. As your painting develops, it will become more accurate. Use as few sweeping brushstrokes as possible.

### *Correct Positioning*

Remember to stand back and hold your brush at the end. Paint through your arm.

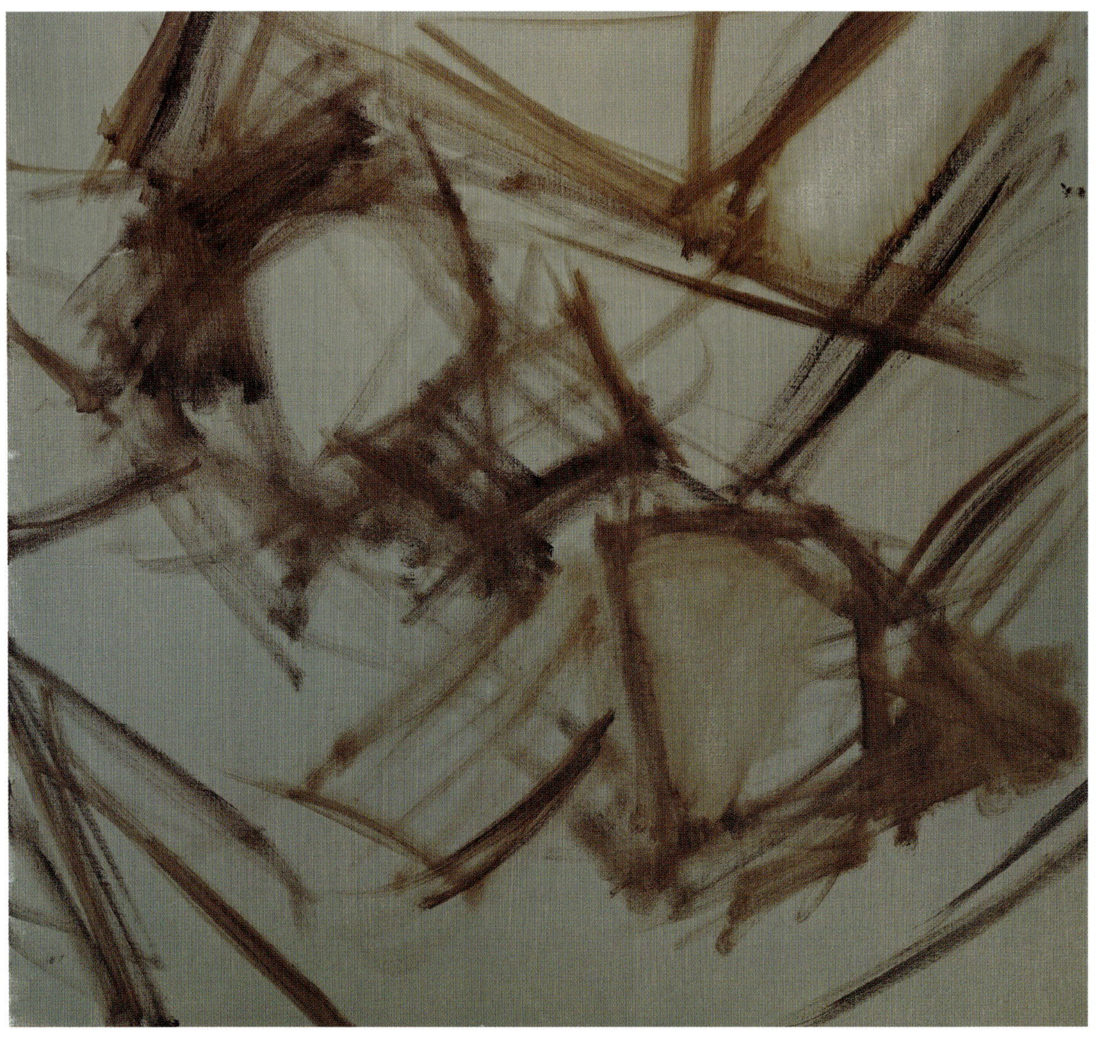

## 4 DEVELOP THE GESTURE

Further develop the gesture. Add more information while still thinking big. Try as hard as you can not to make final proportional decisions.

### *Take Breaks*

When working on a still life or a landscape painting, it is really important to take breaks. Breaks are built in when you're working with a model—you break when your model does. When you don't have this natural rest period, however, it is easy to paint without stopping. You can get exhausted, start losing your focus and find yourself making poor decisions.

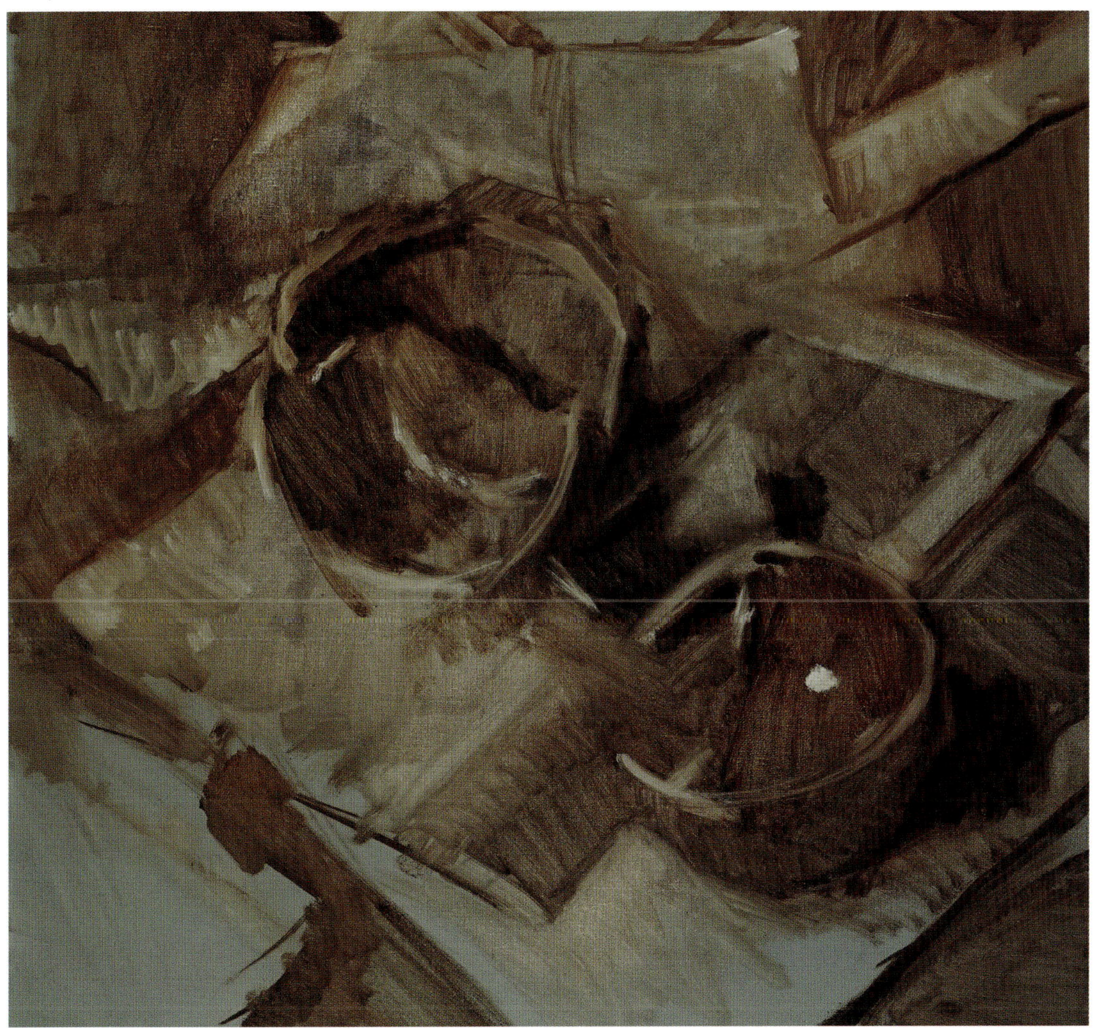

## 5 BLOCK IN SHADOWS AND DARK VALUES

Block in the shadows and dark values. By now you should have decided on the final proportions. Add a note for the brightest bright and the darkest dark. If you paint without these notes, you may paint too dark, which would not leave you with enough value room to show a difference between the dark shadows and the even darker area under that shadow. Or, you might paint too light and not have enough room to show the bright highlight.

### *Value Affects Color*

Remember, if it's not the right value, it can't be the right color.

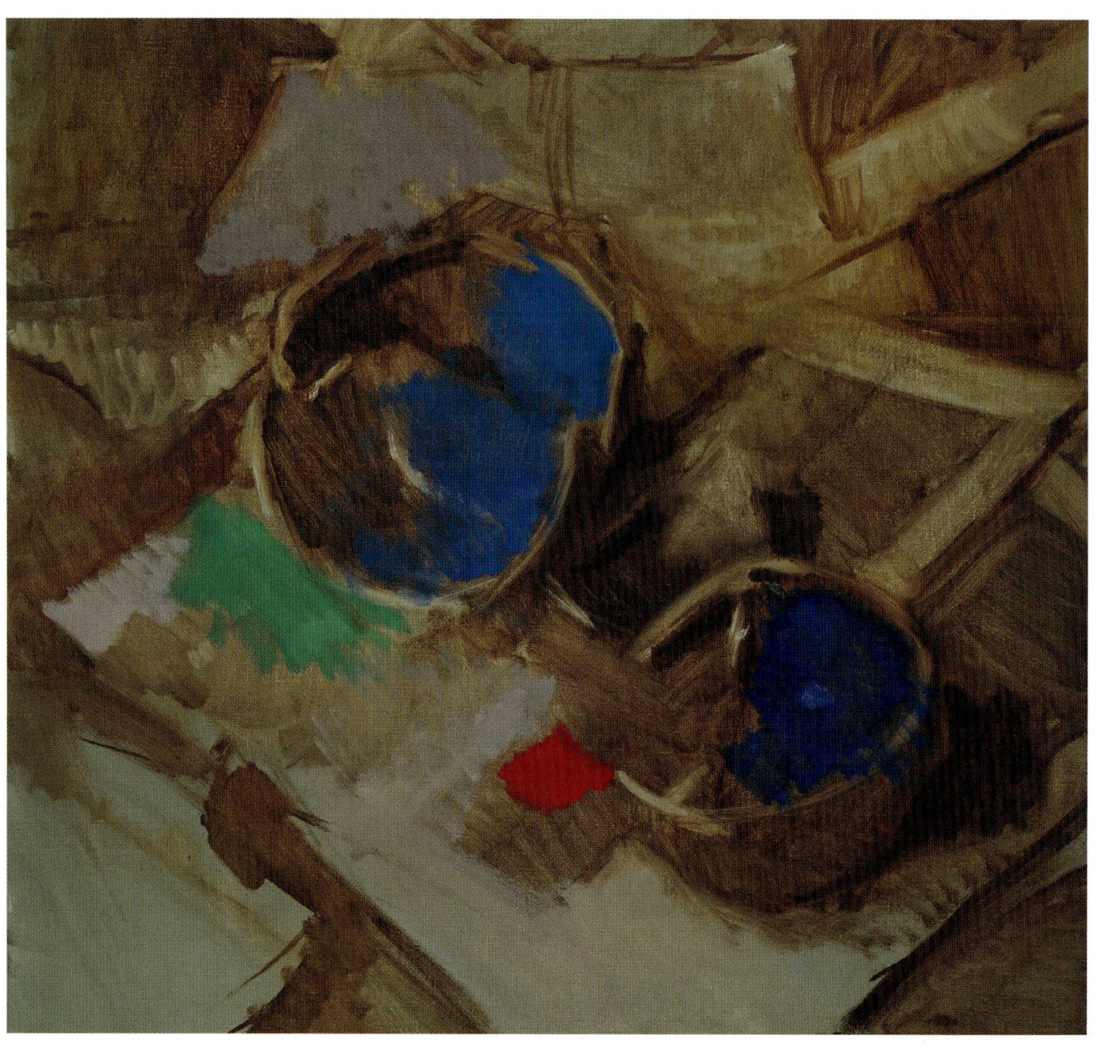

## 6 BEGIN ADDING COLOR

Indicate the first simple, clear colors. In this case, Cobalt Blue, Viridian Green and Cadmium Red Deep. Selecting a strong color like red as a place holder color note. It is going to be the only real color note in the newspapers and an important element in this composition.

Be careful not to overmix your colors.

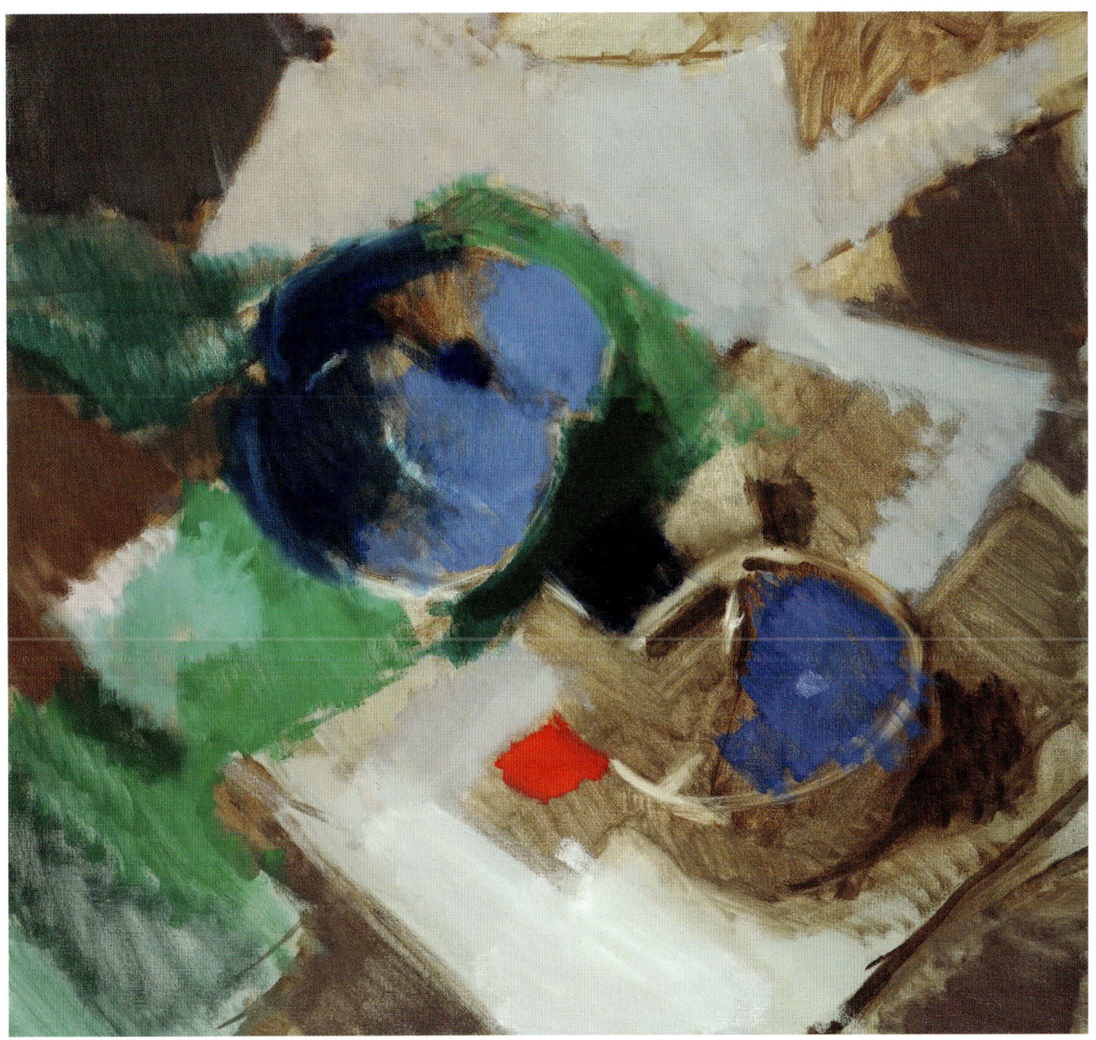

## 7 CONTINUE BUILDING COLOR AND SHARPENING EDGES

Continue building additional colors. Expand your color masses, staying loose with no hard edges. At this stage, you're still able to adjust your drawing shapes. Let the edges that you want to sharpen develop along the way as you bring the painting into focus.

### *Painting Strategies*

As with all multiday paintings, there are multiple strategies for this process. You normally want to have your painting relatively dry so you can paint on top without stickiness. This can mean taking a day off between painting sessions. In the later stages of a painting, you usually want to work on smaller areas one day and larger areas on another day rather than working all over each day.

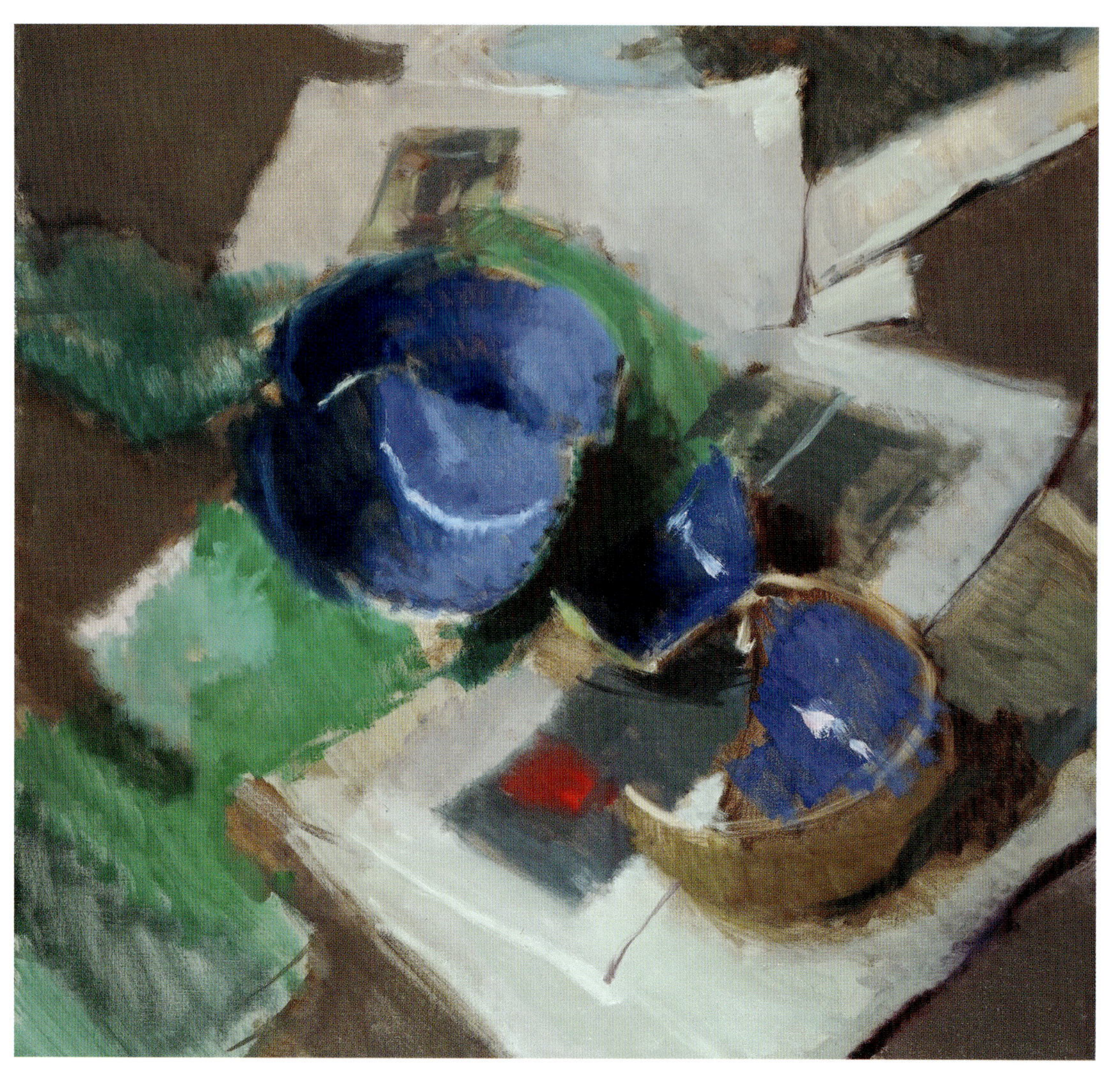

## 8 FINISH THE EDGES AND FOCAL POINTS, ADD DETAILS

The painting is reaching the final phase. Now is the time for decisions about edges and focal points and to reinforce how you want the viewer's eye to move through the painting. Don't rush through this stage; it's important to be objective about how each decision affects the balance and rhythm of the painting. In this case, notice how the red has been adjusted and more information has been developed in the papers. Sharper edges were added on some of the overlapping newspaper pages as a tool to lead the eye around the painting.

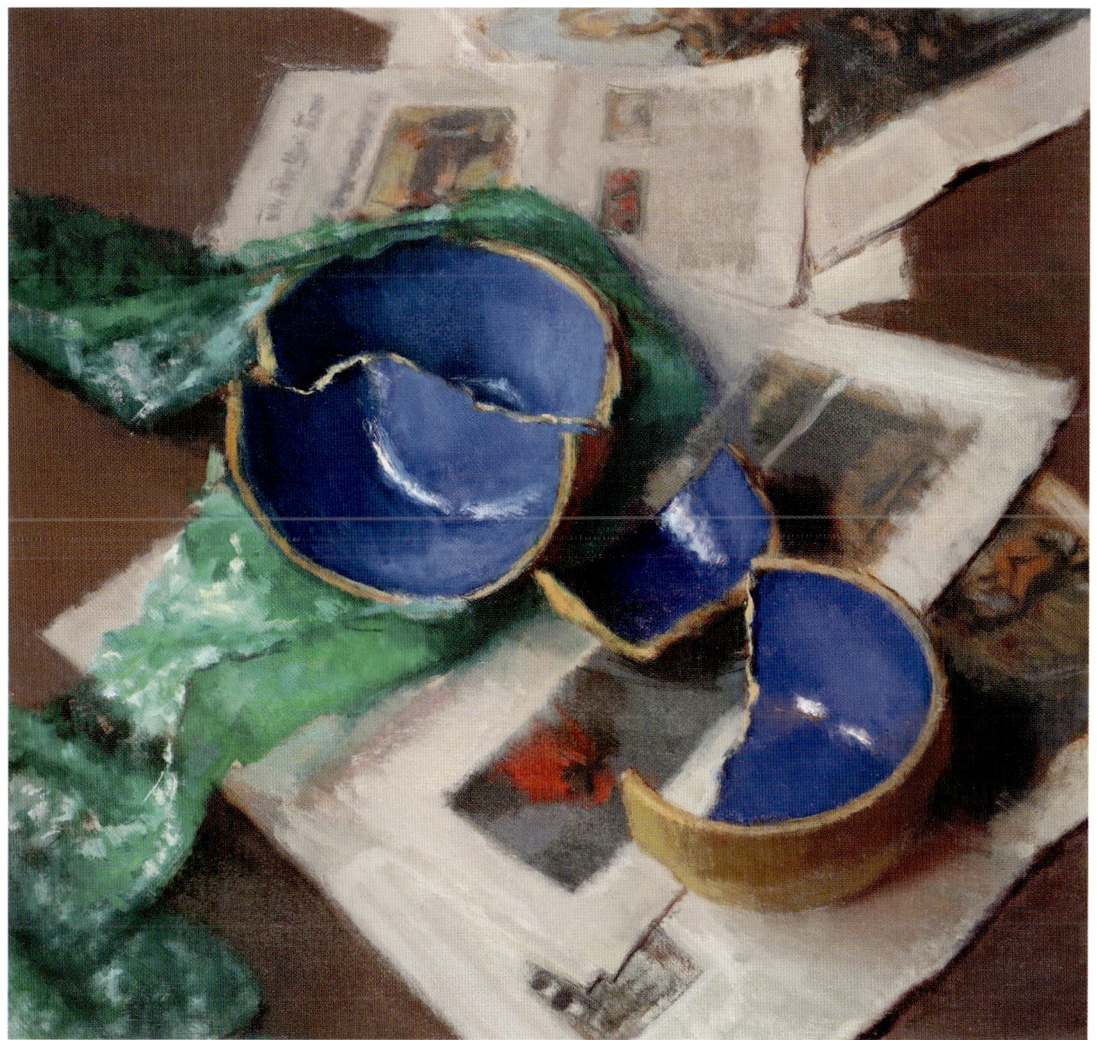

## 9 MAKE FINAL ADJUSTMENTS

When the painting is almost finished, step away from it for a week or two, then go back and study it. The final changes you make may be quite subtle and could be hard to detect by anyone but you.

Here, the shadow cast by the bubble wrap on the left bowl was deepened, and a reflection was added to the bowl. The shadow under the right bowl was worked on, and the value on its rim was lightened to make it stand out a bit more. There were a couple of other changes, which I'll leave you to find. Can you spot them?

# LIGHTING CHALLENGES

This painting had some unique lighting challenges. There is both warm lamp light and cool outside light in the composition, and that relationship changed throughout the day. So I spent a day watching the relationship between the two light sources before deciding that 5:00 P.M. was the right time of day to paint this scene.

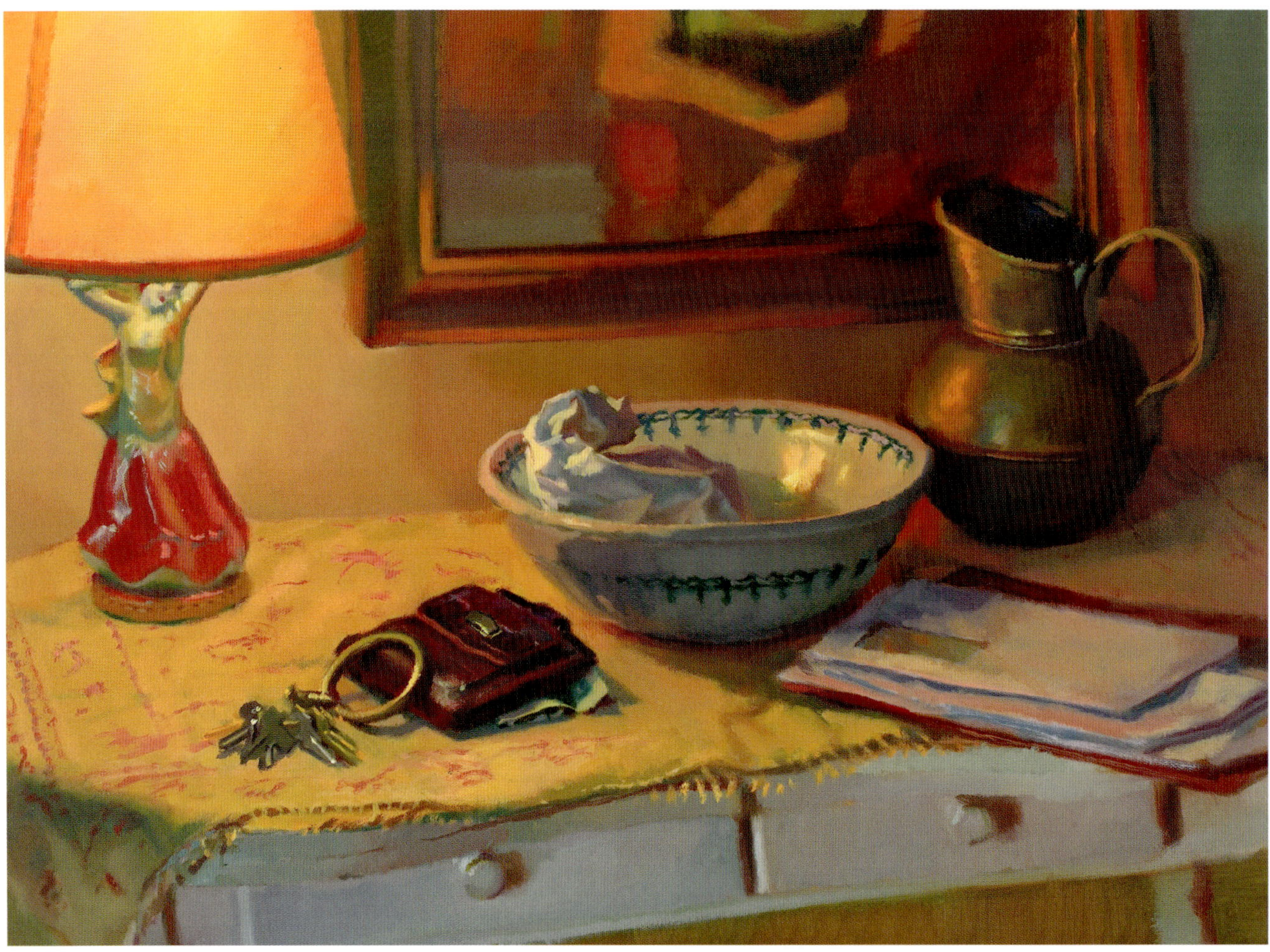

**Running Out**
Lea Colie Wight
Oil on linen
18" × 24" (46cm × 61cm)

## THE PROCESS

I started by blocking in and developing the drawing. Then I blocked in the shadows because they changed during the day, so I knew I needed to get them in right at 5:00.

The next day I blocked in the main colors of the tabletop and the front of the table, since they set up the relationship. (The color of the letters compared with the front of the table is really close but do you notice the pinkish hue on the letters? Bounce your eyes back and forth between them to see this.) Some other important things to get in place were the light on the inside of the bowl, and the shadow on the outside of the bowl. I painted the two areas independent of each other to make sure to stick with the values and colors I had mapped out earlier.

Over the next couple of days, I worked on the painting right around 5:00 P.M. Once I had established the relationship between the two areas and all of the important colors, the time frame to paint spread out, and I could work on the painting from around noon to 7:00 P.M.

# GLASS AND METAL

The key to painting metal, glass and other reflective or transparent objects is to paint what you see, not what you expect to see. Glance quickly and squint to see the value relationships. Then with your eyes wide open, look quickly from one object to another and compare. Don't forget to stand way back from your easel.

In the examples below, both pieces are masterfully painted, although hte artists handled the paint differently

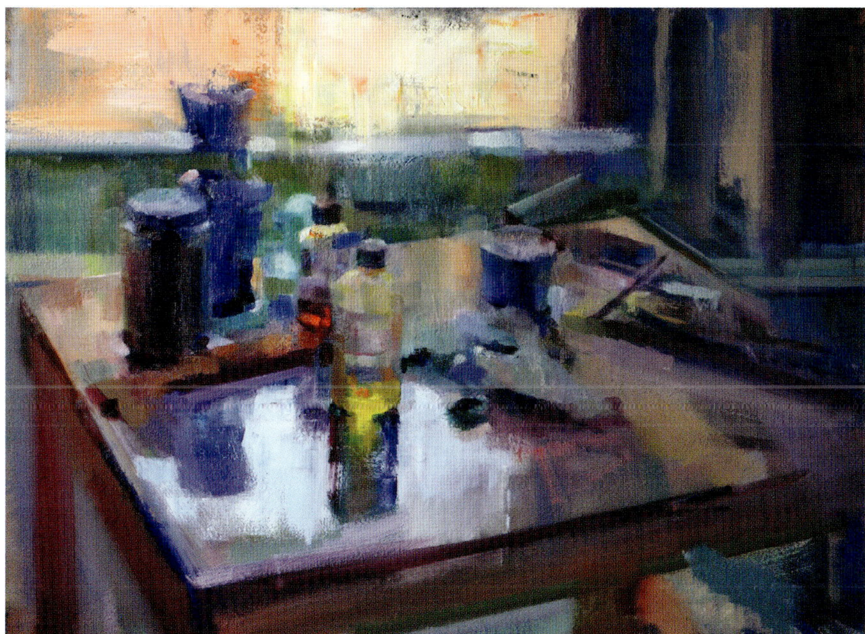

**Limited Palette**
JaFang Lu
Oil on canvas
16" × 20" (41cm × 51cm)

In this painting by JaFang Lu, the yellow color in the bottom of the bottle moves right into the tabletop. Even though we know a bottle has an exact shape, the outline isn't what we notice. Also note the way she handled the reflections on the table.

**Tomatoes and Pumpkins**
Darren Kingsley, 2017
Oil on canvas
20" × 20" (51cm × 51cm)

In Darren Kingsley's painting, you see the same thing. The base of the pumpkins dissolve into the tabletop.

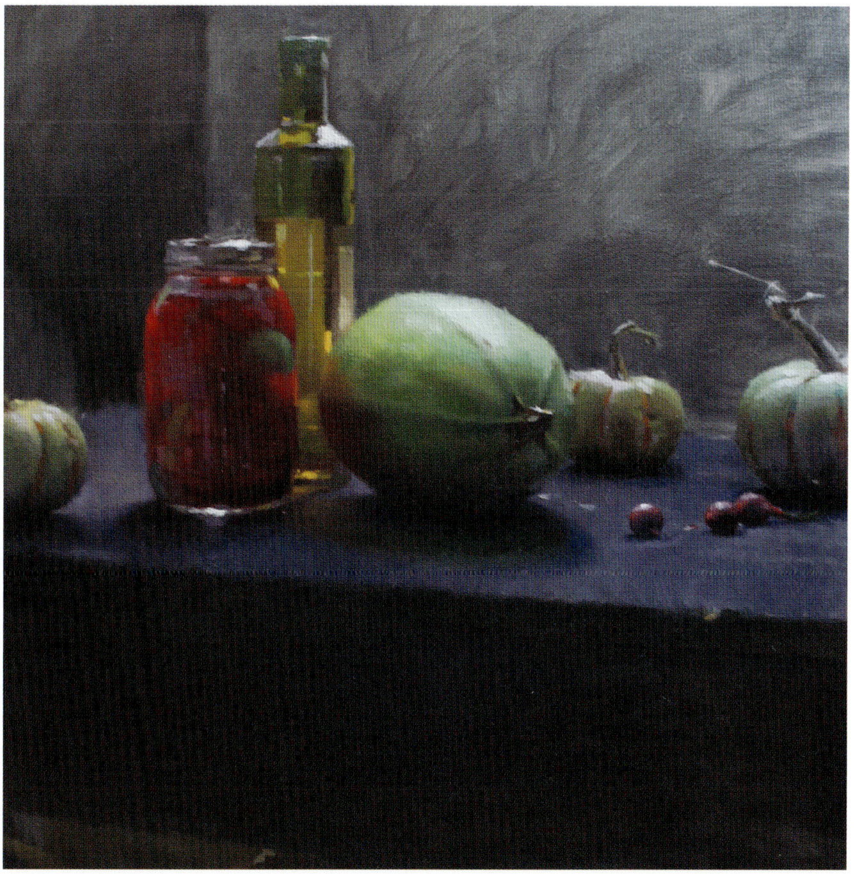

# FABRIC AND PATTERNS

Un-patterned fabric is best started by simplifying it into three or four main colors and blocking those in. Build more detail from there.

Patterns are best painted as large shapes at first. Squint to see the general big pattern. Have a large amount of color for each area mixed on your palette so you can just work back and forth on the painting without having to stop.

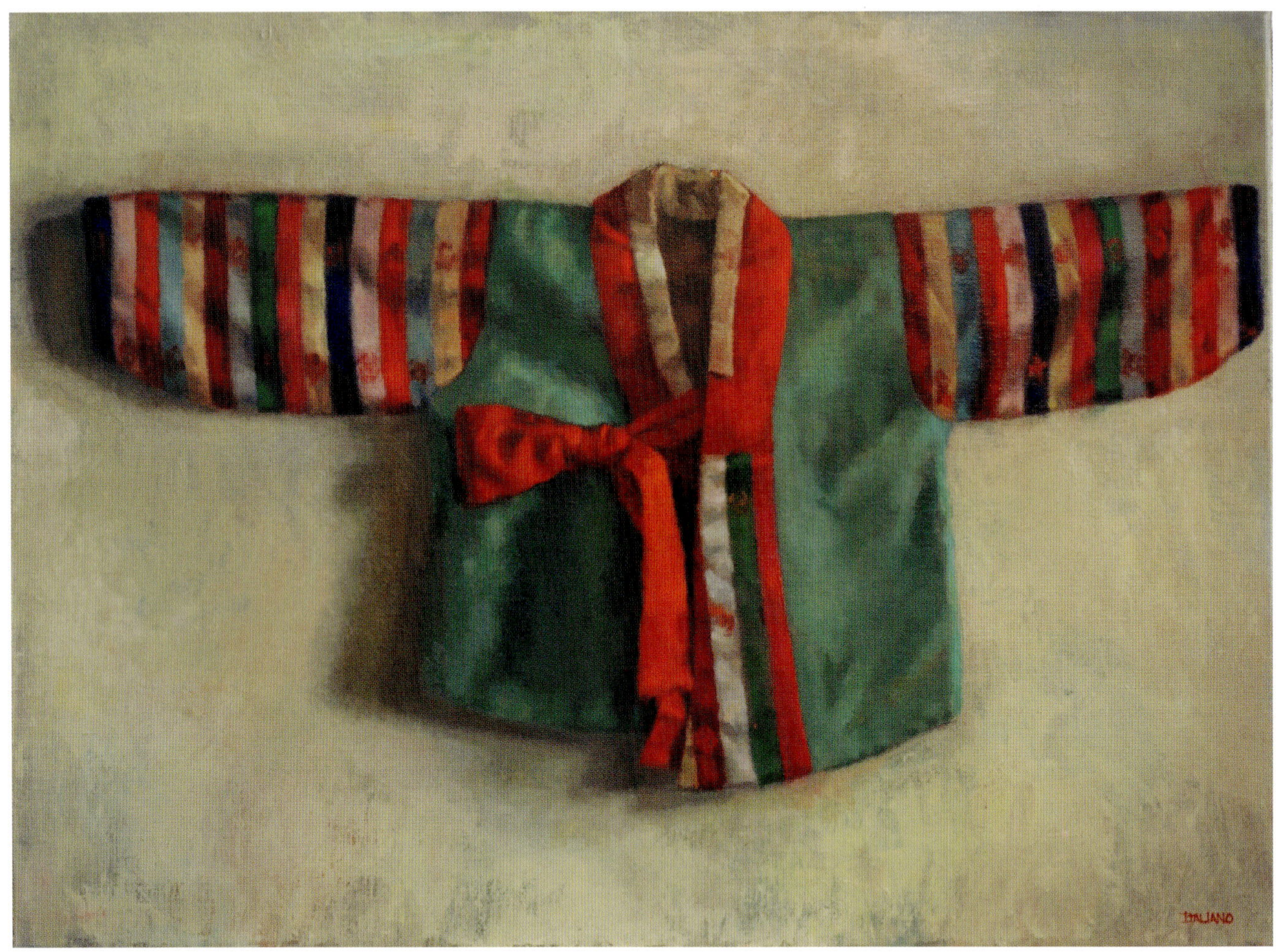


**Korean Child's Hanbok**
Natalie Italiano
Oil on canvas
22" × 30" (56cm × 76cm)

In her painting, Natalie Italiano blocked in the stripes on the sleeves of the jacket first, then painted the shadows on each. She painted different shadow colors on each stripe rather than pulling dark colors across the whole sleeve. It makes a difference in how realistic the jacket seems.

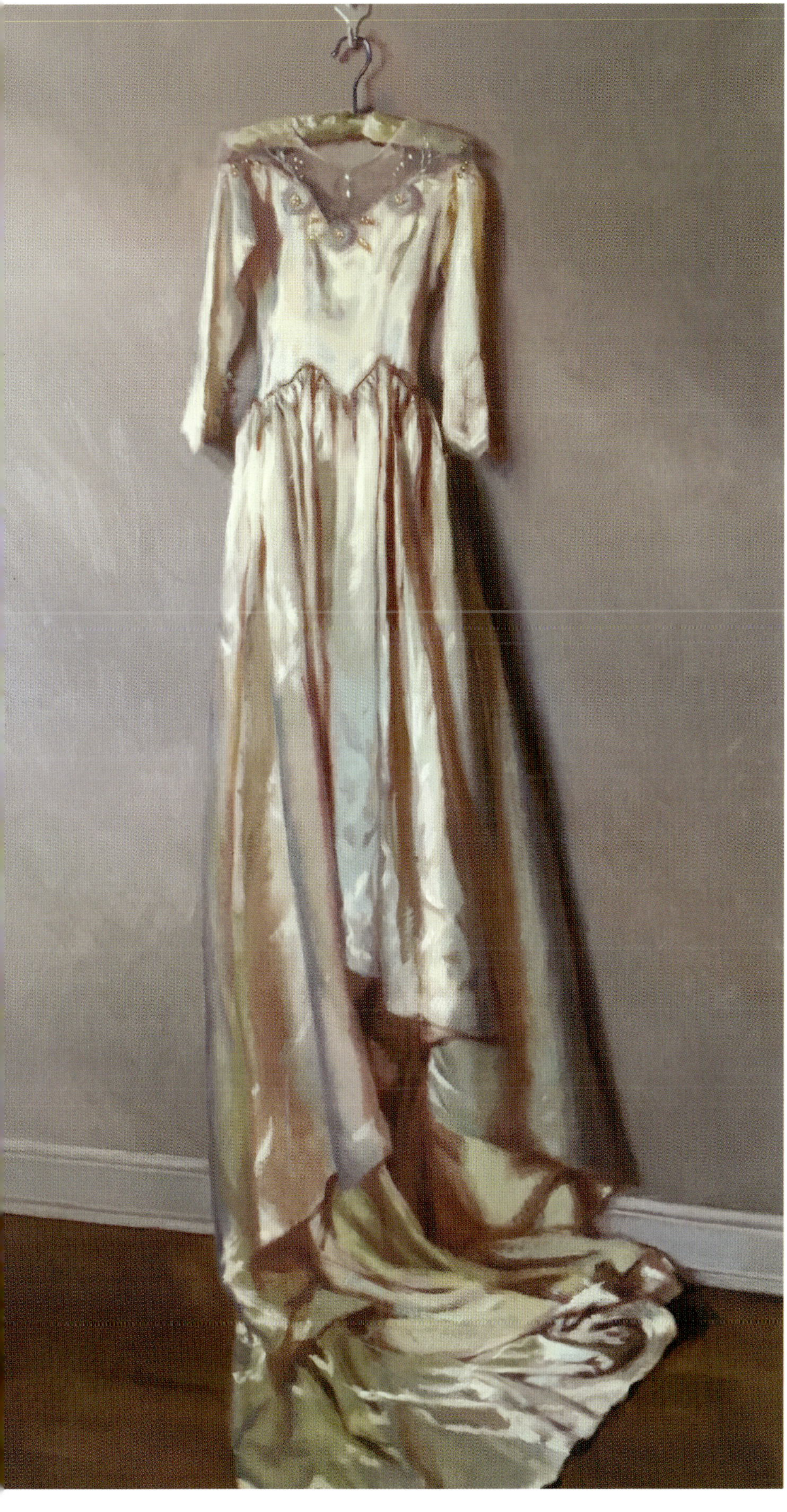

**The Wedding Gown**
Lea Colie Wight
Oil on linen
46" × 26" (117cm × 66cm)

A subject like the dress can be very challenging if you look at all the detail. However, if you break it down into a few main colors and build from there, it becomes much more manageable. Notice my choice of simplified color masses.

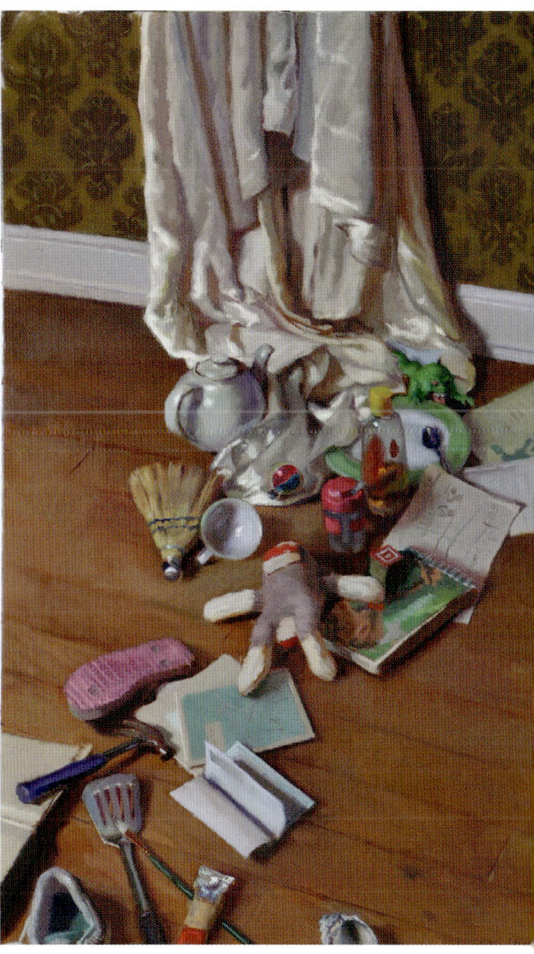

**Chaos**
Lea Colie Wight
Oil on linen
32" × 20" (81cm × 51cm)

I didn't paint information in the shadows. Choose where you want development, either shadow or light areas. If you put in the effort into both the painting gets too chaotic. In nature people look at either one and not both at once.

Observe where the pattern is strong and clear and where it loses its detail as it moves into shadow.

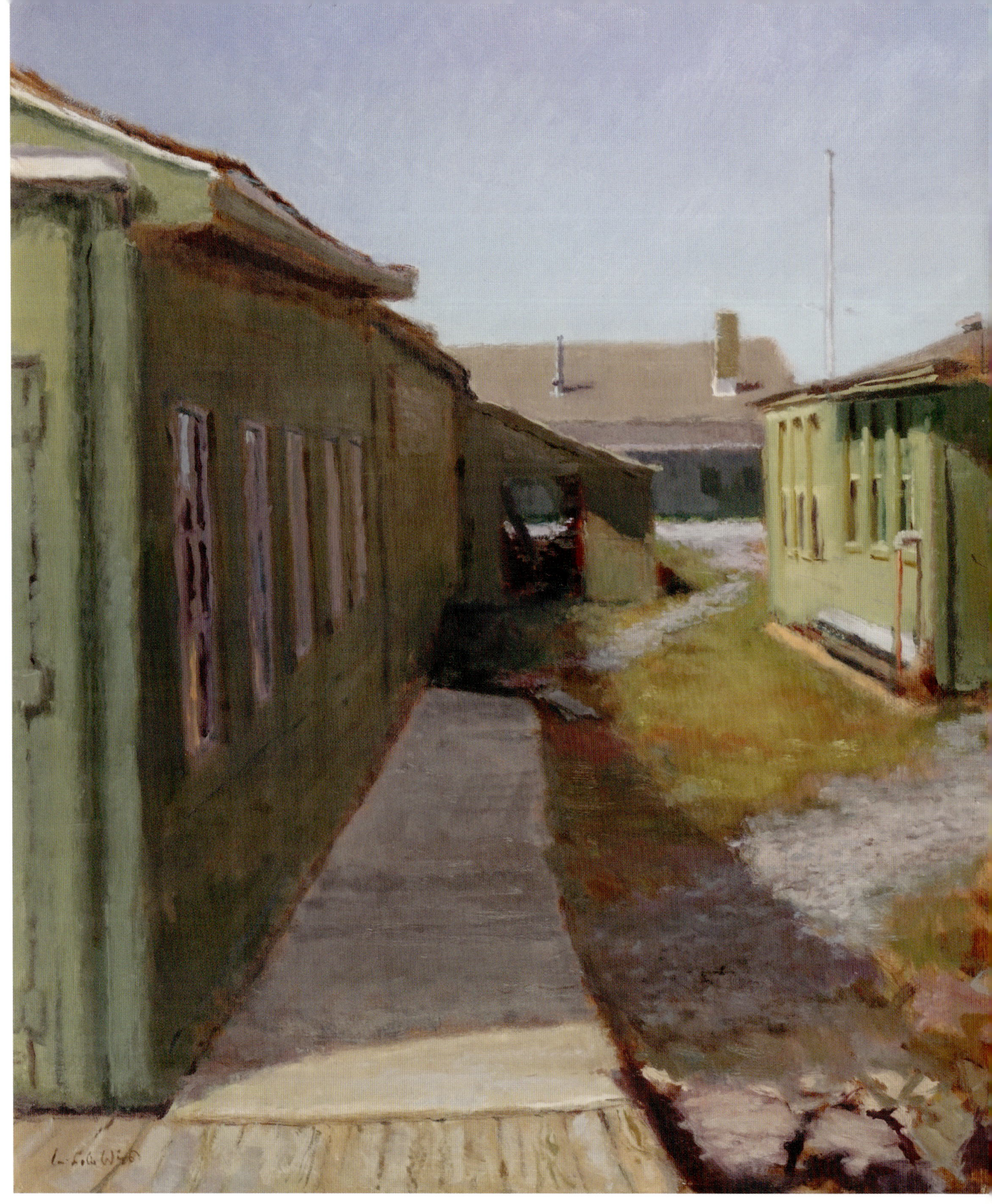

**The Boat Yard**
Lea Colie Wight
Oil on canvas
18" × 24" (46cm × 61cm)

*Demonstration*

# LANDSCAPE PAINTING

When contemplating a landscape painting, try to find a location that is meaningful to you. I don't necessarily mean a place you've been before, but simply a place that holds some allure or stirs something in you. Don't rush this. A painting that doesn't have this connection, no matter how well executed, will usually not be interesting to you or the viewer.

If you've never painted a landscape from life before allow yourself a few practice paintings. Each new ability takes some time to become familiar and second nature. Remember that you have all the artistic tools you need: proportions, value, color. Stand back calmly and look.

## *Materials*

SURFACE
stretched canvas

OIL PIGMENTS
Magenta, Permanent Rose or Quinacridone Red, Cadmium Red Deep, Cadmium Red Medium or Cadmium Scarlet, Cadmium Orange or Cadmium Yellow Deep, Cadmium Yellow Light or Cadmium Lemon, Cadmium Green Light, Viridian or Phthalo Green, Cerulean Blue, Ultramarine Blue, Dioxazine Purple, Cobalt Violet Deep, Yellow Ochre, Indian Yellow, Burnt Sienna or Burnt Umber, Black, Titanium White

BRUSHES
Silver Brush #5001 hake flat or mop brush; Silver Brush #7110 sable cat's tongue sizes 4, 6 and 8; Silver Brush #1034 long bristle filbert sizes 2, 3, 4 and 6; Rosemary brush #278 sizes 2, 4 and 6

OTHER
nitrile or vinyl gloves, odorless mineral spirits or Gamsol, paper towels, spray Retouch varnish

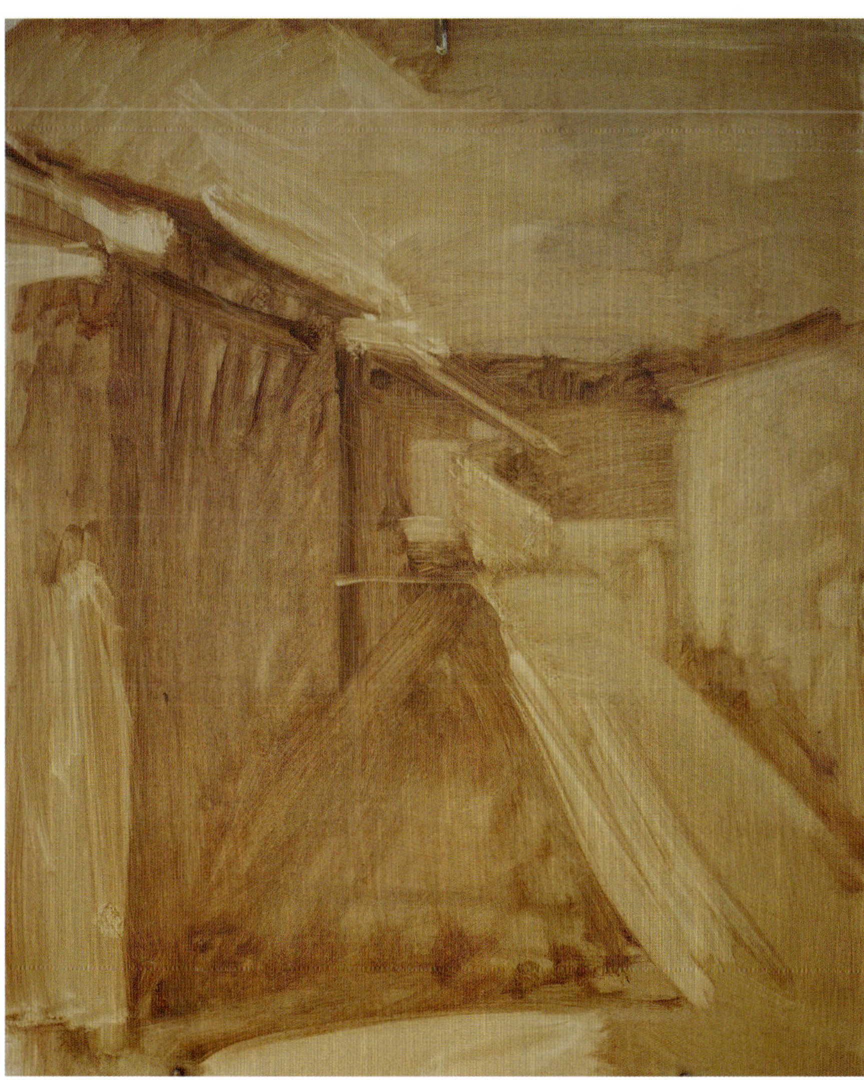

1 BEGIN WITH THE GESTURE
Your first marks should begin with a quick general gesture of the composition, addressing the entire canvas. Think about large proportions, but don't slow down. Move quickly to block in the large value patterns. These will be the bones of your painting.

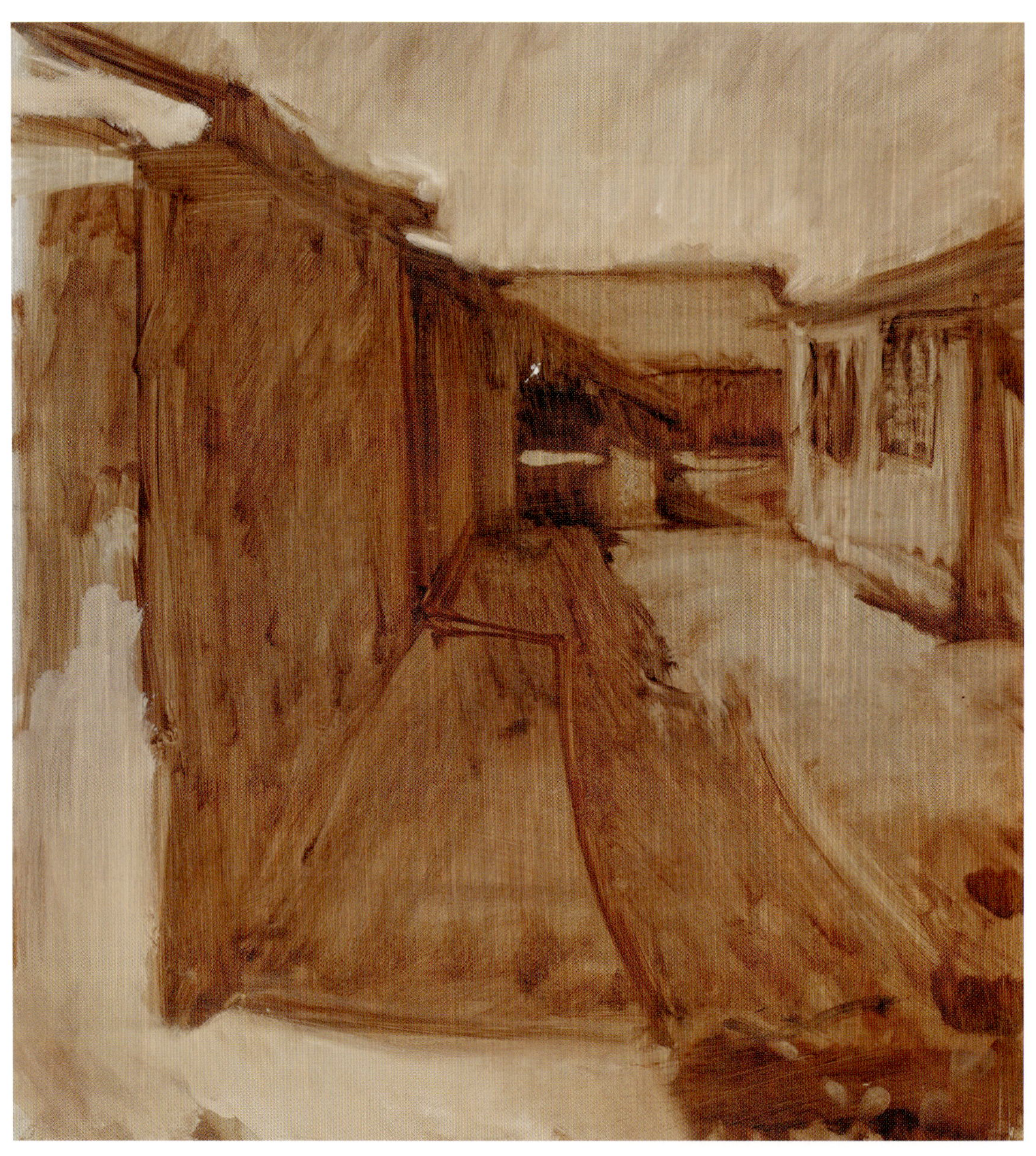

## 2 BLOCK IN THE GRISAILLE

Block in the grisaille. This will allow you to progress through the painting without stumbling over major drawing adjustments, so take as long as you need for this stage.

Take the time now to adjust your drawing while keeping your shapes loose and general. There is a clear vanishing point in a composition like this. All the architectural structures converge at this point. I indicated this with a dot of white to make it simple to find when adjusting the drawing.

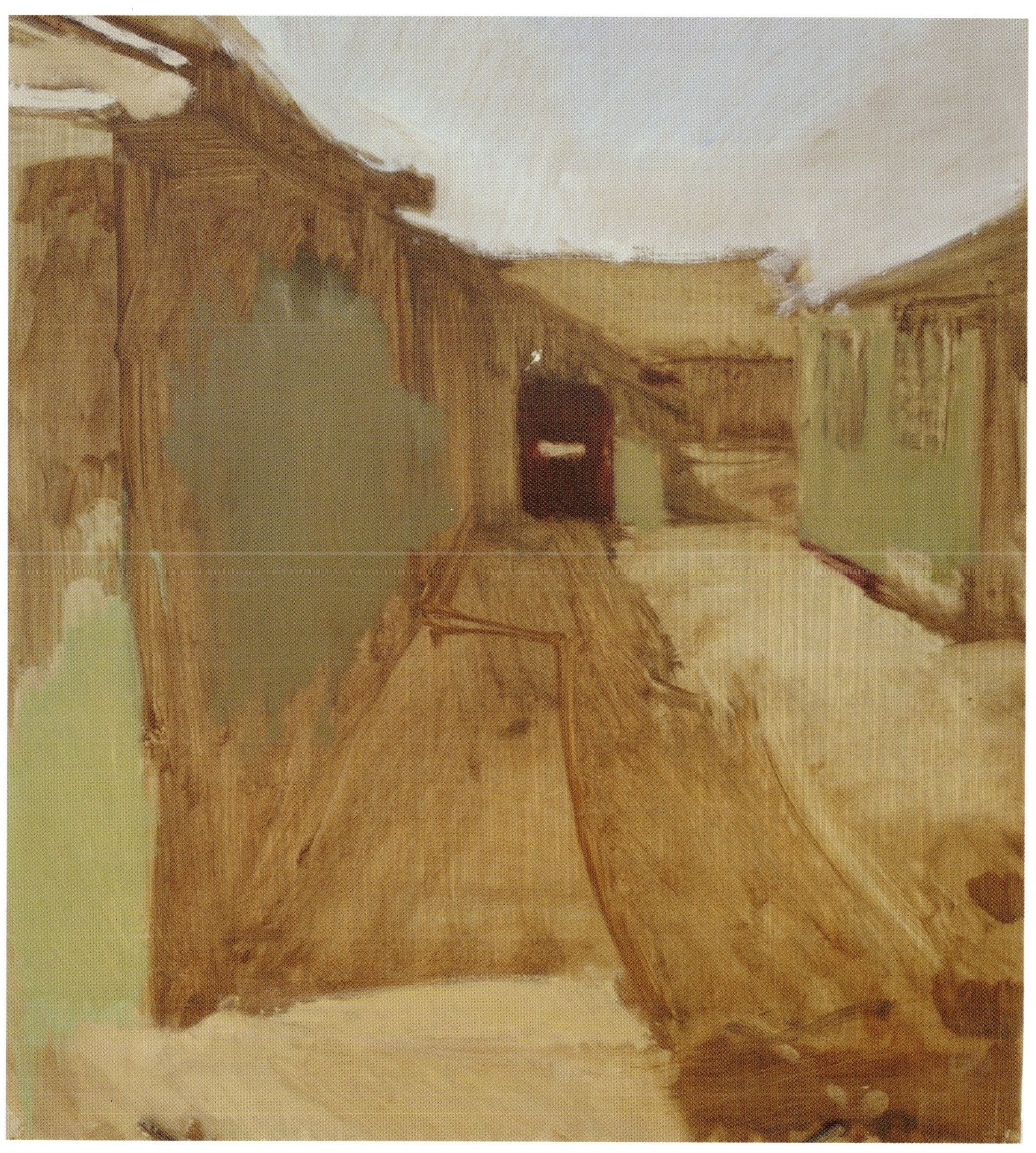

## 3 ADD THE FIRST COLOR NOTES

Begin adding the first color notes. Go for the simplest color notes first because they are the largest masses in the composition. Include the darkest dark as well. In this case, the color notes were adjusted on the canvas. These notes will become deeper and more chromatic as more passes are made on the canvas. As long as the value and color relationships are in the ballpark, they're right for this stage.

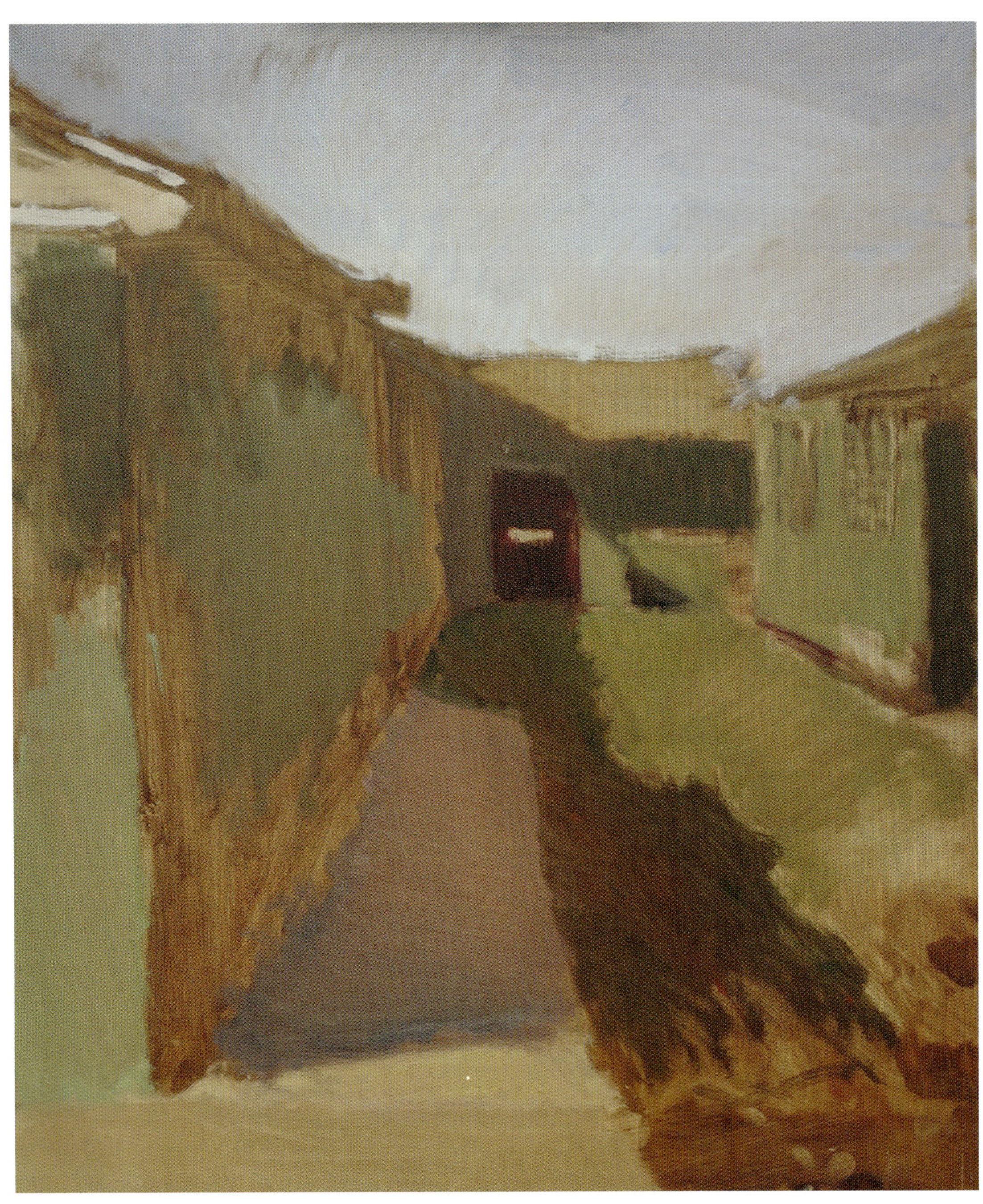

## 4 CONTINUE BUILDING COLOR AND MAKE ADJUSTMENTS

Add more color notes and begin making adjustments where needed. Keep a close eye on the shadow patterns—in this case, they are on the front of the building on the left. The light and shadow patterns change rapidly at this time of day, but I was still not settled on which point I wanted to catch them.

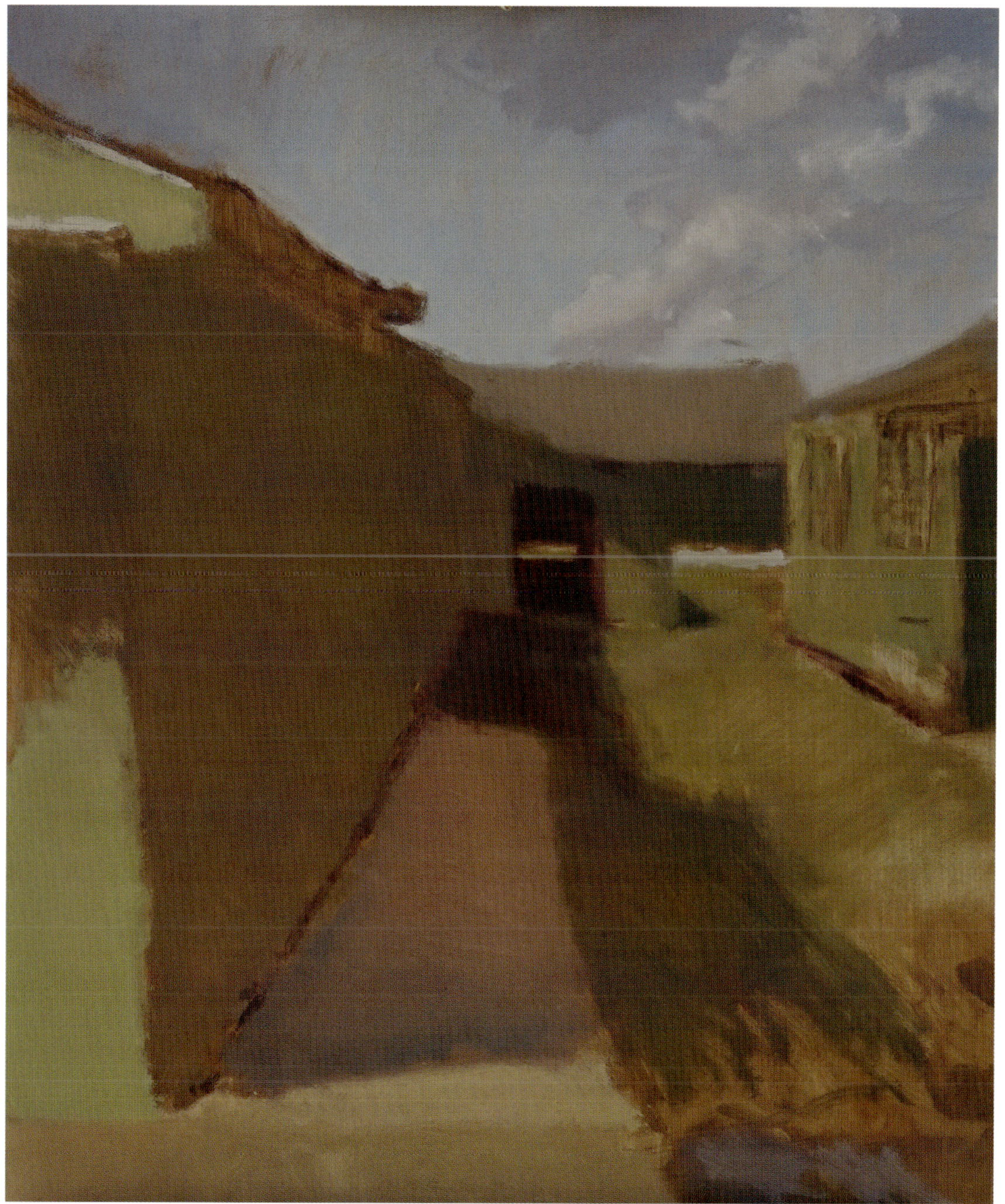

## 5 ADD DARK ACCENTS AND CLOUDS

In addition to working on the large color relationships, add some dark accent lines and the beginnings of some wispy clouds.

Set a goal to try to have the canvas covered by the end of the day. This will allow for a second coat of paint in the next painting session. Step away from the painting for at least a few days to allow time to thoroughly dry.

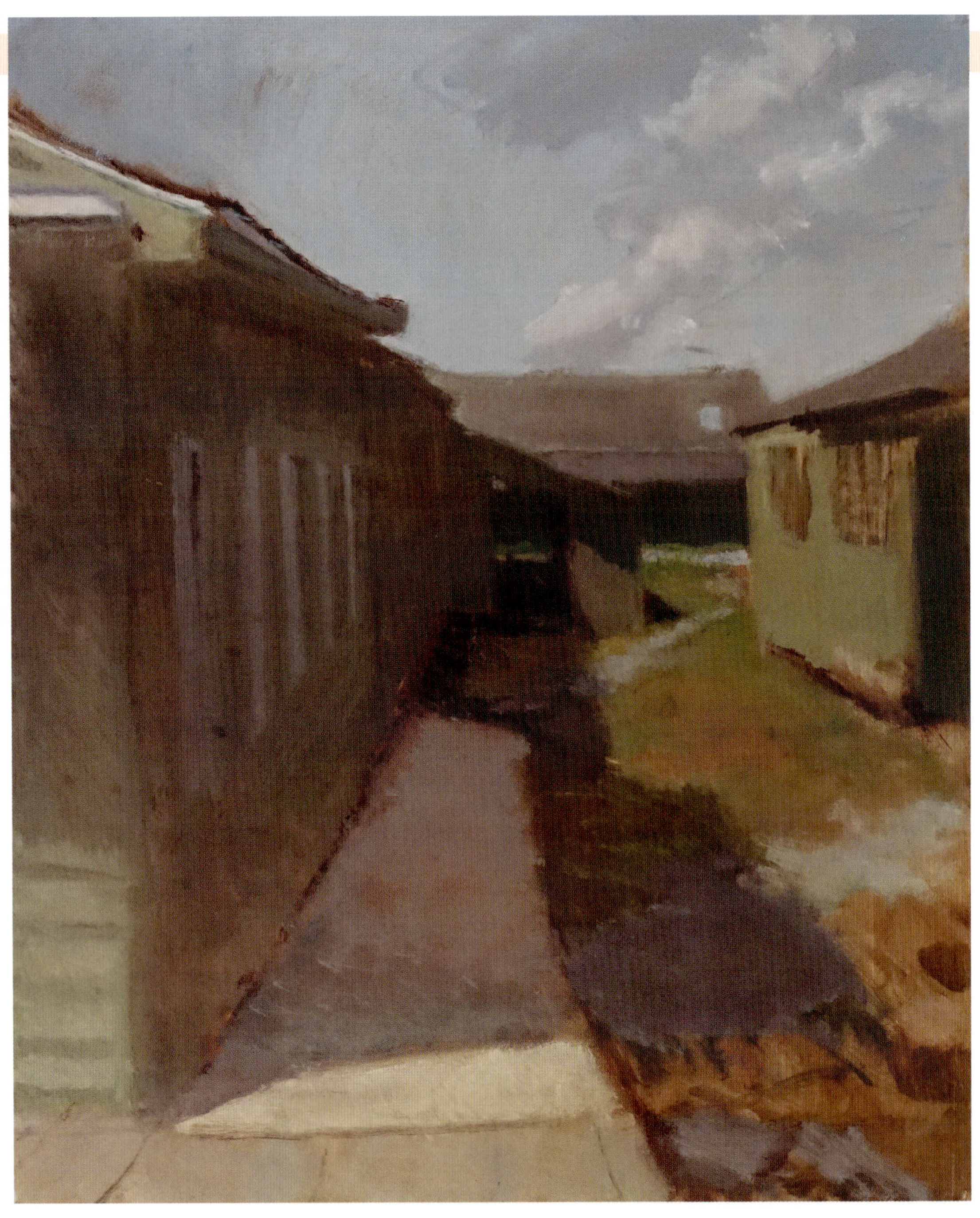

## 6 PUSH THE COLOR DIFFERENCES, MAKE ADJUSTMENTS

After a few days have passed, revisit the painting and push the color differences. For me, that was the area between the two sheds.

I was bothered by the dark shadow within the shed in the middle of the composition. I puzzled over this because it didn't seem as prominent when I looked at the scene. Then I realized that part of the shadow was actually from an open door in the very far shed. For the sake of clarity, I decided to paint this as if that door was closed.

With the exception of the sky, the painting has been worked all over, adjusted and corrected at this point. Notice that with each pass of paint on an area, the thickness and intensity of the paint increases.

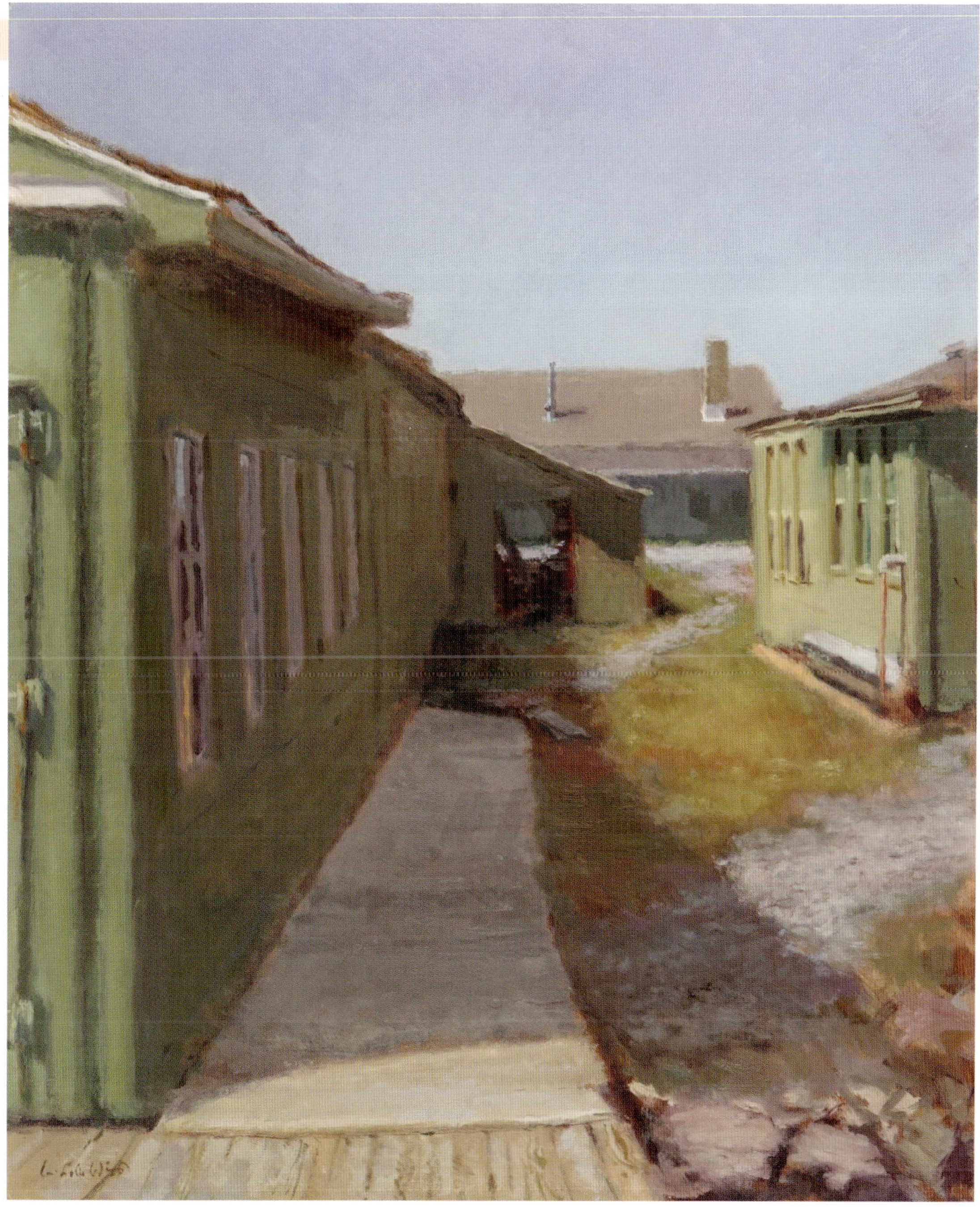

## 7 DEVELOP THE COMPOSITION AND ADD DETAILS

Continue including more color notes to keep the painting from becoming too monochromatic. Here, more notes were added to the windows on the left.

Attack any remaining areas that still need adjustments. In this case, I focused on the relationship between the gravel in shadow and light. I also pushed the far shed into the background to create more of a difference between the two structures.

Then I changed the front of the building on the left, opting to include more information and letting the shadow and light pattern reach the area. A rolling door was added to the front shed, and I wanted to get the detail of the hinges in. I decided this detail was necessary to bring the viewer's eye to the foreground rather than keeping so much information in the distance. It also adds dimension to the painting.

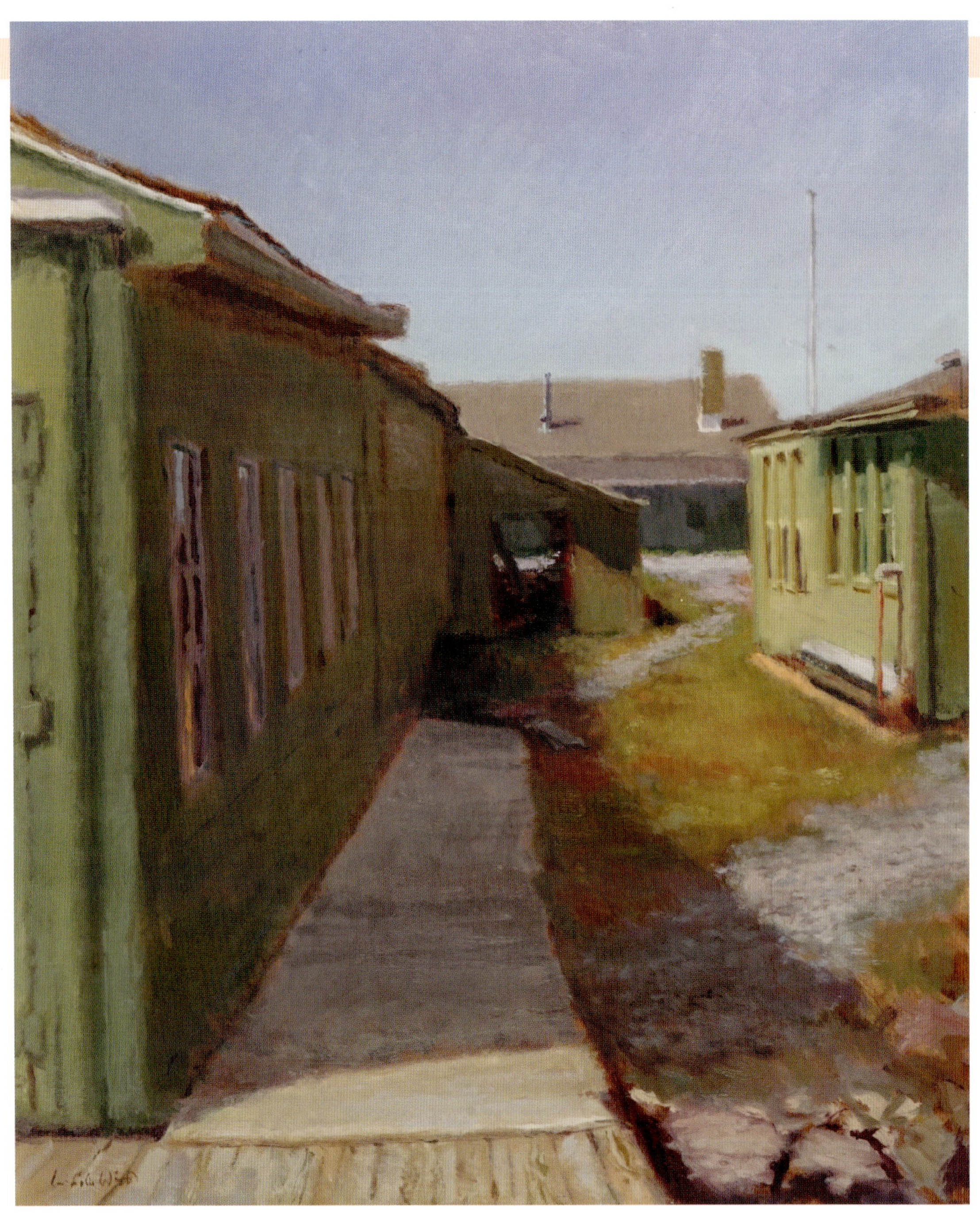

## 8 REFINE THE DETAILS

The windows on the right were corrected and developed. Details were added to the gravel, and the wet area at the end of the walkway was worked over as well.

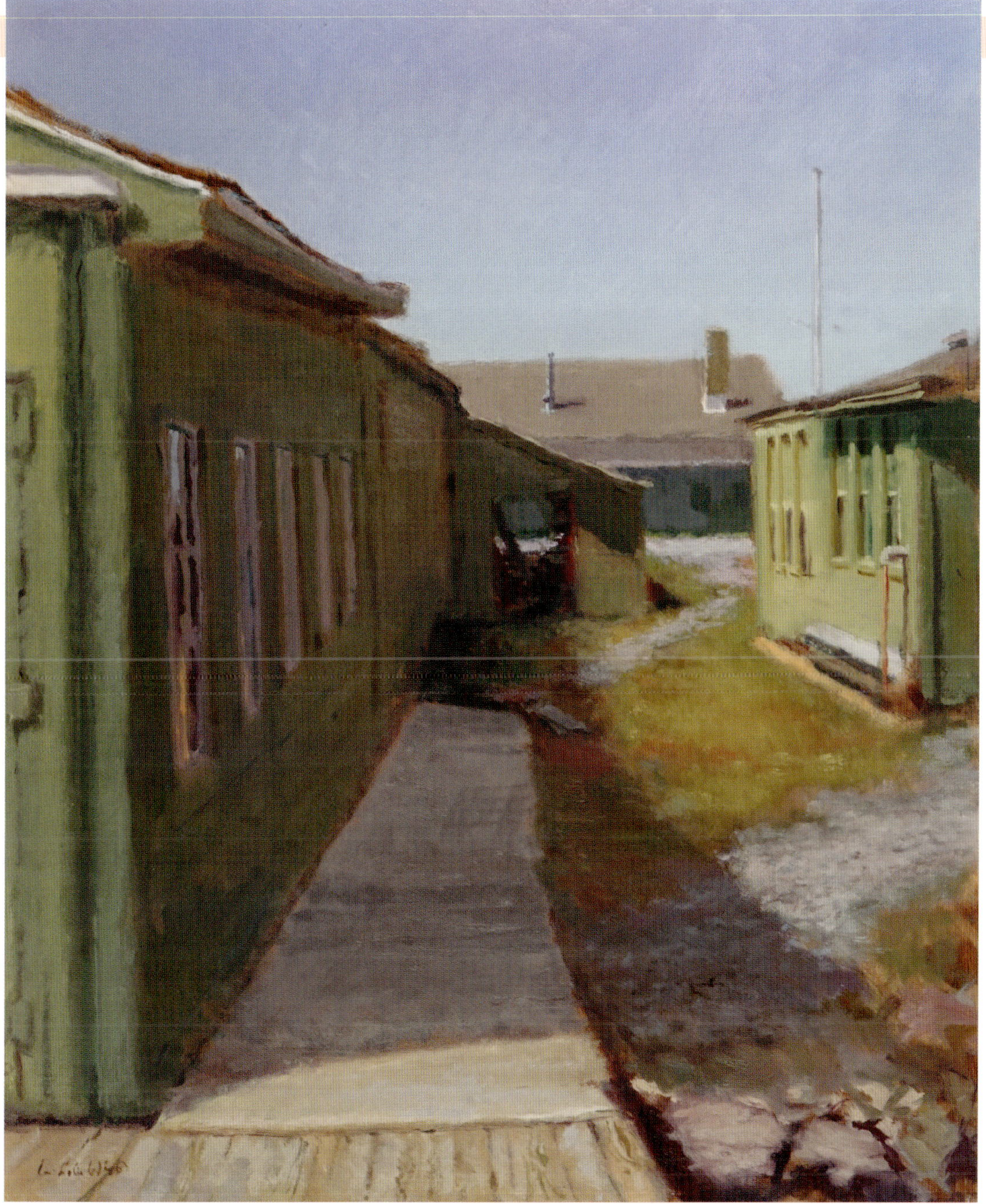

## 9 MAKE FINAL ADJUSTMENTS

Step back and evaluate your work. Make any final additions and adjustments. After I had time to look at the painting objectively, I noticed that the pattern of the clouds and the gravel path had the same angle and were too similar in size and value, so I eliminated the clouds. This gave the painting a clear breathing space to balance out the activity of the main focal point. It's often hard to view a painting objectively when you're in the middle of the process, so if you can, it's best to give yourself a few days away from your painting and then take a fresh look.

## THE WEATHER: SUN VS. SHADE

When painting outdoors, the shadows will be moving across your composition as the sun moves across the sky. The color of the light will change as well. When planning a prolonged painting like the following, it's a good idea to spend a day executing a series of studies catching the different shadow locations. When you decide on one that gives you the composition you like, you can begin. It's important to realize that once you've locked in your shadow locations and color relationships, you can paint for several hours even when they change. You may decide that you want an overcast scene, which will eliminate some of these challenges.

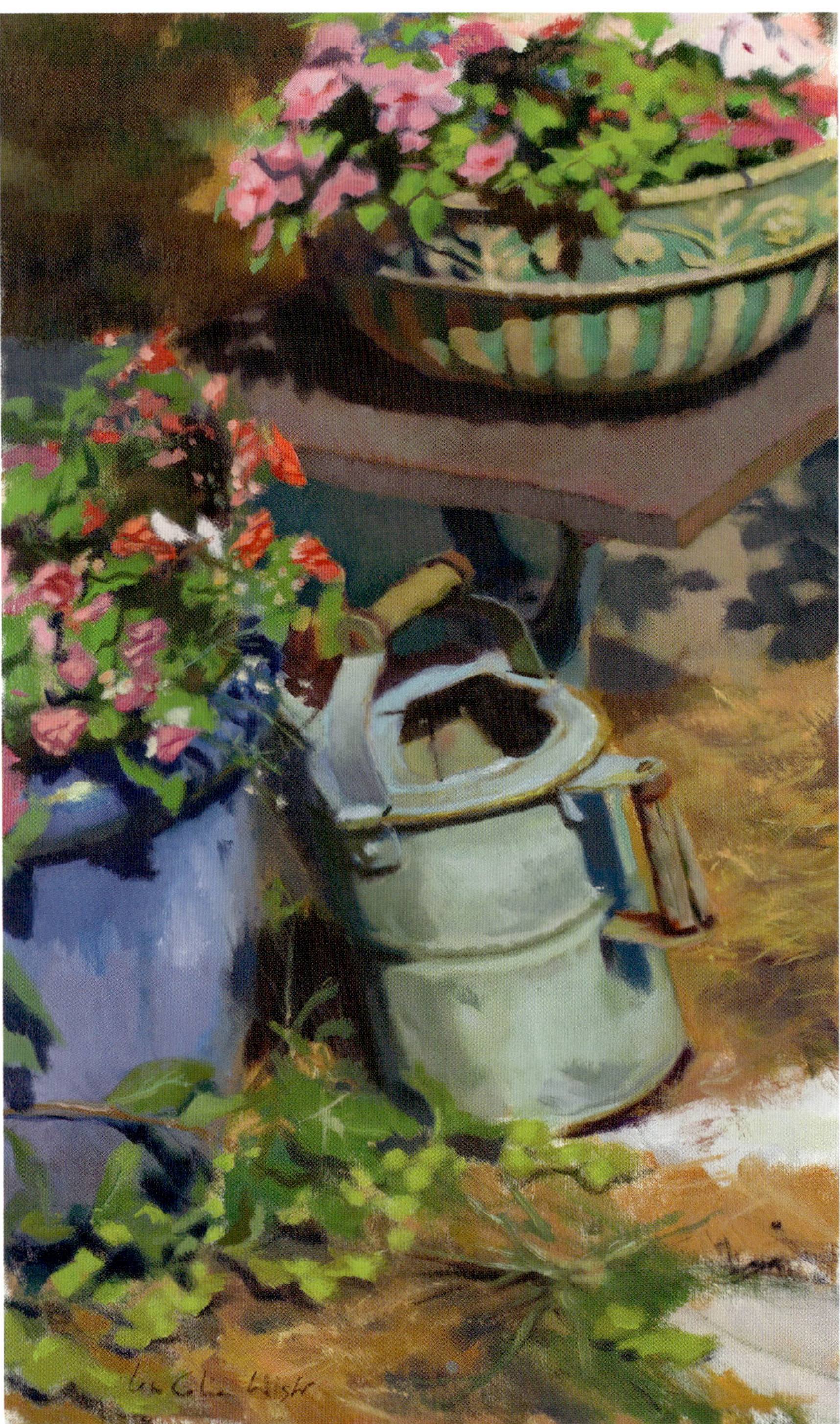

**Summer Morning**
Lea Colie Wight
Oil on linen
28" × 18" (71cm × 46cm)

### *Alla Prima*

Alla prima is the term commonly used for a painting completed on-location in one day. The term alla prima comes from the Italian, meaning "at first attempt."

In a one day alla prima painting there isn't time for a gradual build up of paint. The colors and values need to be fully realized by the end of the painting day. Naturally this results in a much thicker paint application, and the artist paints wet-into-wet.

When painting an alla prima painting, even though there's a time limitation, I've found that it's more important than ever to work out the composition and proportions before any color work. In a painting executed over a few days you have the luxury of time. The goal at the end of the first painting day can simply be a strong start, a developed grisaille and possibly the first color notes.

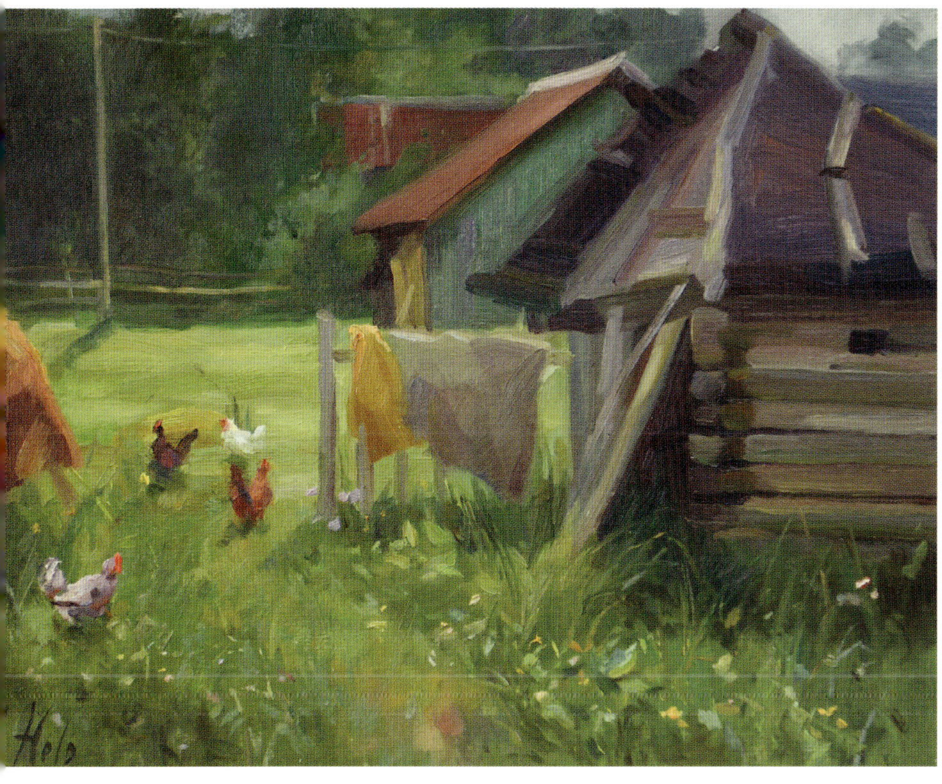

**A Barn**
Katya Held, 2011
Oil on museum board
11" × 11" (28cm × 28cm)

Pay attention to the light you're painting under. Is your canvas in direct sunlight? Is it backlit? Does the sun move across your painting as well as the scene or are you standing under something that blocks the sun? I recommend looking at your painting in different locations to make sure you know how light or dark you're painting. If there's direct sunlight on your canvas you'll probably paint darker because marks look lighter than they really are. The reverse is true if you're in deep shadow. So look at your palette. If the paint in your mixing area is all pastel or all quite dark, that's a warning sign that you're not getting a correct value reading and another reason to establish your highlight and dark accent early on.

## CLOUDS AND WATER

When painting clouds, water or other elusive, ever-changing things, it is especially important to paint your impression of them. If you paint what you think a cloud looks like, it will probably look unnatural. Instead, look for what you notice when you glance. What colors blend into each other. What edges are crisp. If you notice a deeper color, put it in there. Waves and water surfaces are ever-changing. Look for the overall pattern and decide where you want to place it.

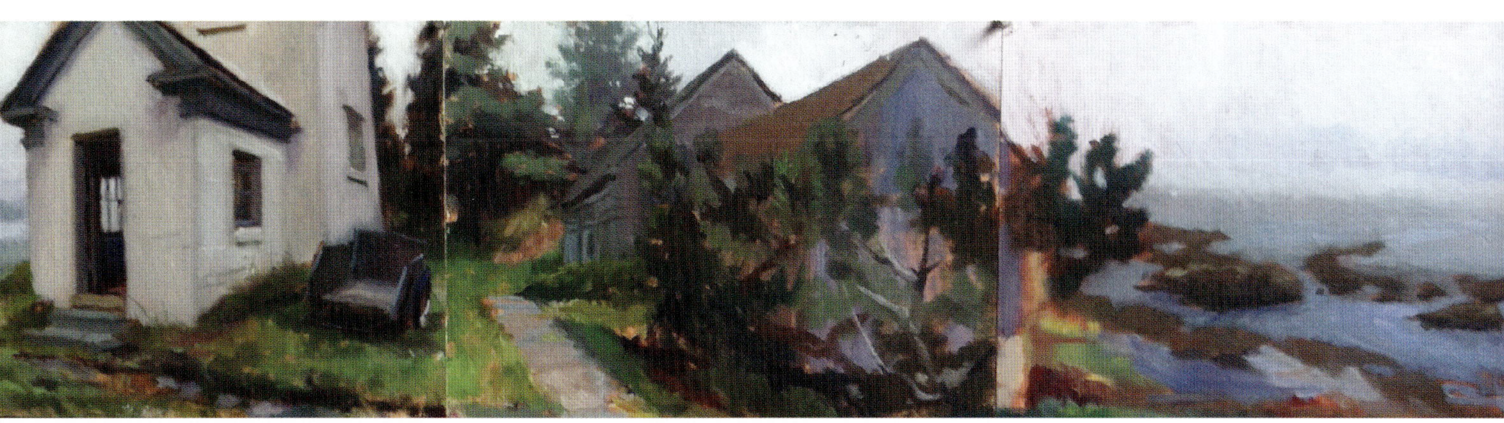

**Indian Island**
Lea Colie Wight
Alla prima triptych
Each panel 7" × 9"
(18cm × 23cm)

Clouds are ever-changing and can be an important compositional element. You have to paint quickly and generally.

# CONCLUSION

My goal in writing this book has been to give you the knowledge to reach your artistic goals. You've been led through the stages of a full-color painting from life and the foundational skills you need. To further advance as a painter it will be necessary to work on these individual stages until you feel you can execute them. All of these exercises have the goal of painting the beauty of nature instinctively and fluidly. Remember that these are skill-building exercises. Your painting practice is yours. Paint with your personal goals dictating how you make use of the knowledge you now have. However you choose to paint will be based on an acquired store of knowledge and not because you don't have the ability.

All great artists started at the beginning. All the artists whose work is hanging in prestigious museums have had the same experience you are having now. Think of that as you look at their work. You share that connection.

A word of warning, though: As you improve, it's more than likely that your goals will keep advancing along with you. You'll probably look back at a level that once thrilled you and realize that you've surpassed that and are much more advanced than you thought possible.

Enjoy the journey!

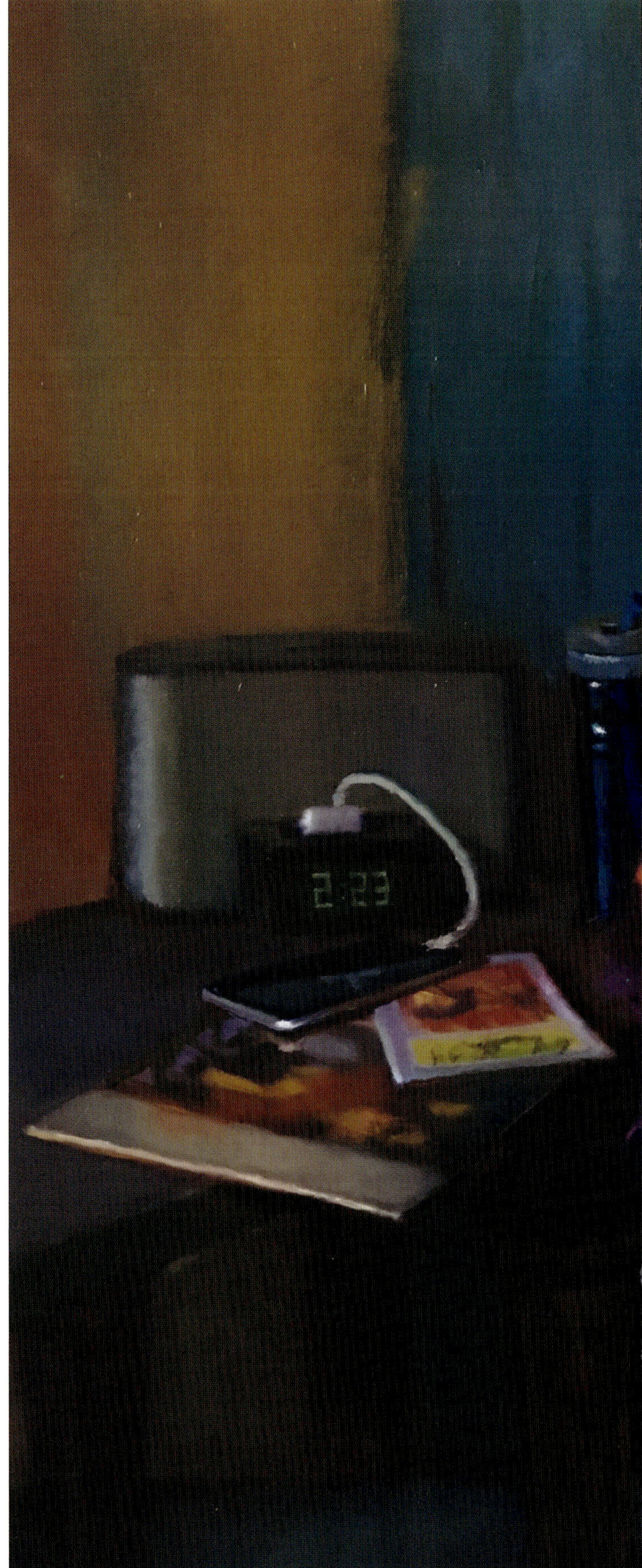

**Contemplation**
Lea Colie Wight
Oil on linen
16" × 20" (41cm × 51cm)

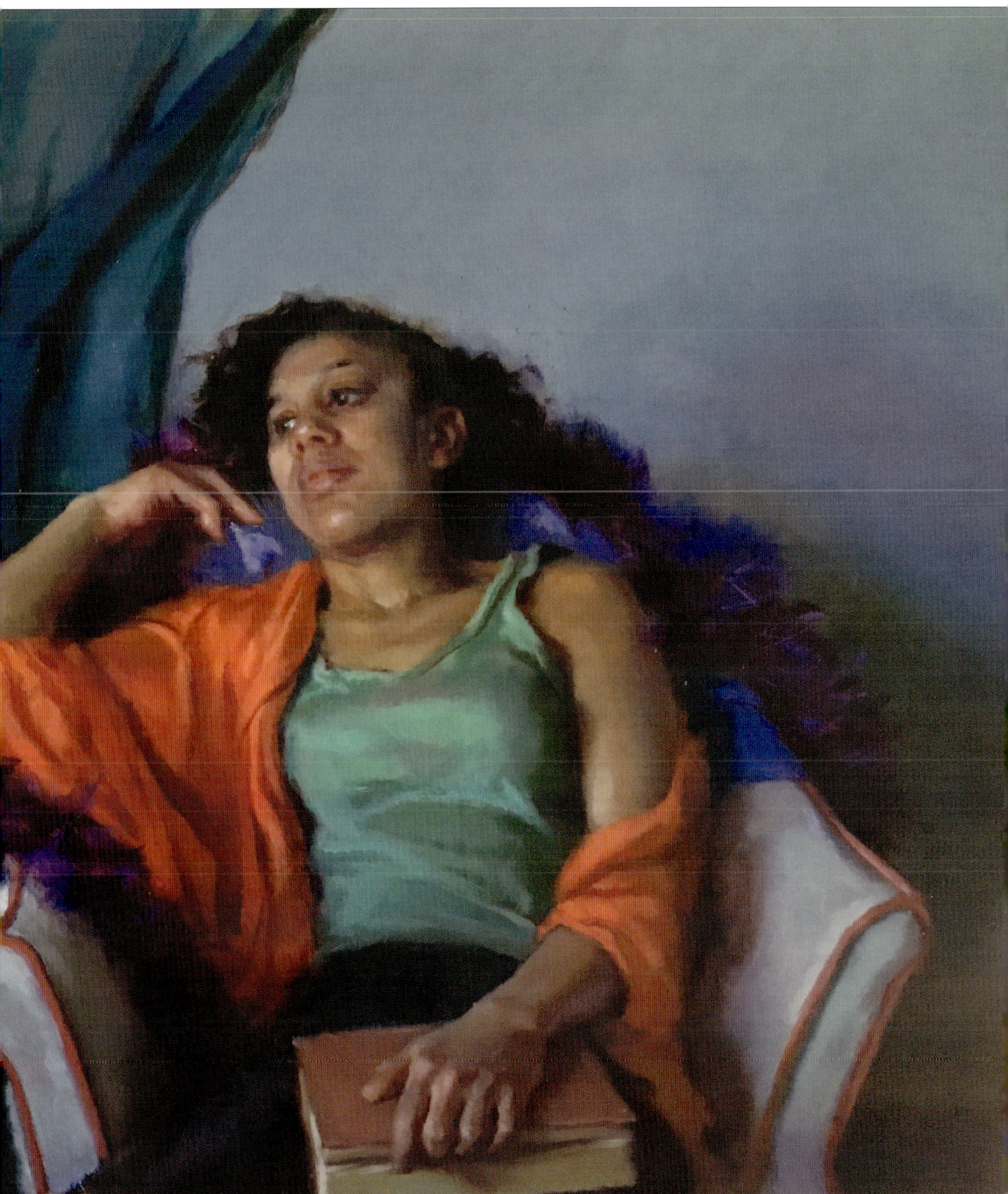

# INDEX

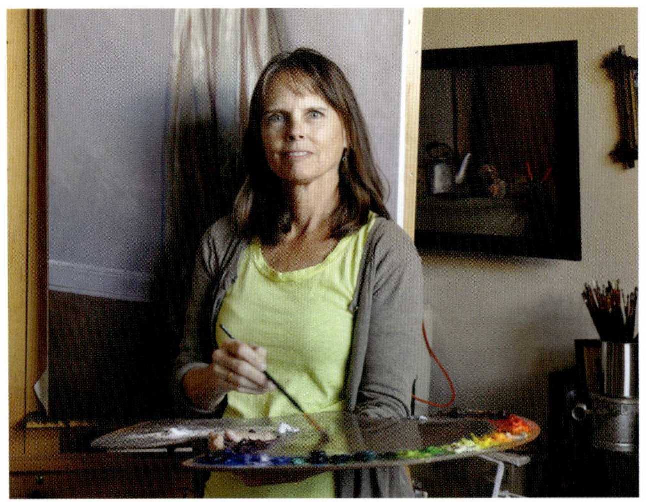

# ABOUT THE AUTHOR

Lea Colie Wight is a realist painter. Born in Philadelphia, she worked primarily in pastels and printmaking until the late 90s, when she began to work in oils. Color has been a focus of Lea's since she began painting, however, it wasn't until she studied with Nelson Shanks at Studio Incamminati that she vigorously pursued the study of color relationships and light keys in oils.

Lea has received numerous painting awards. She was also juried into the the Portrait Society of America's Annual Portrait Competition for three years and was awarded a Certificate of Excellence in 2011.

Lea's paintings have been featured in shows across the country including The Butler Institute of American Art, the Customs House Museum in Tennessee and The National Arts Club in New York City. Her work has also appeared in various magazines and publications. In 2011, she released an art instruction video with American Artist, *Color Essentials: A Painter's Guide.*

Visit leawight.com to learn more about Lea and her events and workshops.

# DEDICATION

This book is dedicated to Nelson Shanks, my mentor, teacher and friend. He taught me everything I know about painting. His encouragement and confidence were immeasurably valuable. Above all, Nelson taught me to explore, push the boundaries, find my own voice and make it joyful.

To my colleagues and dear friends.

To my family—Dick, Tara, David and Nate.

And to my mother, who put down her brush and encouraged me to pick up mine.

 Published by North Light Books, an imprint of F+W Media, Inc. 10151 Carver Road, Suite 300, Blue Ash, Ohio, 45242. (800) 289-0963.

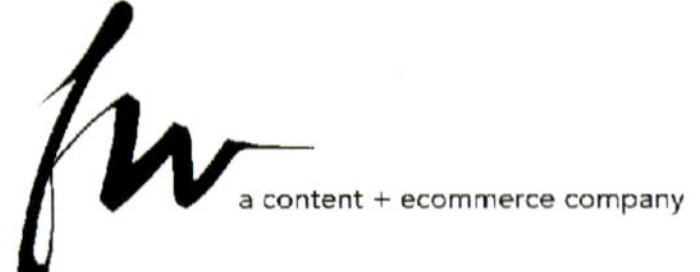


First Edition

Other fine North Light books are available from your favorite bookstore, art supply store or online supplier. Visit our website at fwmedia.com.

22 21 20 19 18 5 4 3 2 1

DISTRIBUTED IN THE U.K. AND EUROPE
BY F&W MEDIA INTERNATIONAL LTD
Brunel House, Pynes Hill Court, Pynes Hill, Rydon Lane, Exeter, EX2 5AZ, United Kingdom
Tel: (+44) 1392 79680
Email: enquiries@fwmedia.com

ISBN 13: 978-1-4403-5242-3

Edited by Christina Richards
Production edited by Jennifer Zellner
Designed by Tara Long

## Metric Conversion Chart

| TO CONVERT | TO | MULTIPLY BY |
|---|---|---|
| Inches | Centimeters | 2.54 |
| Centimeters | Inches | 0.4 |
| Feet | Centimeters | 30.5 |
| Centimeters | Feet | 0.03 |
| Yards | Meters | 0.9 |
| Meters | Yards | 1.1 |

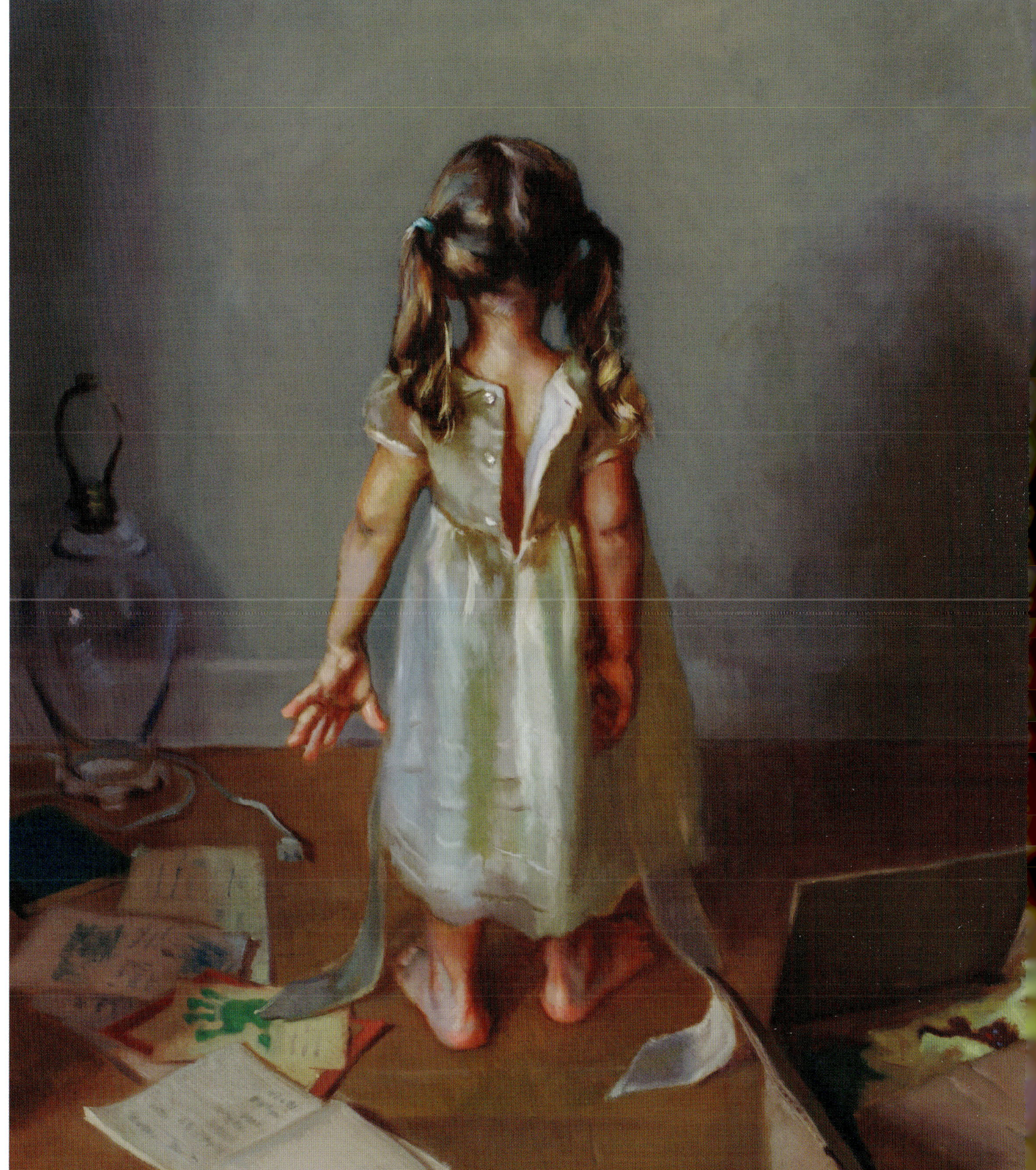

**Loose Ends**
Lea Colie Wight
Oil on linen
30" × 28" (76cm × 71cm)

Artist's Statement

From time to time you notice something unexpectedly beautiful in the most ordinary person; an overlooked corner will tell the story of the people not present; something will tug at you and you take a second look. I hope to provide the viewer with that sort of connection and maybe prompt them to look closer at the world they pass through. I acknowledge the incredible good fortune I have had to be able to spend most of my time as an artist, and I hope to justify it.

# *Ideas. Instruction. Inspiration.*

Receive FREE downloadable bonus materials when you sign up for our free newsletter at artistsnetwork.com/Newsletter_Thanks.

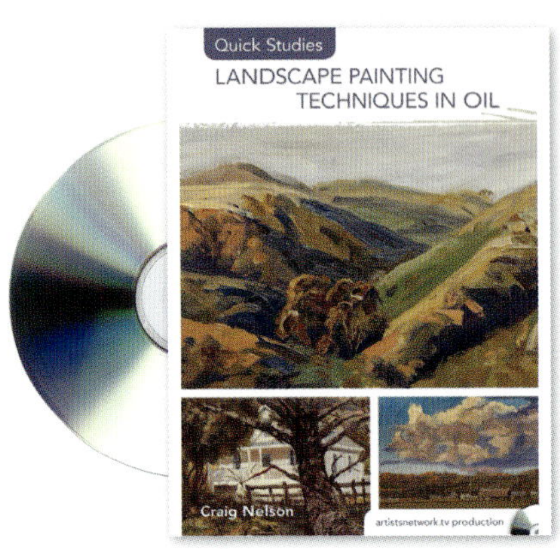


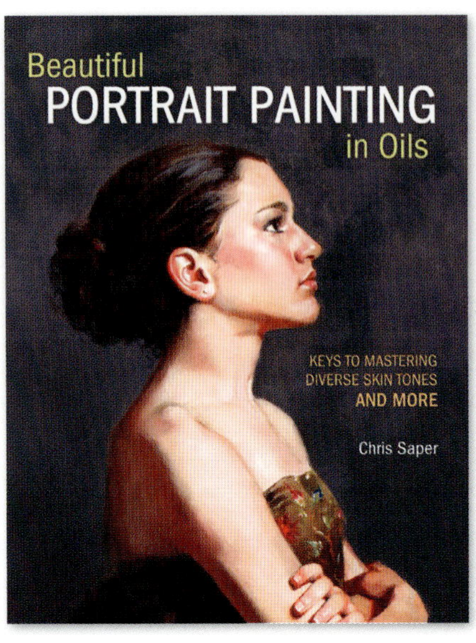


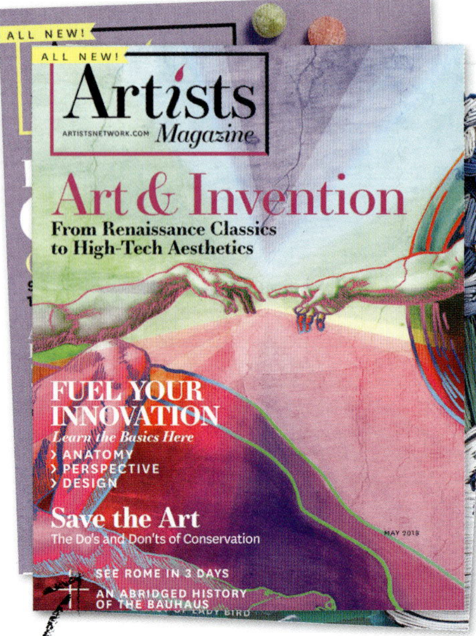


Artistsnetwork
ARTISTSNETWORK.COM

These and other fine North Light products are available at your favorite art & craft retailer, bookstore or online supplier. Visit our websites at artistsnetwork.com and artistsnetwork.tv.

Find the latest issues of ***Artists Magazine*** on newsstands, or visit artistsnetwork.com.

## *Get your art in print!*

Visit **artistsnetwork.com/competitions** for up-to-date information on *Splash* and other North Light competitions.

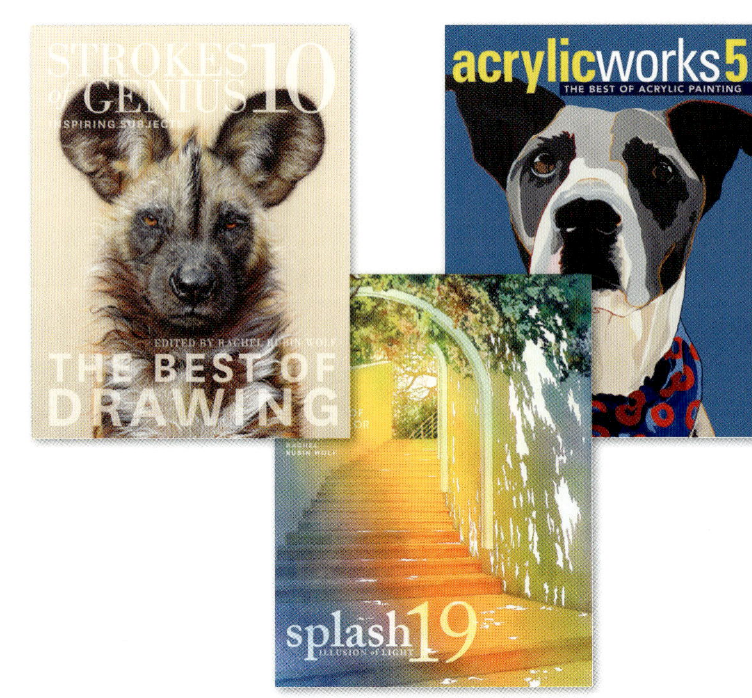


FOLLOW ARTISTS NETWORK FOR THE LATEST NEWS, FREE WALLPAPERS, FREE DEMOS AND CHANCES TO WIN FREE BOOKS!

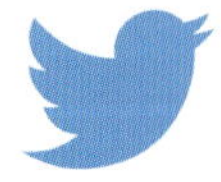
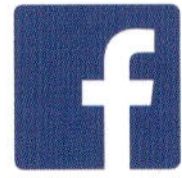